No... included inside
W9-AEA-616

WITHDRAWN

Library & Media Ctr.
Carroll Community College
1601 Washington Rd.
Westminster, MD 21157

JAPANESE GRAPHICS NOW!

GISELA KOZAK &
JULIUS WIEDEMANN

The JAGDA Poster Exhibition JAPAN 2001

T. FUJIMOTO

ジャパニーズ・グラフィックス・ナウ

TASCHEN

KÖLN LONDON LOS ANGELES MADRID PARIS TOKYO

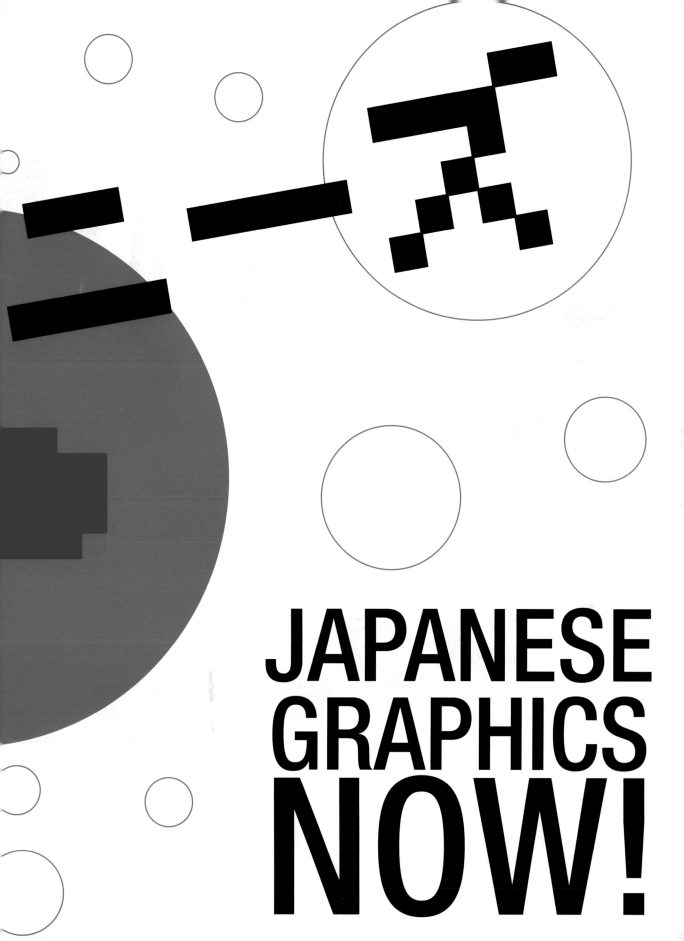

JAPANESE
GRAPHICS
NOW!

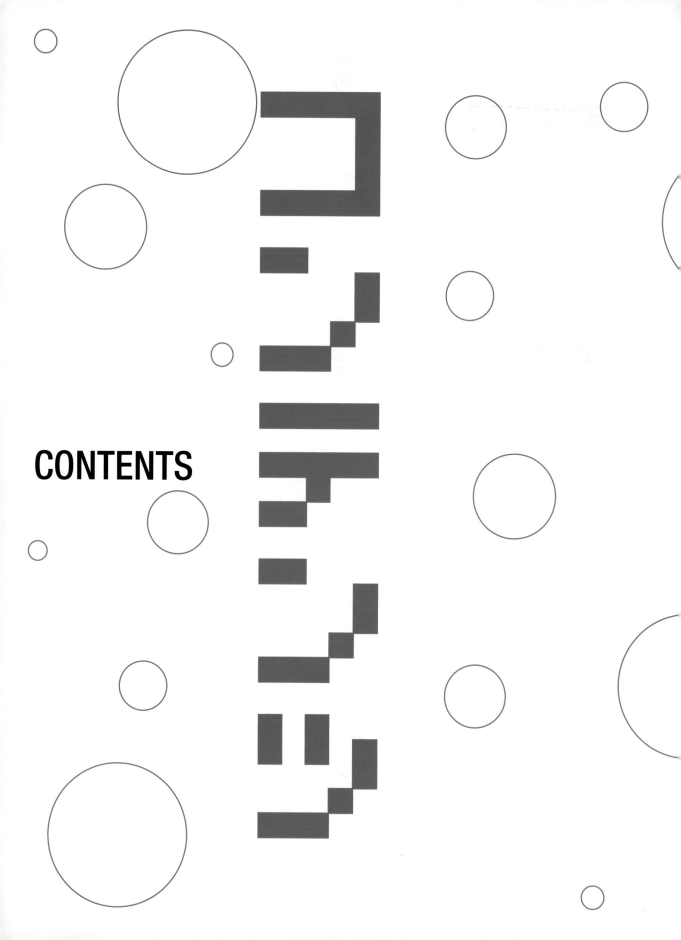

CONTENTS

Packaging パッケージ 034

Posters & Ads ポスターと広告 192

Print プリント 418

Web Design ウェブ・デザイン 552

INTRODUCTION

彼女は20歳になったが、今日が誕生日というわけではない。今日は彼女の「成人の日」なのだ。それで、今年20歳を迎えた他の女の子たちと同じように着物を着ている。彼女は個人的に誕生パーティーを開きたくないわけではないのだが、実を言えば、ここでは個人的な事柄を祝うことがあまりないのだ。一方、他の人たちがしないのなら、自分たちも個別にパーティを開こうとしないらしい人々にとって、伝統的な祭りは祝いごとを合同で済ませるのに適しているようだ。

というわけで、彼女は最新のデジカメ付き携帯電話を使って友人たちの写真や動画を撮りながら、人混みのなかを歩いていく。式典が終わりに近づくと、出席者たちは2次会に向けてどこかへ出かけていく。茶会（茶道の）などまったく計画になく、おそらくどこかのファストフード・レストランに腰を据えるのだろう。あるいはカラオケ・パーティーかも知れない。互いに写真を撮り合う撮影会はまだ終わらないが、彼女たちは移動し始める。お茶しに（ソフトドリンクを飲みに）行く前にちょっとしたショッピングに出かける。ショッピング・リストの上位を占めるのはヨーロッパの高級ブランド品だ。そこには東京のワンルーム・マンションの家賃3ヶ月分に相当する値段のハンドバッグも含まれている。彼女たちは結局のところ、まったく同じタイプのバッグを買うことになる。似たような趣味を共有することが、安心感になるらしい。個別のパーティーを開くよりも、混雑した祭りを共有するのと大して変わらない。パターンは同じだ。ショッピング・タイムが終わる。少なくとも今日のところは。ソフトドリンクを飲み終えると、彼女たちは全員家へ帰りはじめる。最終電車に間に合うように帰らなければならないからだ。これは、いわば鉄道会社に「後援」された日本の戒厳令だ。

日本では、これが当たり前の風景として日常的に見られるのである。着物に携帯電話、伝統的な儀式の仕上げがファストフード・レストラン、高価なブランド・バッグ、身動きも取れないほど混雑した電車。これらすべてが特に違和感もなく肩を並べている。日本の社会では、実に驚嘆すべきことに、新旧の伝統へのリスペクトが特徴のひとつとなっているのだ。

日本のデザインにも、まさにこれと同じ現象が見られる。伝統と新しいものの両者が最も良いところを引き出され、共存するのである。そうした印象的な例の数々を、本書を通じて読者はご覧になれるはずだ。

日本のグラフィックスは見るものが気づかないうちに過去と現在を往来させてくれる能力を持っている。うっかりすれば、どれが過去でどれが現在かに気づくことさえむずかしいかも知れない。それこそが日本様式または「和風」なのである。

何よりも、日本的な感性ではバランスが重視される。この感性が最も端的に見られるのが日本語そのものだろう。日本語には異なる3つの文字種があるが、それが同じ比率で使用されるのである。文章を書くときは、漢字と2種類の音節文字である「ひらがな」と「カタカナ」との組み合わせが使用される。実際には「カタカナ」は基本的に外来語や日本生まれでないものを表すのに使われる。

そして文化を維持しようとするためか、その特殊な習慣がデザインの起源を区別するときにも同じように存在する。日本人が自分たちの作り出したデザインの起源をはっきりさせる必要性を強調するのは、おそらく彼らが「アジア人」と呼ばれるのを嫌うせいかも知れない。グラフィック・デザインは、国産風であろうと外国風であろうと、風合いが商品に与える重要な役割を果たしている。例えば、コーヒーやチョコレートのグラフィックスなら、ロゴやパッケージ、広告までヨーロッパ・スタイルでデザインした方がより理に叶っている。ちょうど「カタカナ」の原則が日本のものと外国産のものとを分ける一線を維持しているかのようだ。それがおそらく製品の起源に敬意を表しつつ、日本のアイデンティティーを維持する方法なのだろう。同じ理由から、昔ながらの和風デザインのパッケージに入っていない「水ようかん」などの和菓子や日本酒にお目にかかることは滅多にない。竹や和紙のような昔ながらの素材が現代的なプラスチック素材に取って代わられるようになった今でも、古いデザインのエッセンスはそのまま残っている。日本のアイデンティティーは国レベルで残されているばかりか、それぞれの地域レベルでも残されている。これは、日本が島国で、独自の文化を維持しやすいことに原因があるのかも知れない。しかし、バランスと釣り合い、あるいはミニマリズム（外国人が日本のデザインについておそらく最も強く抱くイメージだろう）だけが日本のデザインではない。ときにはグラフィック・デザインはたぶん人口の過密な状態に帰因するのだろうが、悪い意味ではなく、いささかごちゃごちゃしたものになる。こうしたデザインの好例は電車の車内広告に見られる。デザイナーたちは忙しく走る電車と「騒々しい」広告で競うつもりはないらしい。むしろ彼らはぎゅうぎゅう詰めの通勤電車で毎日かなりの長時間を過ごさなければならない不幸な乗客を楽しませようとしている可能性がとても高い。乗客は疲弊する通勤中に何か読むものを与えられて感謝さえしているかも知れない。車内広告は、見る人の視力に挑戦しているかのような、たいてい非常に小さなサイズの文字で書かれた情報で埋め尽くされている。信じようと信じまいと、平日午前7時30分の満員電車に乗り合わせたら、それを全部読めるチャンスに遭遇できるにちがいない。もうひとつ見逃せない特徴は、マンガに極めて近く、ときには子供っぽくさえあるユーモアのセンスだ。キュート、または「かわいい」ものが何よりも求められる。望ましい「キュート」なイメージを得ようと、たいてい小さなペットのようなキャラクターやフィギュアがあらゆる商品の販売促進に使われている。仮に商品が大人向けのものであっても、こうした、より「心に触れる」効果を得る方法を使うのがトレンドになっている。

本書は日本の最高のデザイナーたちの作品を巡る旅に読者を誘う。伝統と新しさ、ミニマリストと煩雑さ、バランスの良さとかわいらしさへの感性をどうか楽しんで欲しい。そして何よりも、現代日本文化をより身近に見るという、このユニークなチャンスを満喫していただきたい。

She has turned 20, but today is not her birthday. It is her "coming-of-age ceremony day" (seijin-shiki) and she, like all the other girls who turned 20 this year, is wearing a kimono. It is not that she would not like to have a private birthday party. The truth is you don't really get to celebrate your personal affairs that often here. On the other hand, traditional celebrations (matsuri) seem an ideal way to share the festivities, while assuring people that they will not stand out as much as at a party of their own.

So there she goes, walking among the crowd using the latest mobile phone to take pictures and movies of her friends. The ceremony is almost over and the group is heading somewhere for the second stage of the party. No tea ceremony in their plans… probably some fast-food restaurant will do the trick. Or perhaps a karaoke party? The picture session is not over yet, but they start moving. A little shopping before going for a soft drink. Up-market European brands top the list - including handbags that may cost as much as three months rent for a one-room-flat in Tokyo. They almost end up with the same type of handbag. Sharing a similar taste seems to give them a sense of relief. Not much different from sharing a crowded festival instead of a private party… the pattern is the same. Shopping time is now over - at least for today. After finishing their soft drinks, they all start to head off home. They need to catch the last train, a kind of curfew in Japan "sponsored" by the railway companies.

This could be just a regular day in Japan: kimonos and mobile phones; traditional ceremonies ending at fast food restaurants; expensive branded handbags; and totally packed trains. All of these things occur side by side, without any apparent contradiction. The respect for old and modern traditions marks one of the most astonishing characteristics of Japanese society.

This is exactly the same as you will find in Japanese design. The traditional and the modern coexist, bringing out the best in both. You will get a chance to see impressive examples of this - all the way through Japanese Graphics Now!

Japanese graphics have the ability to let you move between the past and the present without even noticing it. It may even be hard to see the difference between the two. Let's say, rather, Japanese style or "wafu".

The Japanese style sensitivity is based, among other things, on a respect for balance. This sensibility is probably best seen in the Japanese language, in which every character preserves the same proportion throughout the three different Japanesewriting systems. A combination of Chinese characters and two syllabic systems called "hiragana" and "katakana" is used in actual writing. In reality, "katakana" is basically used for foreign words or for things that do not have their origin in Japan. And probably, in an effort to preserve the culture, that peculiarity is also present in order to distinguish the origins of the designs. Perhaps it's because Japanese people dislike being called "Asians" that they emphasize the need to recognize the origin of the design in their products. Graphic design plays an important part in giving their products either a local or foreign flavour. For example, it makes more sense that the graphics for coffee or chocolate – including logo, packaging and advertisement - are designed in a European style. It is as if the "katakana" principle persisted to define the lines between what is Japanese and what is foreign. It is probably a way of keeping the Japanese identity while showing respect for the origin of the products. For the same reason, you will rarely see a Japanese sweet, such as "mizu youkan" (a sort of jelly made from beans) or sake packaged in a way that does not contain a traditionally Japanese design. Even though nowadays the traditional materials such as bamboo or washi paper are sometimes replaced by modern plastic variations, the essence of the old design still remains. Identity is not only being preserved with regard to countries, but also with regard to different areas of the Japanese territory. It is probably because Japan is an island that it has been easier to preserve its own culture. But

Japanese design is not only about balance and proportion, or even minimalism, which is probably the strongest image that people abroad have about Japanese design. Sometimes graphic design gets a little more chaotic – and not in a negative sense - probably due to the overcrowded atmosphere. A good chance to see this kind of design is through the adverts on trains. It is not that the designers are trying to compete with the busy trains by "noisy" advertising. It is quite possible that they are trying to entertain the unfortunate passengers, who have to spend quite a long time everyday commuting to their jobs in packed trains. The passengers might even be grateful to have something to read during such a tiring trip. Train adverts are usually saturated with information written in very small font sizes, sometimes even challenging your eyesight. Believe it or not, you may even get the chance to read it all if you happen to get a crowded 7.30 AM train on a weekday. Another characteristic that will not pass unnoticed is the sense of humor: pretty close to the comic (manga) subculture, and sometimes even close to being childish, with no other claim than to being cute or "kawai". Characters, figures, usually like little pets, are used for promoting all manner of products in an attempt to get that desired "cute" image. Even when the products are supposed to be aimed at adults, the trend is to use this method to achieve a more "touching" effect.

Japanese Graphics Now! will take you on a tour of the works of some of the best Japanese designers. Enjoy the traditional and the modern, the minimalist and the chaotic, the sensitivity to proportion and the cuteness. And, above all, enjoy this unique chance of getting a closer look at today's Japanese culture.

Elle vient d'avoir 20 ans mais ce n'est pas son anniversaire aujourd'hui. C'est le jour de sa cérémonie « de passage à l'âge adulte » (seijin shiki). Elle porte un kimono, comme toutes les autres filles qui ont atteint l'âge de 20 ans cette année. Ce n'est pas qu'elle ne souhaite pas fêter son anniversaire en privé. En vérité, on ne fait pas très souvent de fêtes privées ici. D'un autre côté, les cérémonies traditionnelles (matsuri) semblent être la manière idéale de partager les festivités, tant qu'elles ne donnent pas l'impression de ressembler à des fêtes privées !

Ainsi donc se promène à travers la foule, utilisant un portable dernier cri pour prendre des photos et des vidéos de ses amies. La cérémonie est presque terminée. Le groupe se dirige vers l'endroit où se déroulera la seconde partie de la fête. La cérémonie du thé ne fait pas partie de leurs projets… Un fast-food fera l'affaire. Pourquoi pas un karaoké ? La séance photo n'est pas encore terminée mais elles continuent leur chemin. Elles feront les magasins avant d'aller prendre une boisson sans alcool. Les marques européennes de luxe sont tout en haut de leur liste, et notamment les sacs à main qui peuvent coûter jusqu'à trois mois de loyer d'un appartement d'une pièce à Tokyo. Elles finissent presque par acheter les mêmes modèles. Partager les mêmes goûts les soulage presque autant que d'aller toutes à un concert plein de monde plutôt qu'une fête privée… la tendance est toujours la même. Les courses sont terminées, au moins pour aujourd'hui. Après avoir terminé leur verre, elles retournent chez elles. Elles doivent prendre le dernier train, une sorte de couvre-feu japonais « sponsorisé » par la compagnie ferroviaire.

Ce pourrait être un jour comme les autres au Japon : kimonos et portables, cérémonies traditionnelles se terminant au fast-food, sacs à main de luxe et trains bondés. Tout cela côte à côte, sans contradiction apparente. Le respect des traditions anciennes et modernes est l'un des aspects les plus étonnants de la société japonaise.

C'est exactement ce que reflète le design japonais. Le traditionnel et le moderne coexistent, faisant ressortir ce que les deux ont de meilleur. Vous pourrez en voir des exemples incroyables tout au long de Japanese Graphics Now!

Les représentations graphiques japonaises peuvent vous faire naviguer entre le passé et le présent sans que vous vous en rendiez compte. Vous ne verrez peut-être même pas la différence entre les deux. Disons plutôt qu'il s'agit du style japonais, ou « wafu ».

La sensibilité du style japonais repose, entre autres, sur l'équilibre. Elle est probablement le plus visible dans la langue japonaise, dans laquelle chaque caractère conserve les mêmes proportions à travers des trois systèmes d'écriture japonais. Une combinaison de caractères chinois et de deux systèmes syllabiques appelés « hiragana » et « katakana, » est utilisée pour les mots étrangers ou pour tout ce qui n'a pas ses origines au Japon. Dans un effort pour préserver la culture, cette particularité sert également à distinguer les origines des créations. C'est peut-être parce que les Japonais détestent être appelés « asiatiques » qu'ils mettent l'accent sur la reconnaissance des origines des créations dans leurs produits. La conception graphique est capitale pour donner un aspect local ou étranger aux produits. Par exemple, il est tout à fait logique que le graphisme du café ou du chocolat, dont le logo, l'emballage et la publicité, soit réalisé dans un style européen. C'est comme si le principe du « katakana » persistait pour définir la frontière entre ce qui est japonais et ce qui ne l'est pas. C'est probablement une manière de préserver l'identité nippone tout en respectant l'origine des produits. Pour les mêmes raisons, vous verrez rarement des sucreries japonaises, telles que les « mizu youkan » (une sorte de gelée de haricots) ou du saké, présentés sans graphisme japonais traditionnel. Bien que les matériaux traditionnels tels que le bambou et le papier washi soient aujourd'hui quelquefois remplacés par leurs équivalents en plastique, l'essence du design traditionnel reste présente. L'identité n'est pas seulement préservée par égard pour

les pays, mais également par égard pour les différentes régions du territoire japonais. C'est probablement parce que le Japon a un caractère insulaire qu'il a pu préserver sa propre culture. Les créations japonaises ne sont pas seulement une question d'équilibre et de proportion, ou encore de minimalisme, ce qui est probablement l'image la plus forte que les étrangers aient des créations japonaises. Quelquefois, la conception graphique devient un peu plus chaotique, mais pas dans un sens négatif, probablement à cause de l'atmosphère surpeuplée. Ce type de création est très visible si l'on observe des publicités dans les trains. Ce n'est pas que les publicitaires essaient de concurrencer les trains bondés par des publicités « bruyantes ». Il est très possible qu'ils essaient de divertir les malheureux passagers qui doivent effectuer un long trajet jusqu'à leur lieu de travail dans des trains surchargés. Les passagers peuvent même être reconnaissants d'avoir quelque chose à lire durant ces trajets pénibles. Les publicités dans les trains sont habituellement saturées d'informations rédigées en très petit corps, et sont parfois même quasiment impossible à déchiffrer. Croyez-le ou non, vous aurez peut-être la chance de les lire en intégralité si vous prenez un train en pleine heure de pointe pendant la semaine. Une autre caractéristique qui ne passe pas inaperçue est le sens de l'humour très proche de la culture manga, presque enfantin, et qui n'a pas d'autre but que d'être mignon, ou « kawai ». Des personnages et des silhouettes, habituellement de petits animaux, sont utilisés pour promouvoir toutes sortes de produits en les dotant d'une image « mignonne. » Même lorsque les produits sont destinés aux adultes, cette tendance vise à émouvoir.

Japanese Graphics Now! vous fait découvrir les travaux des meilleurs designers japonais. Nous espérons que vous apprécierez le traditionnel et le moderne, le minimaliste et le chaotique, la sensibilité aux proportions et l'aspect attendrissant. Cet ouvrage vous rapprochera indéniablement de la culture japonaise d'aujourd'hui.

Sie ist zwanzig geworden, doch heute ist nicht ihr Geburtstag. Es ist ihr „Tag der Volljährigkeit" (seijin-shiki) und sie trägt einen Kimono, genau wie all die anderen Mädchen, die in diesem Jahr zwanzig geworden sind. Es nicht so, dass sie sich nicht auch eine private Geburtstagsfeier wünschen würde. Die Realität sieht jedoch so aus, dass man hier nicht sehr oft Gelegenheit findet, etwas privat zu feiern. Andererseits sind traditionelle Feiertage (matsuri) ein idealer Anlass, Feste gemeinsam zu feiern und dabei nicht so sehr im Mittelpunkt zu stehen wie bei einer eigenen Party.

Da läuft sie, bewegt sich inmitten der vielen Menschen, die mit ihren brandneuen Handys Fotos und Videoaufnahmen von ihren Freunden machen. Die Zeremonie ist fast vorbei und die Gruppe wird gleich gehen, um irgendwo anders weiterzufeiern. Eine Teezeremonie ist nicht eingeplant ... wahrscheinlich werden sie sich für ein Fast-Food-Restaurant entscheiden. Oder vielleicht für eine Karaoke-Party? Noch sind nicht alle Fotos geschossen, aber sie setzen sich in Bewegung. Ein bisschen Shopping, bevor sie etwas Alkoholfreies trinken gehen. Teure europäische Marken werden am liebsten gekauft – unter anderem Handtaschen, die bis zu drei Monatsmieten für eine Einzimmerwohnung in Tokio kosten können. Am Ende haben die jungen Frauen praktisch alle die gleichen Handtaschen gekauft. Denselben Geschmack zu haben, scheint ihnen eine Erleichterung zu sein. Wie schon beim gemeinsamen Feiern eines Festes mit vielen Leuten anstelle einer privaten Party ... das Muster ähnelt sich. Jetzt ist man fertig mit dem Shoppen – zumindest für heute. Als alle ihre Softdrinks ausgetrunken haben, machen sie sich auf den Nachhauseweg. Sie müssen den letzten Zug erreichen – eine Art Ausgangssperre, die den Eisenbahnge-sellschaften zu „verdanken" ist.

So könnte ein ganz normaler Tag in Japan aussehen: Kimonos und Handys, traditionelle Zeremonien, die in Fast-Food-Restaurants beschlossen werden, teure Markenhandtaschen und hoffnungslos überfüllte Züge. All das existiert nebeneinander, ohne einen offen-sichtlichen Widerspruch darzustellen. Der Respekt, der sowohl alten wie auch neuen Traditionen entgegengebracht wird, ist eines der erstaunlichsten Merkmale der japanischen Gesellschaft.

Dies gilt auch für das japanische Design. Das Traditionelle und das Moderne existieren nebeneinander, wodurch von beidem das Beste zum Ausdruck kommt. Eindrucksvolle Beispiele für diese Verbindung sind überall in Japanese Graphics Now! zu finden. In japanischen Grafiken sind Vergangenheit und Gegenwart gleich-zeitig präsent, ohne dass sich der Betrachter dessen unbedingt bewusst wird. Es kann sogar schwierig sein zu erkennen, was alt und was neu ist. Vielleicht sollten wir einfach vom japanischen Stil sprechen: wafu!

Das japanische Stilgefühl beruht ganz besonders auf der Wert-schätzung von Ausgewogenheit. Dies lässt sich vermutlich am besten an der japanischen Sprache ablesen, in der jedes Schrift-zeichen in allen drei japanischen Schriftsystemen dieselben Propor-tionen bewahrt. Zum Schreiben selbst wird eine Kombination aus chinesischen Wortzeichen und den zwei Silbenschriften Hiragana und Katakana benutzt. Faktisch wird Katakana zumeist für aus-ländische Wörter oder für Dinge gewählt, deren Herkunft nicht in Japan liegt. Diese Unterscheidung lässt sich auch im Bereich des Designs ausmachen: Im Bemühen um die Bewahrung der eigenen Kultur, so ist zu vermuten, sind „einheimische" und „ausländische" Designansätze jeweils klar zu erkennen. Japaner mögen es nicht, wenn man sie als „Asiaten" bezeichnet – vielleicht erklärt dies das Bedürfnis, die Herkunft eines Designs in ihren Produkten zu verdeutlichen. Grafikdesign spielt eine entscheidende Rolle dabei, ob ein Produkt einen lokalen oder einen globalen Beigeschmack hat. So ist es beispielsweise sinnvoll, dass das grafische Er-scheinungsbild für Kaffee oder Schokolade – einschließlich Logo, Verpackung und Werbung – in einem europäischen Stil entworfen wird. Es ist, als ob das Katakana-Prinzip existierte, um die Grenz-linie zwischen dem Japanischen und dem Ausländischen zu

definieren. Es ist vermutlich eine Methode zur Wahrung der japanischen Identität, die zugleich der Herkunft der Produkte Respekt entgegenbringt. Aus dem gleichen Grund wird man kaum eine japanische Süßigkeit wie mizu-youkan (ein aus Bohnen hergestelltes Gelee) oder Sake finden, deren Verpackung nicht mit traditionell japanischen Designelementen gestaltet ist. Auch wenn heutzutage herkömmliche Materialien wie Bambus oder Washi-Papier manchmal durch moderne Plastikvariationen ersetzt werden, bleibt die Essenz des alten Designs doch erhalten. Identität spielt nicht nur im Hinblick auf Länder, sondern auch im Hinblick auf ver-schiedene Regionen Japans eine Rolle. Die Tatsache, dass Japan eine Insel ist, hat es vermutlich einfacher gemacht, die eigene Kultur zu bewahren. Doch im japanischen Design geht es nicht nur um Ausgewogenheit und Proportion oder Minimalismus, was wohl das vorherrschende Bild ist, das Ausländer vom japanischen Design haben. Das Grafikdesign kann durchaus auch chaotisch werden – und das ist ganz und gar nicht negativ gemeint –, was vermutlich auf das Leben in so großer Enge zurückzuführen ist. Diese Art des Designs lässt sich sehr gut auf den Werbetafeln in den Zügen beobachten. Es ist nicht so, als versuchten die Designer, durch „laute" Werbung mit den überfüllten Zügen zu wetteifern. Es ist sehr gut möglich, dass sie die bedauernswerten Fahrgäste unterhalten wollen, die auf dem Weg zur Arbeit jeden Tag sehr viel Zeit in vollgestopften Zügen verbringen müssen. Vielleicht sind die Passagiere sogar dankbar, dass sie während der ermüdenden Fahrten etwas zu lesen haben. Zugwerbungen sind für gewöhnlich mit Informationen in derart kleiner Schrift vollgepackt, dass sie das Sehvermögen bis zum Äußersten herausfordern. Unglaublich, aber wahr: Wenn man an einem Wochentag um 7 Uhr 30 einen vollen Zug betritt, in dem man die ganze Zeit über stehen muss, hat man womöglich die Gelegenheit, so viel Text auch tatsächlich durch-zulesen. Eine andere, auffällige Eigenschaft ist der Humor: Er ist der Comic-Subkultur (Manga) recht nahe, oft an der Grenze zum Kindischen, mit dem einzigen Anspruch, süß oder „kawai" zu sein. Figuren, für gewöhnlich kleine Tierchen, werden eingesetzt, um alle möglichen Produkte zu bewerben und ihnen das begehrte „süße" Image zu verleihen. Selbst bei Produkten, die auf Erwachsene abzielen, gibt es diesen Trend, der einen „gefühlvolleren" Effekt erzielen soll.

Japanese Graphics Now! nimmt Sie mit auf einen Rundgang zu den Arbeiten von einigen der besten japanischen Designer. Erfreuen Sie sich am Traditionellen und am Modernen, am Minimalistischen und am Chaotischen, am Gefühl für Proportionen und am Süßen. Erfreuen Sie sich vor allem an der einmaligen Gelegenheit, einen näheren Einblick in die japanische Kultur von heute zu gewinnen.

外国から日本を見ると、喧騒に満ちた、あわただしくにぎやかな東京の風景に驚きとショックを感じずにはいられない。単に2000万人以上の人々が往来する大都会というだけではなく、外国人の目からは計り知れない、ほとんど何を意味しているのかわからない看板やポスター、ネオンサインで街中が溢れているからだ。確かに西洋と日本との地理的な距離が、西洋人が自分の目で日本を実際に見ることをむずしくしていることもあるが、しかし現実の東京や日本はそれだけに留まらない。東京の混雑した池袋駅からわずか20分ほど離れた駒場駅のそばには、鯉が池に泳ぐ日本庭園や老人たちが桜を愛でる、信じられないほど静かで穏やかな場所が存在するのだ。それが同じひとつの都市に混在しているのである。

現在の日本は正反対のものが混在する国であり、何もかもが同時に発生する場所だ。日本文化は元来、自分の気持ちを表すにも、食事を供するにも、簡潔さを旨としていた。人々がコミュニケートし合う方法も、しばしばこの簡潔さを強調したものだった。同じことが歌舞伎や浮世絵など、昔ながらの芸術様式にも見られる。ここで最も敬意を払われるのは調和である。同時に、日本にはまったく異なるコミュニケーションのやり方が生まれている。昔ながらの簡潔さとは対照的に、このもうひとつの方法はたいてい、マンガやアニメなど最新の流行に大きく影響され、大胆であわただしく、カラフルである。これらもうひとつの文化は非常に強烈で、それぞれに独自のヒーローが存在する。

日本文化が持つ重要な要素であり、人が何かをしたりコミュニケーションをとったりするために大切なのは文字だ。日本語の書き言葉では規則的に異なる4つの文字種を使う。まず、最も古いのが「漢字」だ。中国を起源とする漢字は日本に少なくとも6世紀頃に入ってきた。漢字は表意文字であり、それぞれ独自の意味を持つ、おびただしい数のシンボルからなり、他の文字との組み合わせによってさまざまな読み方をされる。ふたつ目は46個の音節文字からなる「ひらがな」で、漢字を単純化し、漢字の音を再生する文字だ。ひらがなは奈良時代（710ー794年）に吉備真備によって作られた。みっつ目は奈良時代末期から次の平安時代（794ー1185年）初期の空海という仏教僧が作った「カタカナ」で、ひらがなと類似のものだが、主に外来語を書き表すのに使われる。最後がアルファベットを使ったローマ字である。これはしばしば日本人にとって、西洋人が日本語の文字に対して抱くのと同じ視覚効果を持っている。グラフィック的に言って、日本の活版印刷が使用できる組み合わせは他の多くの文化よりもはるかに多い。

日本人の創作物はこの文字やその他の多様性を探り、どこから導入されたものであろうとメディアやサウンド、ツール、動きなどあらゆるリソースを余すことなく利用する。その一例として、ひらがなの発明なくしては困難だった形式の和歌が平安時代に生まれたことが挙げられる。この環境と日本人の精神性が組み合わさることで、コミュニケーションの方法は常に進化し、新たな適応構造を生み出しては、事実上領域を無限に広げてきたのである。

現代日本で必ず論じられるもうひとつのポイントは、デジタル文化の大きな影響である。この技術は単に利用可能だという域を超えて、当然のように日常的に使われている。携帯電話から家庭用パソコンまで、このハイテク指向の社会は可能な限りのコミュニケーション・ツールすべてを利用するのだ。天気予報を知りたい、本を買いたい、ピザを注文したい――どんなことでも電子的に処理できる。この結果、多くの創造物が業界の規模や影響に、またこうした思考方法の拡大に対応するようになってきたと思われる。それで、日本が生み出す作品スタイルは主にふたつに分けられるようになった。ひとつは非常に煩雑で、単語や色彩、イメージが豊かなもの、そしてふたつ目は大きな絵にわずかなメッセージを持たせた、明瞭でシンプルなものだ。しかも両者共にそれぞれユニークなオリジナル・スタイルを持っている。

生産面から言えば、日本市場は大きいので、大多数のクリエーターが海外へ進出する必要がない。それで、時間のほとんどを極めて日本的なアプローチに注ぎ込むことができる。これが日本のデザインのアイデンティティーをいっそう色濃くすることに繋がるのである。本書はポスターや広告、ロゴ、デザイン印刷、印刷物やウェブ・デザインの形態を見ることができる、大多数のものの見方やライフスタイルを表す断片として捉え、さらにこの活気に溢れた文化を商業的な対応物の一部として解釈した。

本書には、CMを数本と、アートディレクターやデザイナー、CMディレクターたちのインタビューを収録し、日本人クリエーターたちの考えを紹介する興味深い特集DVD が付いている。また、最近オープンした東京広告博物館が制作した日本の広告や西洋の影響、そして最も重要な時代の歴史的ミニ・ドキュメンタリーも収録されている。DVD は地域「0」、つまり地域制限がないので、世界中どこの地域コードでも使用できるようになっている。

日本のデザイン・スタイルについては好き嫌いがあるだろうが、全体像として、このユニークなコミュニケーション方法の重要性に気づく必要性はあるはずである。何よりも、世界中のデザイナーやコミュニケーションの専門家にとって、日本のデザインはヴィジュアルの参考書としての役割をこれまで長らく演じてきている。本書は日本のデザイン事務所およそ80社の最新作を収録し、コミュニケーションや広告、デザインに新たな方法を模索する人たちへのヴィジュアル・ガイドとして役立つようにした。どうか楽しんでいただきたい。

D:デザイナー／デザインオフィス
d:デザイン
ad:アートディレクター
adv:広告主
pr:PR
art w:作品
a:アート
cg:コンピュータグラフィック
p:写真
c:コピーライト
cc:クリエイティブディレクター
cl:クライアント
i:イラスト

When Japan is seen from abroad, inevitably people are both amazed and shocked by scenes dominated by the clamour of busy, bustling Tokyo. The capital is not only big, with its more than 20 million people coming and going, but also inscrutable in the eyes of the non-Japanese. The city is packed with signboards, posters, and light boxes that can be hardly understood. Moreover, the physical distance between western countries and the islands of Japan makes it hard for people to come and see what the country is about with their own eyes. But the city of Tokyo and Japan itself is not only that. Just 20 minutes away from Tokyo's crowded Ikebukuro Station, you will find the quietest and most peaceful place imaginable, with carp swimming in a lake, and elderly people contemplating cherry blossoms - a Japanese Zen garden in the very centre of the city.

Today Japan is a country of contrasts, a place where everything occurs simultaneously. Japanese culture is originally based on the simplicity of things, whether in the way you express your feelings or serve the food. The manner in which people communicate also often highlights this simplicity. The same can easily be seen in traditional art forms, such as Kabuki theatre and Ukiyo-e woodcuts. Harmony is the most respected value here. At the same time, another completely different approach to communication has emerged in Japan. In contrast to the traditional simplicity, this other approach is usually brash, busy, colourful, and mainly influenced by other, more recent popular currents in Japan, such as Manga, the comic magazine scene, and Anime, the animated movies. These other cultures are very strong and have their own national heroes. Among the many important aspects of Japanese culture, and the consequences it has for how one does things and communicates, is the written language. Japanese writing regularly uses four different alphabets. The first and oldest is Kanji, originating from China and introduced to the island around the 6th century, if not earlier. Kanji is an ideographic system consisting of thousands of symbols each with its own meaning, which can be read as representing a variety of sounds, depending on the combination in which they appear. Secondly, the Japanese also use Hiragana, a phonetic alphabet that consists of 46 symbols for writing Japanese words, as well as for simplifying and reproducing the sounds of Kanji. It was created by Kibi-no-Makibi during the Nara Period (710 to 794). Thirdly, they use Katakana, which is similar to Hiragana but mainly used to write foreign words. It was created by a Buddhist priest known as Kuukai, who lived at the end of the Nara Period and at the beginning of the subsequent period, named Heian (794 to 1185). Finally, they also use the Roman alphabet, which often has the same aesthetic appeal for them that the Japanese symbols have for Westerners. Graphically speaking, the possibilities for combination offered by Japanese typography are far greater than those available in most other cultures.

The Japanese creations explore this and other diversities, and make full use of all the resources in terms of media, sounds, tools, movements, etc, no matter where they are from. One example is the Heian Period, which saw the invention of Japanese poetry, a literary form that was difficult before the invention of Hiragana. This environment, combined with the Japanese mind set, has generated a virtually boundless territory for exploration, where the way of communicating is always in evolution and undergoing new adaptations.

Another point constantly discussed today is the strong presence of digital culture in Japan. Technology is not simply available but also used on a daily basis. From mobile phones to home computers, this high-tech-oriented society makes use of all the possible communication tools. No matter what you do, if you want to see a weather forecast, buy a book or order a pizza, it all can be done electronically. The result can also be seen in the way many creations have responded to the size and influence of the industry, and to the spread of this way of thinking. So the works from Japan can be mostly divided into two main styles. One that is very busy, full of words, colour, and images, and the second one that is clear and simple, having one big picture and few words. Yet both in their own ways are original and unique.

In terms of production, the market in Japan is big enough that most creators do not need to go outside for jobs, and can most of the time adopt a very local approach - which reinforces the identity of the design in the region. Almost every conceivable vision of Japan and every consequence of its lifestyle has been captured in this book in the form of posters, ads, logos, print designs, printed media and web design. It is a showcase not only of works, but above all of the way this vibrant culture is translated into its commercial counterpart.

This book also comes with a DVD, which has many interesting features to give an inside view of the Japanese creators, including interviews with art directors, designers, a commercial movie director, as well as some commercial movies. The DVD also features a historic mini-documentary on advertising in Japan, the influences of the West, and its most important periods. It was done in the recently opened Advertising Museum Tokyo. The DVD is region "0" or region-free, so it works with all region codes.

One may or may not like the style of many of the Japanese designs, but it is crucial to realize the importance of this unique approach to communication as a whole. More than that, for a long time now it has served as a visual reference for designers and communication professionals worldwide. Japanese Graphics Now! showcases recent works from about 80 design offices in Japan, and intends to serve as a visual guide for those who seek new ways in communications, advertising and design. Have a nice trip.

Symbols for the captions:
D: Designer /Design Office
d: design
ad: art direction
adv: advertiser
pr: public relationship
art w: art work
a: art
cg: computer graphics
p: photography
c: copywrite
cd: creative direction
cl: client
i: illustration

Lorsqu'ils regardent le Japon de loin, les gens sont inévitablement impressionnés et choqués par la clameur d'un Tokyo très affairé. La capitale n'est pas seulement gigantesque, avec ses quelque 20 millions de gens qui vont et viennent, elle est également insondable aux yeux des non-Japonais. La ville est remplie de panneaux publicitaires, d'affiches et de néons difficiles à comprendre. De plus, la distance physique entre les pays occidentaux et les îles du Japon ne facilite pas la découverte du pays. Mais Tokyo et le Japon ne se limitent pas à cela. A 20 minutes à peine de la gare toujours pleine de monde d'Ikebukuro à Tokyo se trouve l'endroit le plus calme et le plus paisible qu'on puisse imaginer, avec des carpes nageant dans un lac, un jardin zen, et des personnes âgées contemplant des cerisiers en fleur, près de la gare de Komagome, dans la même ville.

Le Japon d'aujourd'hui est un pays de contrastes, un endroit où tout se déroule en même temps. La culture japonaise repose à l'origine sur la simplicité des choses, que ce soit dans la manière d'exprimer des sentiments ou dans la manière de servir la nourriture. La façon dont les gens communiquent met souvent l'accent sur cette simplicité. Il en va de même pour les formes artistiques traditionnelles, telles que le Kabuki et l'Ukiyo-e. L'harmonie est la valeur la plus respectée ici. Parallèlement, une autre manière de communiquer tout à fait différente émerge au Japon.

Contrastant avec la simplicité traditionnelle, cette autre approche est plutôt tape-à-l'œil, affairée, colorée et principalement influencée par d'autres courants populaires plus récents au Japon, tels que les Manga, les bandes dessinées, et l'Anime, les dessins animés. Ces autres cultures sont très présentes et ont leurs propres héros nationaux.

Le langage écrit est l'un des aspects les plus importants de la culture japonaise, avec ses conséquences sur la manière dont les gens communiquent et font les choses. L'écriture japonaise utilise régulièrement quatre jeux de caractères différents. Le premier et le plus ancien est le Kanji, originaire de Chine et introduit sur l'archipel aux environs du 6e siècle, ou plus tôt encore. Le Kanji est composé de milliers d'idéogrammes, chacun ayant un sens propre et pouvant être lu comme représentant une variété de sons, en fonction des combinaisons dans lesquelles ils sont ordonnés. Les Japonais utilisent ensuite les 46 caractères de l'Hiragana pour écrire les mots japonais, et pour simplifier et reproduire les sons du Kanji. Il a été créé par Kibi no Makibi pendant la période Nara (de 710 à 794). Ils utilisent également le Katakana, similaire à l'Hiragana, mais employé principalement pour écrire des mots étrangers. Il a été créé par un moine bouddhiste appelé Kuukai, qui a vécu à la fin de la période Nara et au début de la période suivante, appelée Heian (de 794 à 1185). Enfin, ils utilisent l'alphabet romain, pour lequel ils éprouvent le même attrait esthétique que les occidentaux pour les symboles japonais. Graphiquement parlant, les possibilités offertes par la typographie japonaise sont nettement plus importantes que celles qu'offrent la plupart des autres cultures.

Les créations japonaises explorent cette diversité ainsi que d'autres, et tirent pleinement parti de toutes les ressources en termes de supports, de sons, d'outils, de mouvements, etc. quelles que soient leurs provenances. La période Heian en est un bon exemple, qui a vu l'invention de la poésie japonaise, une forme littéraire difficile à exprimer avant l'arrivée de l'Hiragana. Cet environnement, combiné au mode de pensée japonais, a généré un territoire à explorer virtuellement sans limites, où les moyens de communiquer évoluent en permanence et s'adaptent aux nouvelles situations.

Un autre point que l'on ne cesse de discuter aujourd'hui est la forte présence de la culture numérique au Japon. La technologie n'est pas seulement disponible, elle est également utilisée quotidiennement. Des portables aux ordinateurs, cette société orientée sur les technologies de haut niveau utilise tous les outils de communication possibles. Quoi que vous fassiez, que ce soit consulter la météo, acheter un livre ou commander une pizza, tout peut être fait électroniquement. On peut également constater cela dans la manière dont les créations ont réagi à l'importance et l'influence de ce marché, et à cette nouvelle manière de penser. Ainsi, les travaux provenant du Japon peuvent être divisés en deux styles essentiels. Un style dynamique, plein de mots, de couleurs et d'images, et un style clair et simple avec une image principale et quelques mots. Tous deux, à leur manière, sont pourtant originaux et uniques.

En termes de production, le marché japonais est suffisamment vaste pour que la plupart des créateurs n'aient pas besoin de rechercher un emploi à l'extérieur, mais puissent la plupart du temps adopter une approche très locale, qui renforce l'identité des créations de la région. Quasiment toutes les visions imaginables du Japon et les conséquences de son mode de vie ont été recueillies dans cet ouvrage, sous forme d'affiches, de publicités, de logos, d'imprimés et de contenus web. C'est une vitrine de créations, mais c'est avant tout la façon dont cette vibrante culture est traduite dans un but commercial.

Cet ouvrage est fourni avec un DVD contenant de nombreux éléments intéressants qui donnent un aperçu des travaux des créateurs japonais, et notamment des interviews avec des directeurs artistiques, des designers, un réalisateur de films publicitaires, ainsi que des films publicitaires. Le DVD comprend également un mini-documentaire sur l'histoire de la publicité au Japon, les influences de l'Occident et ses périodes les plus importantes. Récemment réalisé dans le cadre de l'ouverture du Musée de la publicité de Tokyo, le DVD est configuré en région 0 (pas de région) pour être visionné dans tous les pays.

Que l'on apprécie ou non le style de certaines créations japonaises, il est crucial de réaliser l'importance de cette approche unique de la communication en un tout. Plus important encore, ces créations ont depuis longtemps déjà servi de référence visuelle aux designers et aux professionnels de la communication du monde entier. Japanese Graphics Now! illustre les travaux récents de 80 agences de design japonaises et compte servir de guide à ceux qui recherchent de nouvelles manières de communiquer, de faire de la publicité ou de concevoir. Bon voyage !

D : Designer / Agence de design
d : design
ad : direction artistique
adv : publicitaire
pr : relations publiques
art w : graphique
a : art
cg : image
p : photographie
r : rédaction publicitaire
cd : direction de création
cl : client
i : illustration

Wer Japan von außen betrachtet, ist unweigerlich erstaunt und erschreckt zugleich vom Gewühl des betriebsamen, geschäftigen Tokio. Die Stadt mit ihren mehr als 20 Millionen Einwohnern und Pendlern ist nicht nur groß, sondern für den Nichtjapaner auch undurchschaubar. Überall hängen unverständliche Wegweiser, Plakate und Leuchtreklamen. Bedingt durch die enormen Entfernungen zwischen den japanischen Inseln und den westlichen Ländern ist es darüber hinaus schwer, selbst zu kommen und mit eigenen Augen zu sehen, wie das Land nun wirklich ist. Täte man dies, würde man merken, dass Tokio und Japan ganz anders sind, als es der erste Eindruck vermittelt. Nur zwanzig Minuten von der hektischen U-Bahn-Station Ikebukuro in Tokio entfernt, befindet sich der stillste, friedlichste Ort, den man sich nur vorstellen kann: Karpfen schwimmen im Teich, ältere Leute erfreuen sich an der Kirschblüte - ein japanischer Zen-Garten mitten in der Stadt.

Das heutige Japan ist ein Land der Kontraste, ein Ort, an dem verschiedenste Dinge zugleich geschehen. Die ursprüngliche Grundlage der japanischen Kultur ist die Einfachheit, sei es in der Art, wie man seinen Gefühlen Ausdruck verleiht oder wie man das Essen serviert. Einfachheit spielt auch in der Kommunikation eine große Rolle. Dieses Ideal lässt sich auch in traditionellen Kunstformen wie dem Kabuki-Theater und dem Ukiyo-e-Holzschnitt leicht erkennen. Harmonie ist der Wert, der am höchsten geschätzt wird. Gleichzeitig hat sich jedoch in Japan ein weiterer Ansatz in der Kommunikation herausgebildet. Im Gegensatz zum traditionellen Kult der Reduktion geht es hier laut, hektisch und bunt zu, gewinnen andere, jüngere Strömungen in der japanischen Populärkultur wie etwa die Manga, Comicbücher, oder die Anime, Zeichentrickfilme, großen Einfluss. Sie sind weit verbreitet und haben ihre eigenen, im ganzen Land bekannten Helden.

Zu den wichtigen Facetten japanischer Kultur zählt die geschriebene Sprache, die einen großen Einfluss darauf hat, wie Dinge gemacht und kommuniziert werden. In der japanischen Schriftsprache werden vier verschiedene Alphabete nebeneinander benutzt. Das älteste ist Kanji, das im 6. Jahrhundert, wenn nicht früher, aus China auf die Inseln kam. Kanji ist ein ideografisches System, das aus Tausenden von Symbolen mit jeweils verschiedener Bedeutung besteht, die auch als verschiedene Laute gelesen werden können, je nachdem, in welcher Reihenfolge sie auftreten. Als zweites verwenden die Japaner die Schrift Hiragana, ein phonetisches Alphabet, das aus 46 Silbenzeichen besteht. In dem japanische Wörter geschrieben und die Lautwerte des Kanji vereinfacht nachgeahmt werden. Die Schrift wurde in der Nara-Zeit (710-794) von Kibi-no-Makibi geschaffen. Als drittes gibt es das Katakana, das dem Hiragana verwandt ist, jedoch hauptsächlich zum Schreiben ausländischer Wörter benutzt wird. Es wurde von einem buddhistischen Mönch namens Kukai erfunden, der am Ende der Nara-Zeit und am Anfang der darauf folgenden Heian-Zeit (794-1185) lebte. Schließlich wird auch das lateinische Alphabet benutzt, das für die Japaner einen ähnlichen ästhetischen Reiz besitzt wie japanische Schriftzeichen für Europäer und Amerikaner. Vom grafischen Gesichtspunkt aus betrachtet bietet die japanische Typografie weit mehr Kombinationsmöglichkeiten als fast alle anderen Kulturen der Welt.

Die kreativen Arbeiten Japans feiern diese Vielgestaltigkeit und machen sich sämtliche Ressourcen zunutze, die an Medien, Klängen, Hilfsmitteln, Bewegungen usw. zur Verfügung stehen, ungeachtet ihrer Herkunft. Ein Beispiel dafür ist die Heian-Zeit, in der die japanische Dichtung ihren Ursprung nahm, eine literarische Form, die vor der Entwicklung des Hiragana kaum denkbar gewesen wäre. Dieses Umfeld hat zusammen mit dem japanischen Geist ein praktisch grenzenloses Spielfeld für neue Ideen geschaffen, in dem sich die Kommunikation in ständiger Evolution befindet und immer wieder von neuem wandelt und anpasst.

Ein anderer Punkt, über den heute sehr viel gesprochen wird, ist die starke Präsenz digitaler Kultur in Japan. Hochtechnologie ist weit verbreitet und im täglichen Leben allgegenwärtig. Von Handys bis zu PCs nutzt diese stark hightech-orientierte Gesellschaft alle möglichen Hilfsmittel zur Kommunikation. Alles lässt sich elektronisch erledigen, ob man die Wettervorhersage sehen, ein Buch kaufen oder eine Pizza bestellen möchte. Das Resultat lässt sich auch an der Art ablesen, wie das Design auf die Größe und den Einfluss der Elektronikindustrie sowie auf die Verbreitung der mit ihr einhergehenden Denkweise reagiert. Kreative Arbeiten aus Japan können also zum Großteil in zwei Hauptstile unterteilt werden: einen sehr geschäftigen Stil, der in Wörtern, Farben und Bildern schwelgt, und einen zweiten, der klar und einfach ist und aus einem großen Bild mit wenigen Wörtern besteht. Beide sind auf ihre Weise originell und einzigartig.

Der japanische Markt ist so groß, dass die meisten Kreativen nicht im Ausland nach Arbeit zu suchen brauchen und zumeist eine stark lokal gefärbte Herangehensweise praktizieren können – was wiederum zur Verstärkung der Identität des japanischen Designs führt. In diesem Buch ist nahezu jede denkbare Vision von Japan und seinen Lebensstilen in der Form von Plakaten, Anzeigen, Logos, Druckgrafiken, Printmedien und Webdesign zu finden. Es ist ein Kompendium nicht nur der Arbeiten, sondern insbesondere der Art, wie diese höchst lebendige Kultur in kommerzielles Design übersetzt wird.

In diesem Buch ist auch eine DVD enthalten, deren viele interessante Beiträge einen Insiderblick auf die japanischen Kreativen erlaubt; geboten werden Interviews mit Art Directors, Designern, dem Regisseur eines Werbefilms sowie einige Beispiele von Werbefilmen. Auf der DVD gibt es auch einen Minidokumentarfilm über die Geschichte der Werbung in Japan mit ihren wichtigsten Phasen und den Einflüssen des Westens. Er wurde im neu eröffneten Advertising Museum in Tokio erstellt. Die DVD hat den Regionalcode „0", ist also codefree und kann daher auf allen DVD-Playern abgespielt werden.

Ob einem nun der Stil des japanischen Designs gefällt oder nicht: Es ist sehr wichtig, die enorme Bedeutung dieses einzigartigen Ansatzes für die Kommunikation insgesamt zu erkennen. Darüber hinaus dient die japanische Grafik seit langem als visueller Bezugspunkt für Designer und Kommunikationsexperten auf der ganzen Welt. Japanese Graphics Now! bietet einen Überblick über neue Arbeiten aus ca. 80 Designagenturen in Japan und soll denjenigen als visueller Reiseführer dienen, die nach neuen Wegen in Kommunikation, Werbung und Design suchen. Wir wünschen eine angenehme Reise.

Symbole für die Bildunterschriften:
D: Designer /Designagentur
d: Design
ad: Art Director
adv: Advertiser
pr: Public Relations
art w: Kunstwerk
a: Kunst
cg: Computergrafik
p: Fotografie
c: Texter
cd: Creative Director
cl: Kunde
i: Illustration

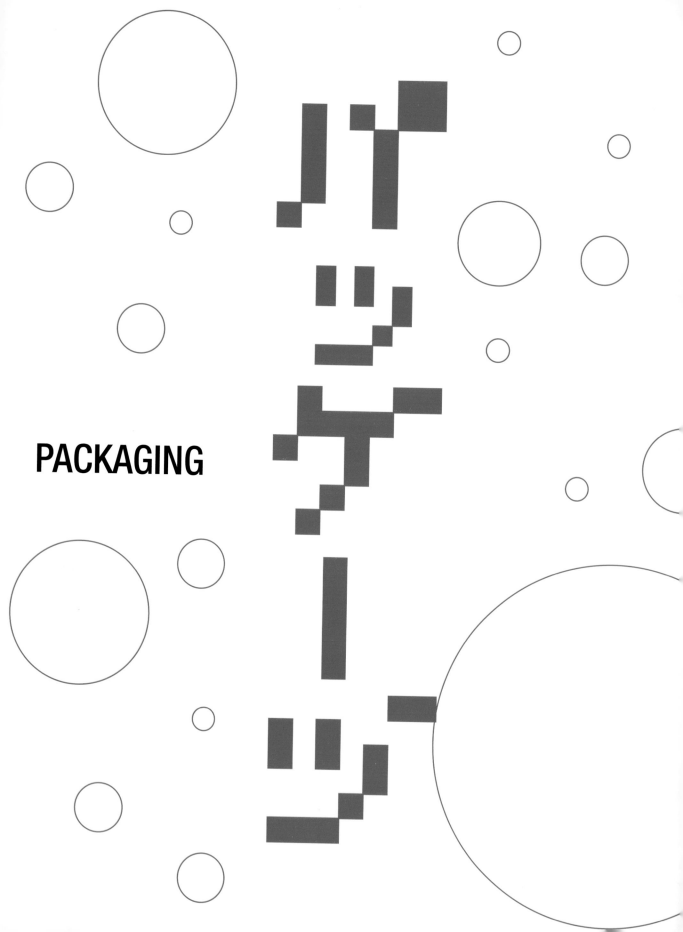

PACKAGING

ポテトフィリング

（調理パン・サンドイッチ用）

北海道士幌農協の責任指導により、
ていねいに栽培された高品質の馬鈴薯だけを使用しています。

http://www.ajinomoto-catering.com/

1kg

ゆで卵フィリング

（調理パン・サンドイッチ用）

指定農家から直送された国産の鶏卵だけを使用した、
ゆで卵本来の風味が特長の調理パン・サンドイッチ用のフィリングです。

http://www.ajinomoto-catering.com/

1kg

ふんわり
スクランブルエッグ
フィリング

（調理パン・サンドイッチ用）

ふんわりと柔らかいスクランブルエッグと、マヨネーズがほどよくなじんだ、
調理パン・サンドイッチ用のフィリングです。

http://www.ajinomoto-catering.com/

1kg

しこしこ
スパゲティサラダ

当社の技術をいかし、パスタのコシに持続性があります。

当社の技術をいかし、しこしことした歯ごたえのあるスパゲティと、マイルドな味つけのマヨネーズが
ほどよくなじんだサラダです。スパゲティは食べやすい長さにカットしました。

http://www.ajinomoto-catering.com/

1kg

しこしこ
たらこスパゲティ

当社の技術をいかし、パスタのコシに持続性があります。

当社の技術をいかし、しこしことした歯ごたえのあるスパゲティと、クリーミーでコクのあるたらこ風味の
ソースがほどよくなじんだサラダです。スパゲティは食べやすい長さにカットしました。

http://www.ajinomoto-catering.com/

1kg

士幌ポテト

大きなポテトの彩りサラダ

北海道士幌農協の責任指導によりていねいに栽培された高品質の馬鈴薯だけを使用しています。

http://www.ajinomoto-catering.com/

1kg

士幌ポテト

うすあじサラダ

北海道士幌農協の責任指導により、ていねいに栽培された高品質の馬鈴薯だけを使用しています。

http://www.ajinomoto-catering.com/

1kg

士幌ポテト

男爵サラダ

（減農薬栽培 男爵いも、たまねぎ、にんじん使用）

北海道士幌農協の責任指導により、ていねいに栽培された高品質の馬鈴薯だけを使用しています。

http://www.ajinomoto-catering.com/

1kg

しこしこ
マカロニサラダ

当社の技術をいかし、パスタのコシに持続性があります。

当社の技術をいかし、しこしことした歯ごたえのあるエルボーマカロニと、
マイルドな味つけのマヨネーズがほどよくなじんだサラダです。

http://www.ajinomoto-catering.com/

1kg

↓ Mitsukan "Bistro vinegar":
Seasoning vinegar
D: Toru Ito
cd: Kenji Urabe

Mitsukan "2033": vinegar
D: Toru Ito
cd: Kenji Urabe

→ Benibana Brand Grape Oil
D: Minato Ishikawa

パッケージ

38

Dole

アスパラガスとしめじの
炒め物用

野菜たっぷりヘルシー料理

新鮮素材で、かんたん手作り。
Cookin'工房

■ アレンジ自在、素材のおいしさ生きています！

P-プラス

調理時間 約10分
1〜2人前

要冷蔵

香りもおいしいコンビネーションです。
グリーンアスパラガス・しめじ

Dole

イタリア風野菜煮込み
カポナータ用

野菜たっぷりヘルシー料理

新鮮素材で、かんたん手作り。
Cookin'工房

■ みずみずしいおいしさ
■ 洗わずに安心してそのまま使えます

調理時間 約35分
3〜4人前

要冷蔵

トマトを加えて煮込むだけです。
なす・パプリカ・ズッキーニ・ペコロス・ローリエ

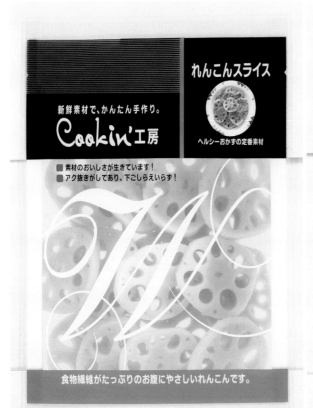

新鮮素材で、かんたん手作り。
Cookin'工房

れんこんスライス

ヘルシーおかずの定番素材

■ 素材のおいしさが生きています！
■ アク抜きがしてあり、下ごしらえいらず！

食物繊維がたっぷりのお腹にやさしいれんこんです。

里芋

ヘルシーおかずの定番素材

新鮮素材で、かんたん手作り。
Cookin'工房

■ 素材のおいしさが生きています！
■ アク抜きがしてあり、下ごしらえいらず！

要冷蔵

煮物、炒め物に、ほくほくのおいしさです。

Calbee

本場上海中華味
Chinese Okoge

ジュワッと広がるおこげの香ばしさ。

期間限定

賞味期限

中華おこげ

Calbee

うまさピリ辛!
Nori Tougarashi

海苔と唐辛子の刺激的なおいしさ。

期間限定

賞味期限

のり唐辛子

← Chinese okoge for Calbee
  D: Emiko Shibasaki

↓ Karada kaicho for Meiji
  D: Emiko Shibasaki

Nori tougarashi for Calbee
D: Emiko Shibasaki

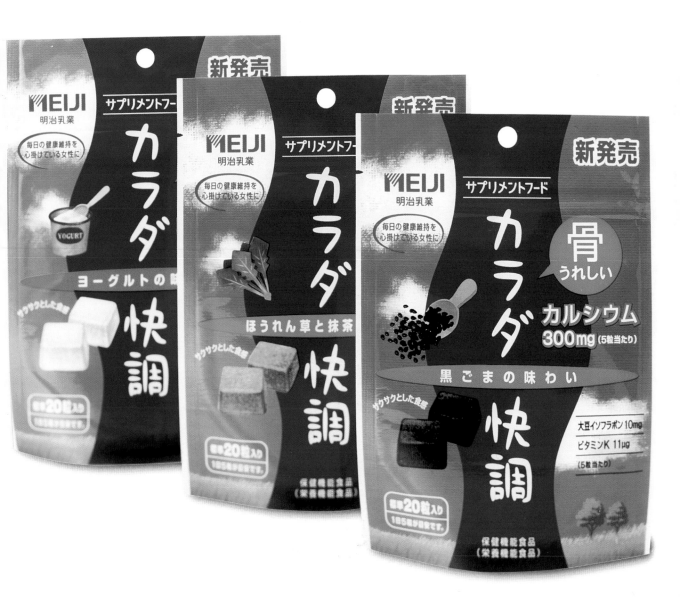

Calbee

Café au Lait

Café de Cereal

カフェオレ
Café au Lait

牛乳をかけると広がる
カフェオレ風味
のシリアル

for your
for your

NET

Calbee

Royal Milk Tea

Café de Cereal

ロイヤルミルクティー
Royal Milk Tea

牛乳をかけると広がる
ロイヤルミルクティー風味
のシリアル

for your fine morning
for your healthy life

NET100g

↓ Kajitsuryoku (Candy)　　　　→ Lotte Mint Blue Gum
　 D: Sio Design Co. Ltd.　　　　　Lotte Xylitol Gum, Pink mint
　　　　　　　　　　　　　　　　　Lotte Green Gum
　　　　　　　　　　　　　　　　　Lotte Xylitol Gum
　　　　　　　　　　　　　　　　　D: Taku Satoh

46

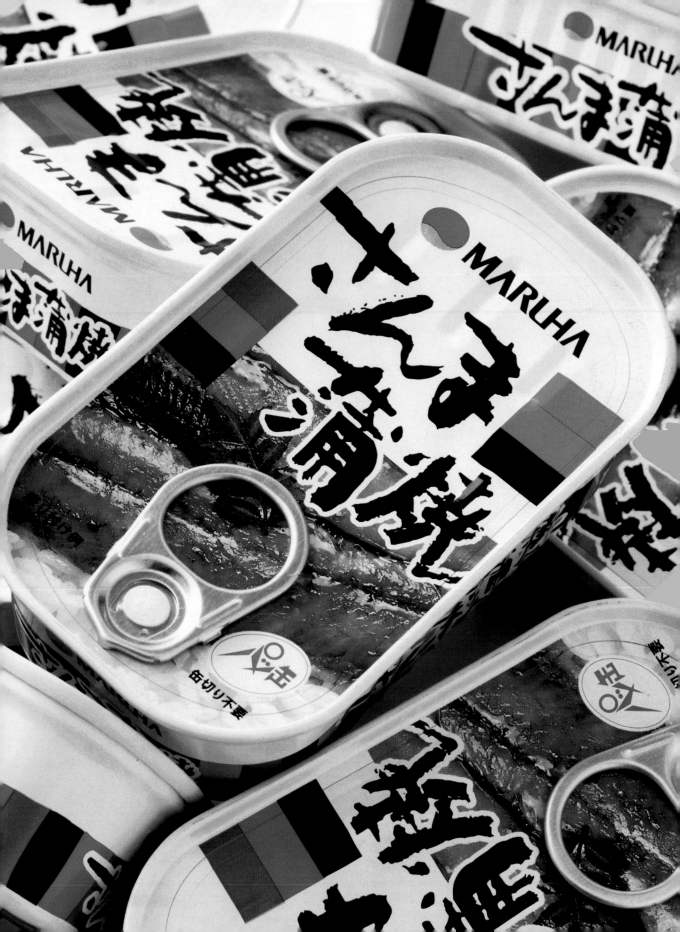

Apple pudding
D: Aquas

↓ Ice-cream
D: Aquas

➜ Bone-biscuits for pets
D: Aquas

Bonito-jerky for pets
D: Aquas

58

犬用おやつ

ONE LAC

お気にッ
低カロリー

ボーンビスケット

骨を丈夫にする
3つの特長

乳性カルシウム配合
グルコサミン配合
ビタミンD強化

合成保存料・着色料は使用しておりません

国産品

ONE LAC

～ネコちゃんのおつまみ～
かつおジャーク
猫用

うまくてヘルシー
かつおだ
ニャン！

ONE LAC

～ワンちゃんのおつまみ～
かつおジャーク
犬用

うまくてヘルシー
かつおだ
ワン！

↓ Figure-Package
　To-fu oyako 400% kubrick pack
　D: Devilrobots Inc.

→ To-fu box
　D: Devilrobots Inc.

→ Chinese Diet Tea for Gourmet house
　D: Minato Ishikawa

パッケージ　60

Figure-Package
To-fu oyako kubrick pack
D: Devilrobots Inc.

自然の恵みがつまってます

木屋平村のニワトリは、高原に放し飼いにされています。
ヒナの時から天然の緑餌を食べて大切に育てられました。
その健康なニワトリから産まれた高原たまごは、
卵黄の色が濃く、卵白の粘りが違います。
ビタミンが豊富で栄養価が高いのも特徴です。

頭のよくなる卵

「高原たまご」には世界が注目のDHA（ドコサヘキサエン酸）を
普通の卵の2倍以上含んでいます。
DHAは目をよくし、コレステロールをコントロールしたり、
脳の記憶・学習機能を高めます。
また、がんの抑制・抗アレルギー作用（アトピー性皮膚炎）
などに効果があるのでは、と研究が進められています。

← Eggs Package
D: Takaaki Fujimoto
cl: Koyadaira Village

Package for food boiled down in soy
D: Takaaki Fujimoto

↓ Kikuya Japanese cake
D: Takaaki Fujimoto

↓ Baked confectionery gift
D: Mihiko Hachiuma

→ Ice cream
D: Mihiko Hachiuma

Ice cream gift package
D: Mihiko Hachiuma

パッケージ

64

← Betty's Sweet Cheese cake
D: Mihiko Hachiuma

↓ Ice dessert for families
D: Mihiko Hachiuma

Potato confectionery bag
D: Mihiko Hachiuma

Betty's Sweet roll cake gift
D: Mihiko Hachiuma

← Tempura gift
D: Mihiko Hachiuma

Assortment of tempura for souvenir
D: Mihiko Hachiuma

↓ Potato confectionery
D: Mihiko Hachiuma

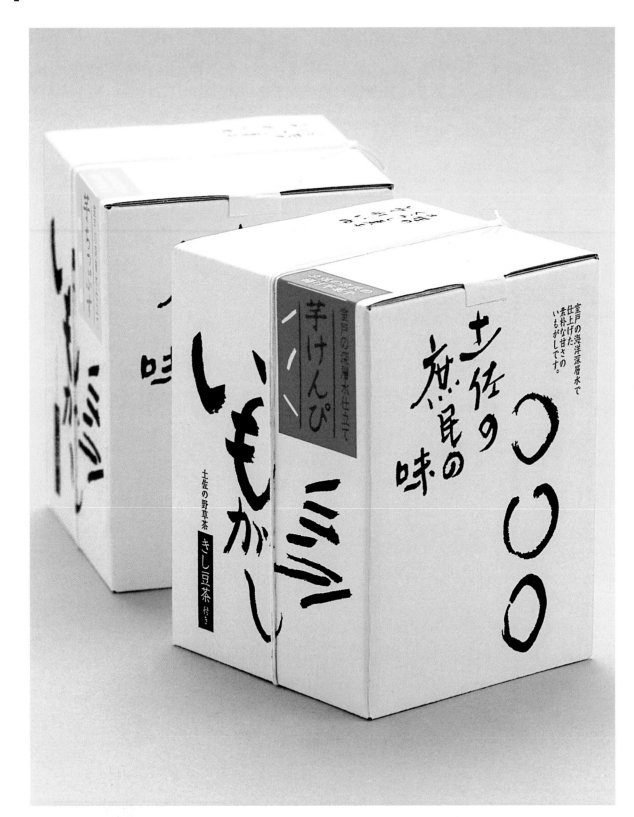

Sweet bean paste and
natural Japanese tea gift
D: Mihiko Hachiuma

Rice cracker
D: Mihiko Hachiuma

Sweet bean paste for souvenir
D: Mihiko Hachiuma

↓ Joyeux nöel
D: K note

→ Chocolat ride
D: K note

Honey lemon jelly
D: K note

パッケージ 72

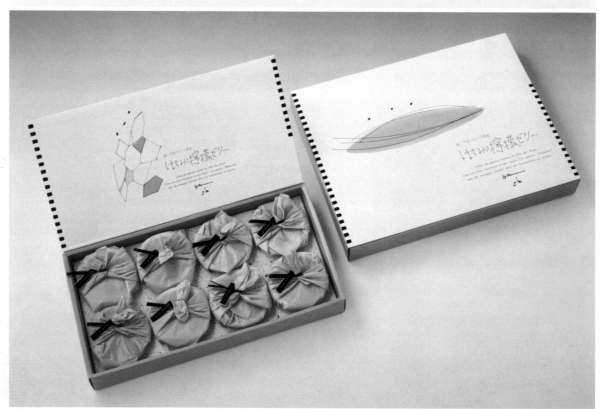

CHOCOLAT RIDE

B Billancourt

Chocolat Ride HIGH MILK

Chocolat Ride HIGH MILK

Chocolat Ride SWEET

Chocolat Ride SWEET

Chocolat Ride SWEET

ビアンクール

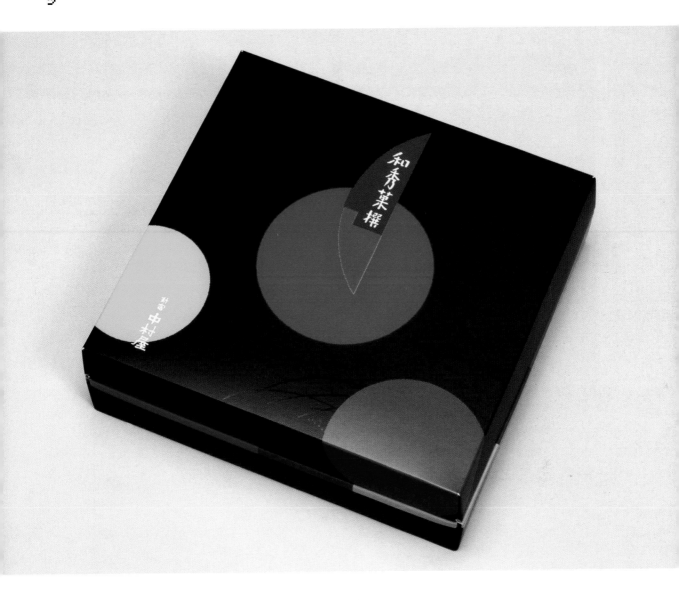

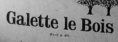

← Innocence
D: K note

Truffes
D: K note

↓ Juliette
D: K note

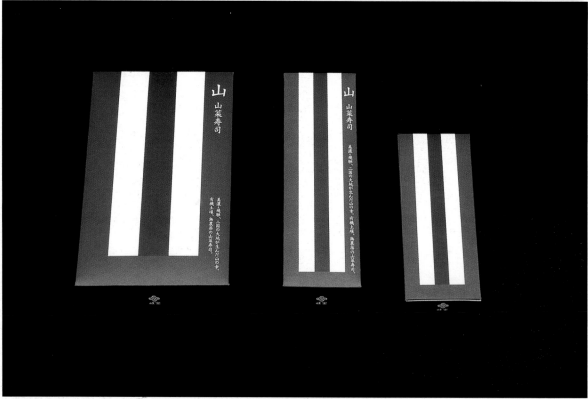

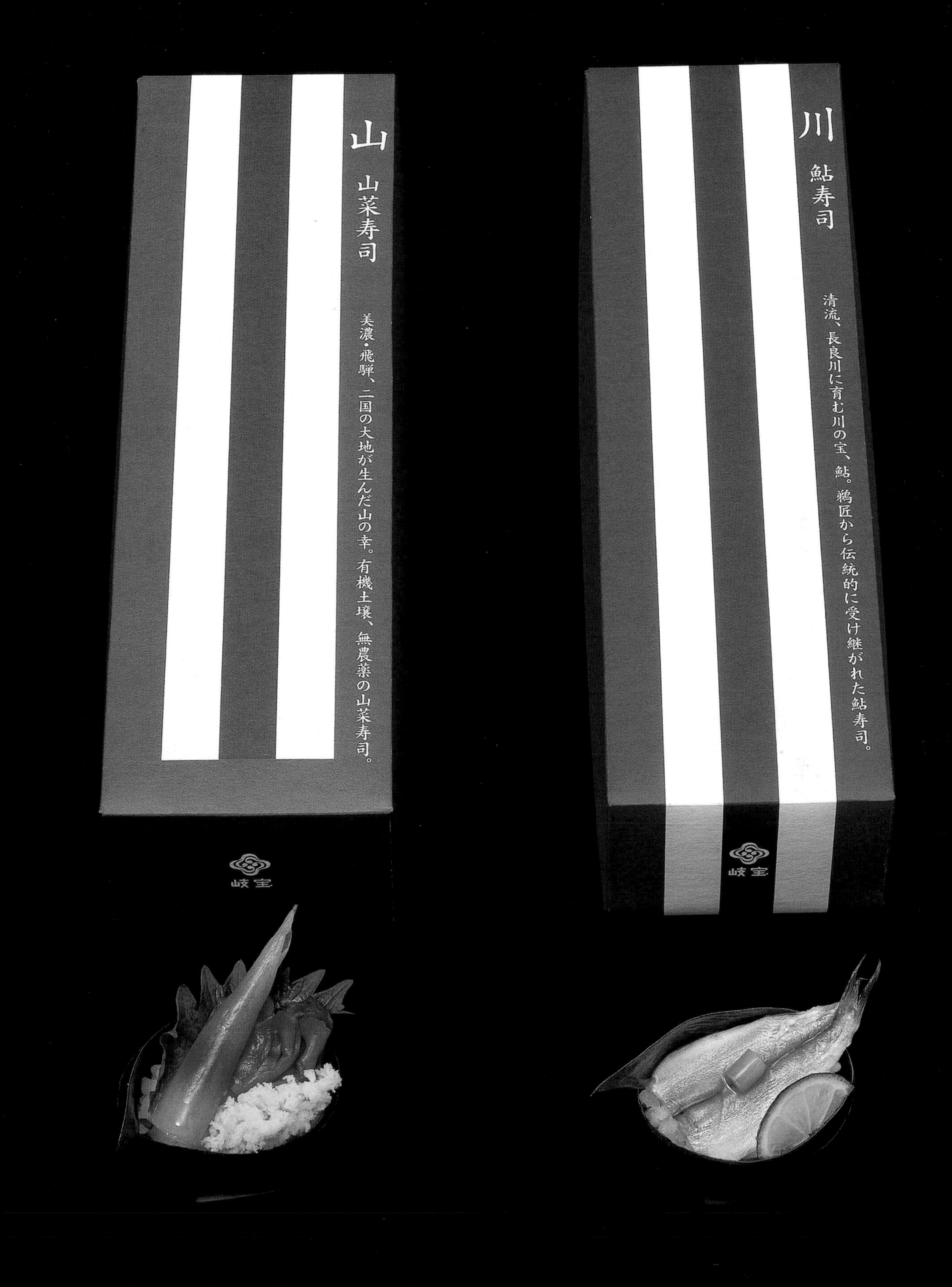

山 山菜寿司

美濃・飛騨、二国の大地が生んだ山の幸。有機土壌、無農薬の山菜寿司。

岐宝

川 鮎寿司

清流、長良川に育む川の宝、鮎。鵜匠から伝統的に受け継がれた鮎寿司。

岐宝

バッケージ

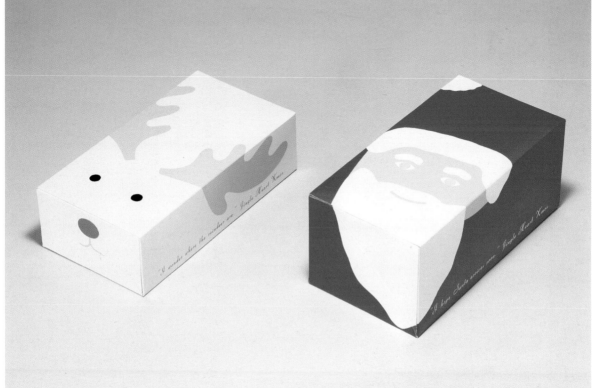

↓ Package for boiled fish pastes
   D: Takaaki Fujimoto
   cl: Awaji Kamaboko Akiyama
   d: Takaaki Fujimoto

→ Tokyo Azuki Glaces
   D: Taku Satoh

88

パッケージ

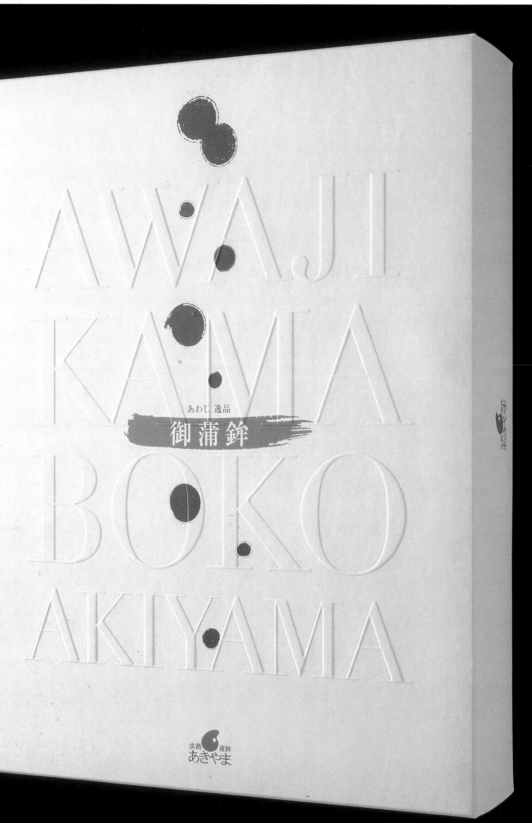

東京
あずき
グラッセ

← Beverages
D: Aquas

↓ Jelly to drink
D: Aquas

Baby beverage
D: Aquas

Kirin Lager Beer
Soccer Design Can Package
D: Butterfly Stroke Inc.
cl: Kirin Brewery Co.,LTD.
cd+ad+d: Katsunori Aoki
cd: Hidenori Azuma
d: Kana Takakuwa
i: Bunpei Yorifuji

→ Kirin Maroyaka Kobo
D: Minato Ishikawa

BREWED BY KIRIN BREWERY COMPANY, LIMITED
MELLOW
TASTE
まろやか酵母
酵母が生きてる生ビール
Kirin's Premium
KIRIN'S PREMIUM BREW
MAROYAKA KOBO
KIRIN

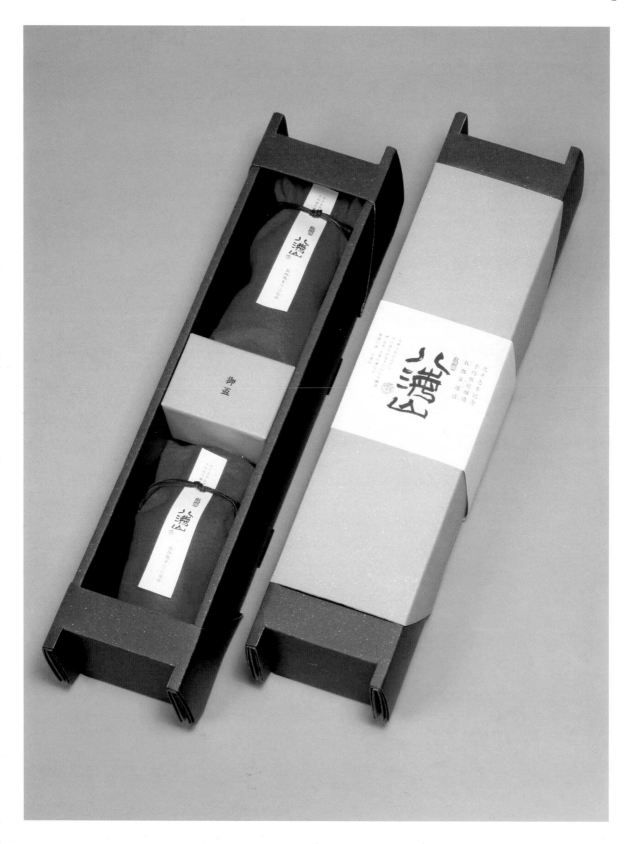

↓ Spirits: Kannoko
D: Hiroshi Mitsuishi

→ Nikka Whisky pure malt
D: Taku Satoh

102

バッケージ

← Hakutsuru Sake New Year Gift Set
Hakutsuru Sake Brewing Co., Ltd.
D: TCD

↓ Zena
D: Taku Satoh

↓ Spirits: Banshoko
D: Hiroshi Mitsuishi

→ Spirits: Kannoko 300ml
D: Hiroshi Mitsuishi

パッケージ

106

↓ Kei Japanese Sake
  D: Sio Design Co., Ltd.

→ Hakkin Japanese rice wine
  D: Kenya Hara
  ad+d: Kenya Hara

パッケージ 108

Hakutsuru Sake Wafujin series
D: TCD
cl: Hakutsuru Sake Brewing Co., Ltd.

Hakutsuru Sake Jousen
D: TCD
cl: Hakutsuru Sake Brewing Co., Ltd.

Hakutsuru Sake Honnori kaoru
D: TCD
cl: Hakutsuru Sake Brewing Co., Ltd.

112

パッケージ

↓ The Cup 200 Sake
D: Akio Okumura

→ Spirits: Isshasenri
D: Hiroshi Mitsuishi

Sake: Gekkeikan
D: Hiroshi Mitsuishi

パッケージ

114

↓ Gekkeikan Petit Moon
D: Hiroshi Mitsuishi

→ Sake Bottle
D: Akio Okumura

116

パッケージ

← Coco Farm & Winery
D: Yoshie Watanabe

↓ Medicinal Liquor: Juntokushu 30ml
D: Hiroshi Mitsuishi

Medicinal Liquor: Juntokushu
D: Hiroshi Mitsuishi

↓ Spirits: Orraqua
D: Hiroshi Mitsuishi

→ The 360th Anniversary Of Gekkeikan
D: Akio Okumura

パッケージ

120

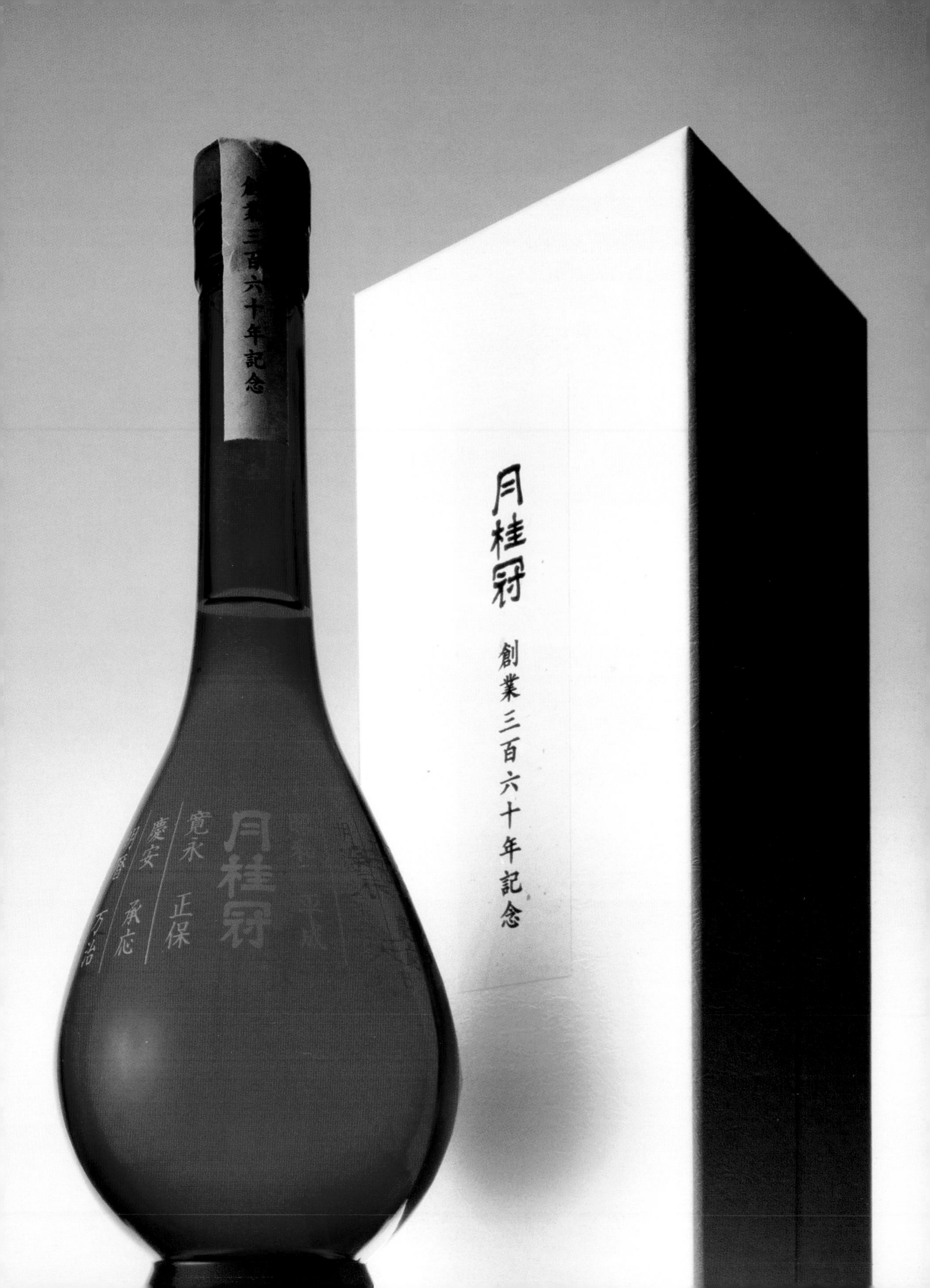
月桂冠
創業三百六十年記念
月桂冠
寛永 正保
慶安 承応

← Sokenbicha
D: Sio Design Co., Ltd.

↓ Meiji Oishii Gyunyu
D: Taku Satoh

Stylish Blue Natural Mineral Water
D: Taku Satoh

Carame NOIR
キャラメ・ノ
UCC
Latteccino
ラテチーノ
〈MILK & BITTER CAFÉ〉
UCC
Mocha LATTE
モカ・ラテ
〈BITTER & SWEET〉
コーヒー
スチール

← Kirin Beverage G,G, Tea
D: TUGBOAT

↓ Kirin Coffe Can Fire
D: TUGBOAT

↓ Kirin Chibi Lemon
D: Samurai

Drink! Smap!
D: Samurai

Kirin Brewery Gokunama
D: Samurai

Kirin Brewery Namakuro
D: Samurai

パッケージ

130

↓ Fan Tee
D: Sio Design Co., Ltd.

Beauté de Kosé
D: Kosé
ad: Fujio Hanawa

Rutína Vital Force
D: Kosé
ad: Fujio Hanawa

→ Stylism
D: Kosé
ad: Fujio Hanawa

STYLISM SHOWER
KOSÉ STYLISM
STYLISM
STYLISM
KOSÉ STYLISM FOOT

← Carté
D: Kosé
ad: Fujio Hanawa

↓ Cosme Decorte Celestial G
D: Kosé
ad: Fujio Hanawa

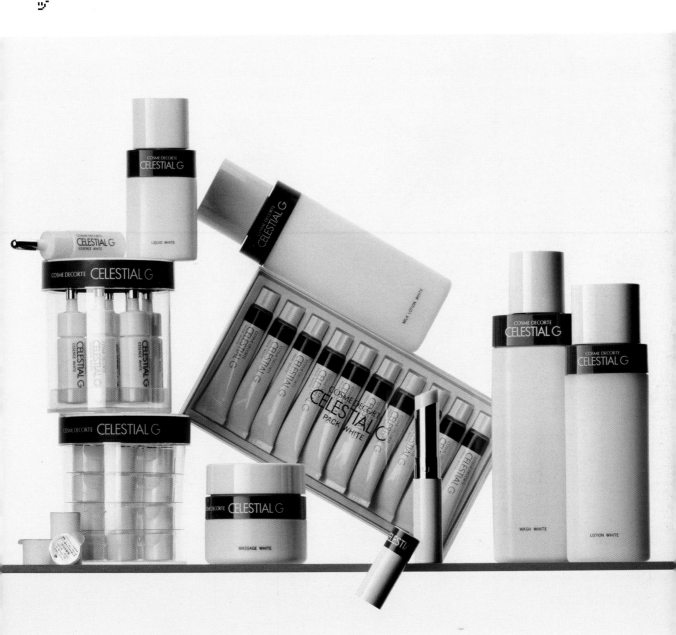

↓ Sekkisei Series
D: Kosé
ad: Fujio Hanawa

→ Beauté de Kosé
D: Kosé
ad: Fujio Hanawa

Selfconscious wéek-end estherapy
D: Kosé
ad: Fujio Hanawa

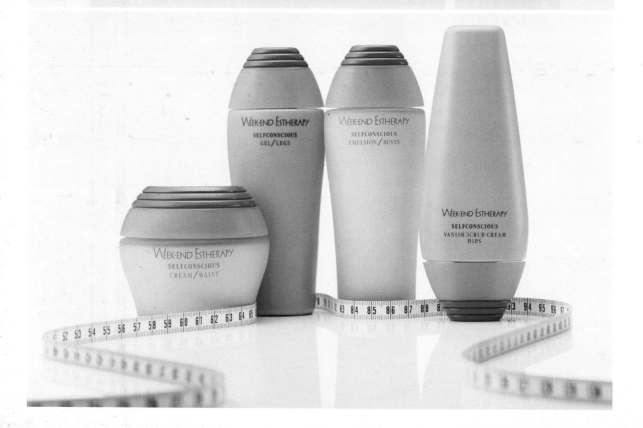

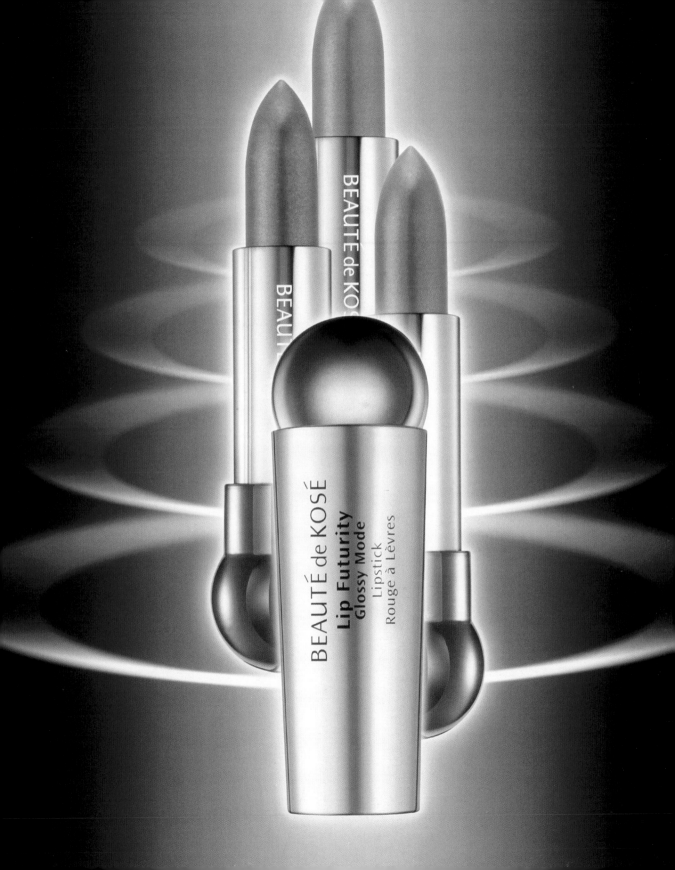

Awake
D: Kosé
ad: Fujio Hanawa

Rutína Pure White
D: Kosé
ad: Fujio Hanawa

Luminous
D: Kosé
ad: Fujio Hanawa

パッケージ

← Styling
D: Kosé
ad: Fujio Hanawa

↓ Tarzan
D: Kosé
ad: Fujio Hanawa

Sports Beauty
D: Kosé
ad: Fujio Hanawa

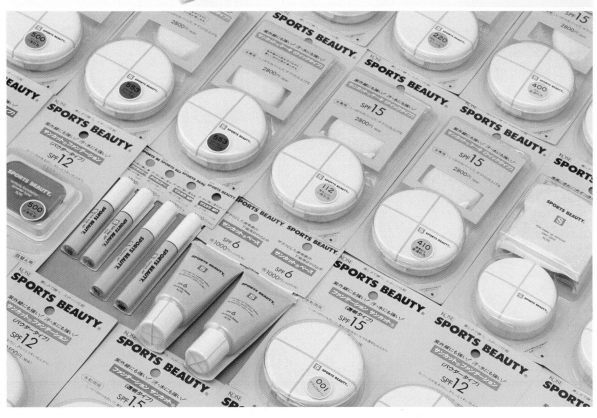

← Deuxseize
D: Kosé
ad: Fujio Hanawa

Intelligé
D: Kosé
ad: Fujio Hanawa

↓ Infinity
D: Kosé
ad: Fujio Hanawa

← Luminous
D: Kosé
ad: Fujio Hanawa

Fasio
D: Kosé
ad: Fujio Hanawa

↓ Phytorium
D: Kosé
ad: Fujio Hanawa

← Minä perhonen
Shopping bag
D: Bluemark Inc.

↓ Afloat-f
D: Buttterfly Stroke Inc.
cl: Eternal co.,Ltd.
cd+ad+d: Katsunori Aoki

↓ Round box for confectionery gift
D: Mihiko Hachiuma

→ Tomitaro Makino Museum shop
D: Mihiko Hachiuma

Betty's Sweet sprinng gift
D: Mihiko Hachiuma

↓ Poeta
D: Ken Miki

→ Two tops
D: Ken Miki

パッケージ

152

← Float
D: Sayuri Studio, Inc.

↓ Candle 0015/0017
D: Sayuri Studio, Inc.

↓ H2O Fluid
D: Sayuri Studio, Inc.

Shiseido 5S
D: Sayuri Studio, Inc.

→ Remede
D: Sayuri Studio, Inc.

パッケージ

156

← B·E
D: TCD
cl: Naris Up Cosmetics Co., Ltd.

↓ Prirism
D: TCD
cl: Naris Up Cosmetics Co., Ltd.

I Wish, Skin care products
D: Toru Ito
cd: Minoru Shiokawa
ad: Benoit Higel

Carita "Le corps", Body care products
D: Toru Ito

Carita "Le cheveu", Hair care products
D: Toru Ito

162

パッケージ

Shiseido Relaxina, Fragrance water
D: Toru Ito
cd: Minoru Shiokawa

➜ RMK skincare series
D: Taku Satoh

Taihei Chemical Industrial Co., Ltd.
Washing liquid for dentistries
D: TCD

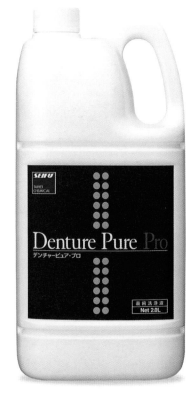

RMK CLEANSING GEL

RMK CLEANSING OIL

RMK CLEANSING MLK

RMK SOAP BAR

RMK SKINTUNER 1

RMK SKINTUNER 2

RMK SKINTUNER 3

RMK SKINTUNER 4

RMK NIGHT DEW

RMK CREAMY SOAP

fec.
pre make-up
formula
3

↓ Shiseido Agree
D: Taku Satoh

→ Neue Men'S
D: Taku Satoh

Neue
D: Taku Satoh

168

neue
MEN'S
WILD TWIST WAX

neue MEN'S
SUPER HARD MOUSSE

neue
HAIR STYLING MOUSSE

neue
HAIR STYLING GEL

moisture
MILD

lotion-l

KOSÉ
COSMEPORT

moisture
MILD

milk lotion

KOSÉ
COSMEPORT

moisture
MILD

lotion-m

KOSÉ
COSMEPORT

MOISTURE MILD
white
lotion-l

さっぱり

KOSÉ
COSMEPORT

MOISTURE MILD
white
milky lotion

KOSÉ
COSMEPORT

MOISTURE MILD
white
lotion-m

しっとり

KOSÉ
COSMEPORT

◀ Moisture, body lotion
D: Taku Satoh

↓ P.G.C.D Protection Integrale Tendre
D: Taku Satoh

GUEST & ME

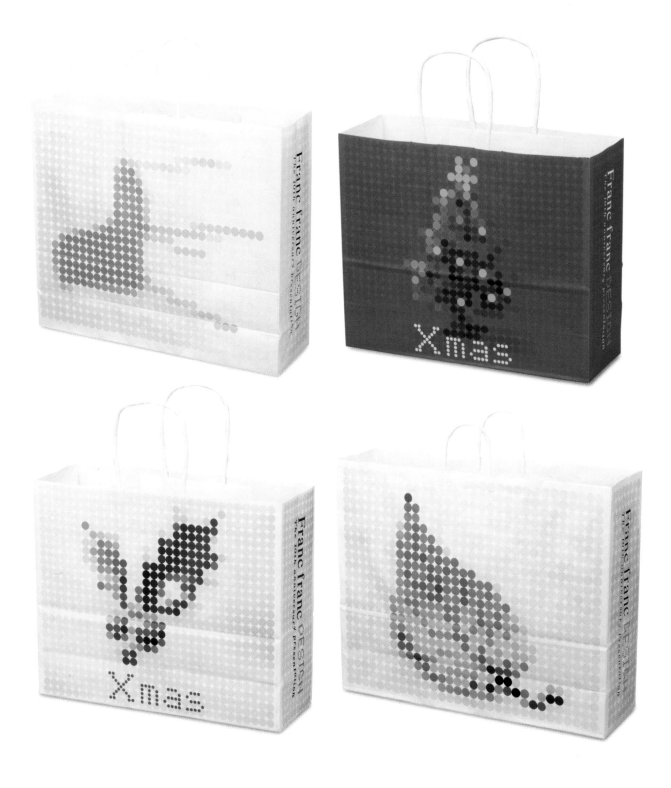

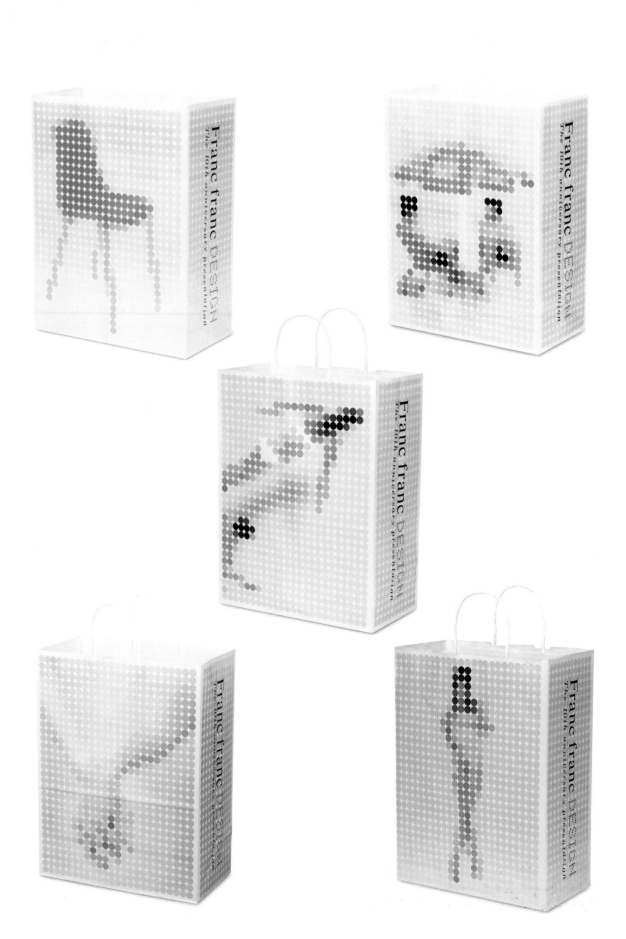

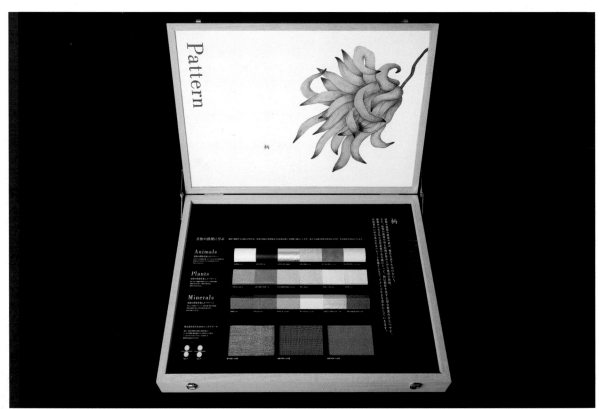

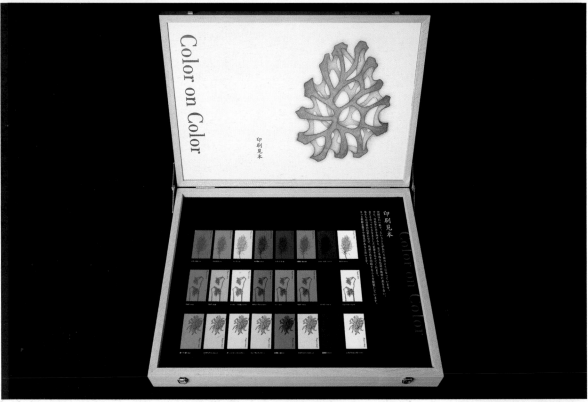

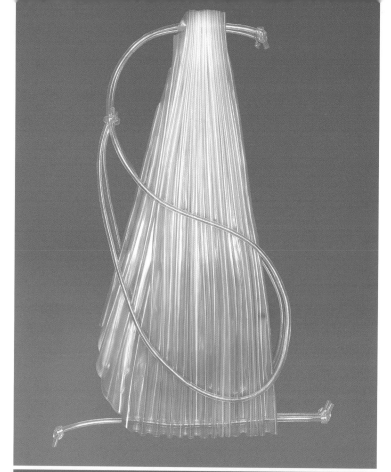

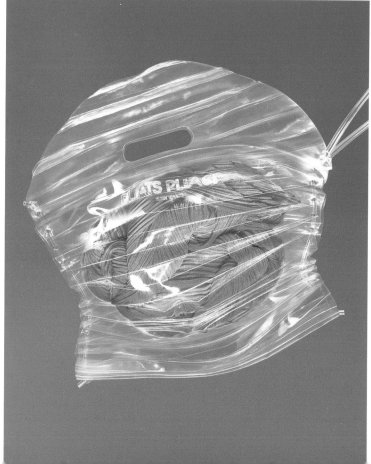

← Pleats Please shopping bag
↓ D: Sayuri Studio, Inc.

← Product packaging for an
image-processing software company
D: Shinnoske Sugisaki

↓ The 360th Anniversary of Gekkeikan
D: Akio Okumura

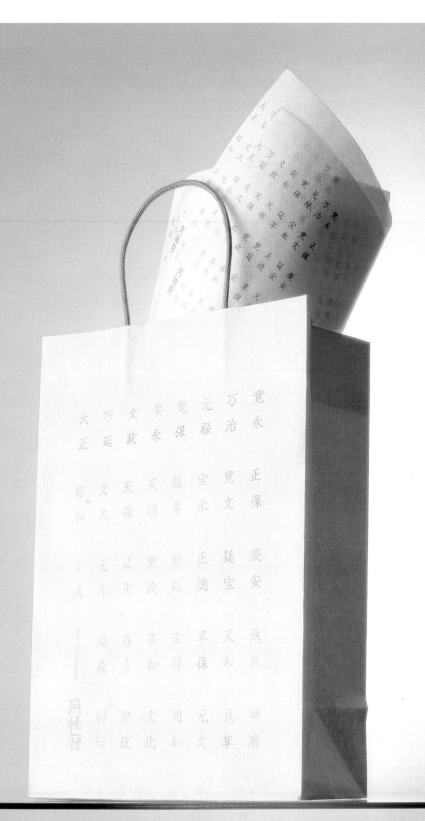

↓ Human Intellect
　 D: Akio Okumura

→ Shopping bag
　 D: Akio Okumura

　 Kintetsu
　 D: Akio Okumura

パッケージ

188

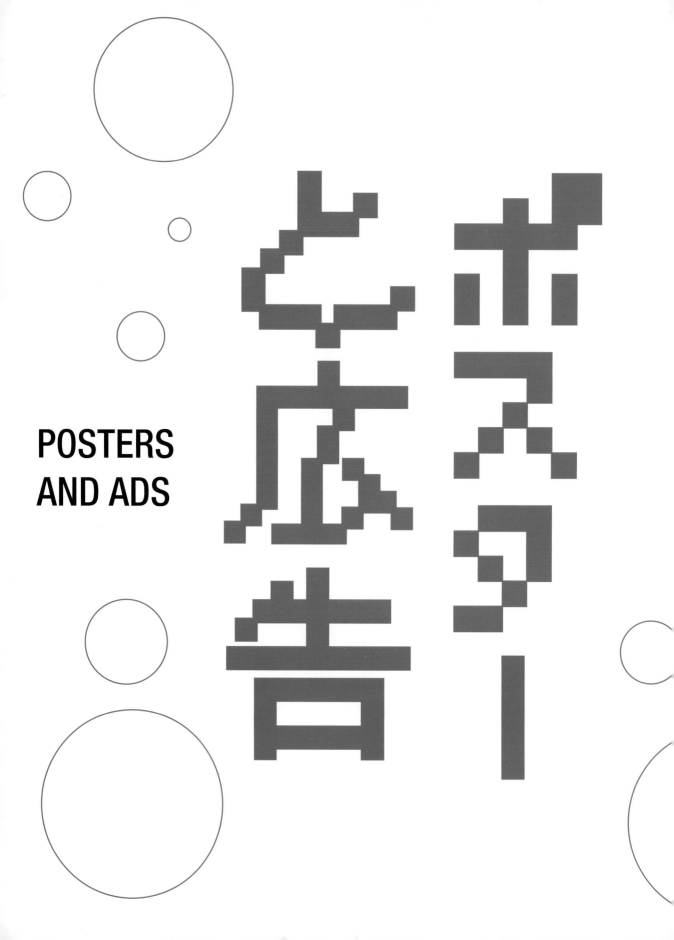

POSTERS
AND ADS

ポスター広告

The JAGDA Poster Exhibition: JAPAN 2001

← Japan
D: Gaku Ohsugi
ad+d: Gaku Ohsugi
d: Kenji Iwabuchi
cl: JAGDA

↓ Vitality of peacock
D: Gaku Ohsugi
ad+d: Gaku Ohsugi
d: Eiji Sunaga
cl: Megahealth Japan Co., Ltd.

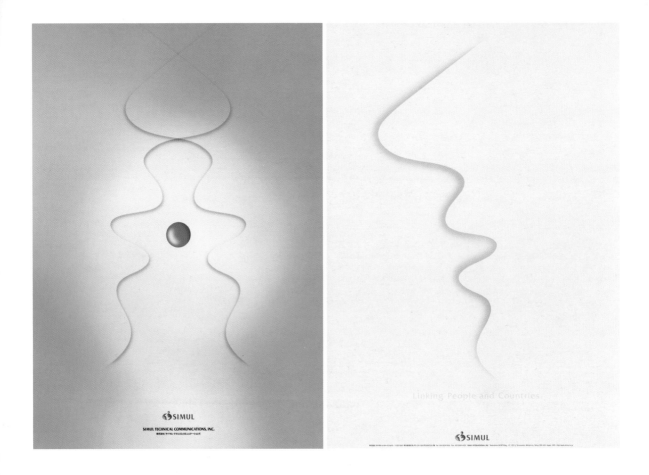

Linking People and Countries

← Simul Technical
D: Gaku Ohsugi
ad+d: Gaku Ohsugi
d: Eiji Sunaga
cl: Simul Technical Communications

Linking people and countries
D: Gaku Ohsugi
ad+d: Gaku Ohsugi
d: Kenji Iwabuchi
cl: Simul International Inc.

↓ Linking people and countries
D: Gaku Ohsugi
ad+d: Gaku Ohsugi
d: Kenji Iwabuchi
cl: Simul International Inc.

Linking People and Countries

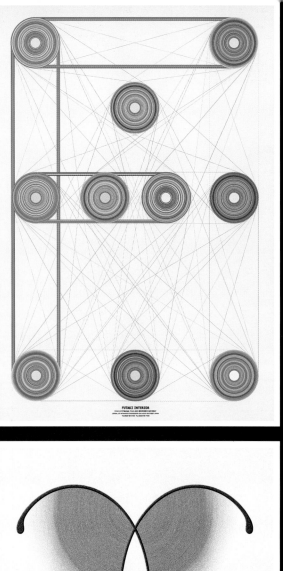

FUTAKI INTERIOR

[70] NANAMARUNI DESIGN WORKS CO.,LTD.

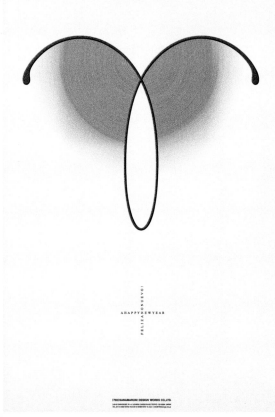

AHAPPYNEWYEAR

FELIZAÑONUEVO!

[70] NANAMARUNI DESIGN WORKS CO.,LTD.

[70] NANAMARUNI DESIGN WORKS CO.,LTD.

ポスターと広告

← Futaki Knit "F"
D: Gaku Ohsugi
ad+d: Gaku Ohsugi
d: Yuko Takaba
cl: Futaki Interior Co.Ltd.

702 Design Invitation '03
ad+d: Gaku Ohsugi
d: Eiji Sunaga

Mikako Wada Invitation
D: Gaku Ohsugi
ad+d: Gaku Ohsugi
d: Yuko Takaba

Message
D: Gaku Ohsugi
ad+d: Gaku Ohsugi
d: Mika Shinozaki

↓ Asia Collection Invitation
D: Gaku Ohsugi
ad+d: Gaku Ohsugi
d: Mika Shinozaki
cd: Murase Shumei
cl: Asia Collection Executive Committee

ASIA COLLECTION
MAKUHARI
GRAND PRIX

INVITATION TO FASHION DESIGN COMPETITION!

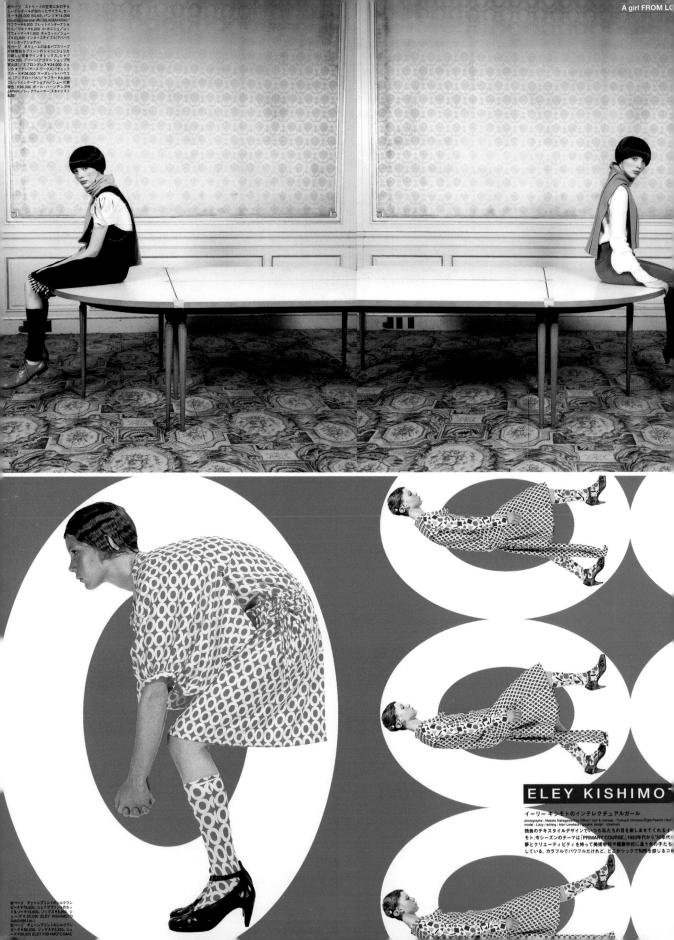

ELEY KISHIMO

イーリー キシモトのインテレクチュアルガール

ポスターと広告

↓ Is it beer cold at a refrigerator? Kanpai!!
↓ LAGER

↓ Kanpai!! LAGER

Kanpai!! LAGER TOKIO Version

ポスターと広告

202

D: Butterfly Stroke Inc.
cl: Kirin Brewery Co.,LTD.
cd+ad+d: Katsunori Aoki
cd+c: Hidenori Azuma
d: Kana Takakuwa
i: Bunpei Yorifuji

D: Butterfly Stroke Inc.
cl: Kirin Brewery Co.,LTD
cd+ad+d: Katsunori Aoki
cd+c: Hidenori Azuma
d: Kana Takakuwa
i: Bunpei Yorifuji

D: Butterfly Stroke Inc.
cl: Kirin Brewery Co.,LTD
cd+ad+d: Katsunori Aoki
cd+c: Hidenori Azuma
d: Yuji Sakai
i: Bunpei Yorifuji

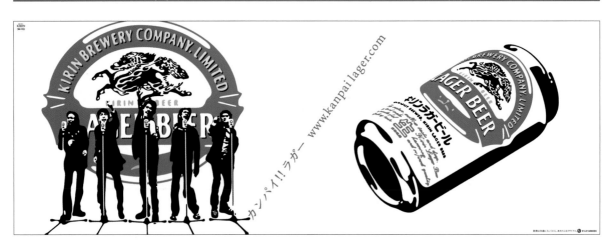

ポスターと広告

↓ Kanpai!! LAGER Hirosue Version1.
D: Butterfly Stroke Inc.
cl: Kirin Brewery Co.,LTD.
cd+ad+d: Katsunori Aoki
cd+c: Hidenori Azuma
d: Yuji Sakai
p: Kaoru Ijima/Hiroyoshi Koyama
i: Bunpei Yorifuji
p: Tomoyuki Inoue

Kanpai!! LAGER Hirosue Version2.
D: Butterfly Stroke Inc.
cl: Kirin Brewery Co.,LTD.
cd+ad+d: Katsunori Aoki
cd+c: Hidenori Azuma
d: Yuji Sakai

Laforet Grand Bazar '96 Spring
D: Butterfly Stroke Inc.
cd+ad+d+c: Katsunori Aoki
cd+c+cg: Ichiro Tanida

← Laforet Grand Bazar '97 Summer
D: Butterfly Stroke Inc.
cl: Laforet Harajuku
cd: Katsunori Aoki/
Ichiro Tanida / Yasuhiko Sakura
ad+d: Katsunori Aoki
cg: Ichiro Tanida

↓ Tokyo Art Directors Club Annual Exhibition '99
D: Butterfly Stroke Inc.
cl: Tokyo Art Directors Club
ad+d: Katsunori Aoki
i: Bunpei Yorifuji

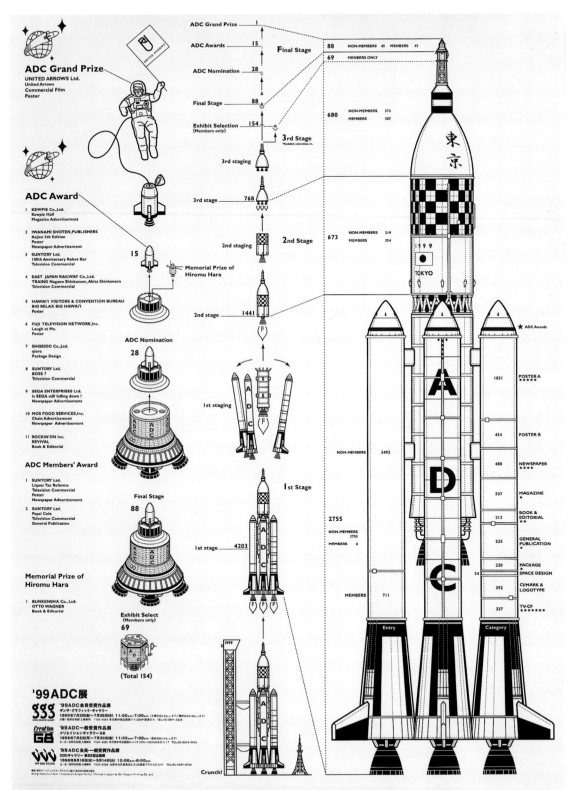

1999 Tokyo Art Directors Club Exhibition

↓ VenusFort Bargain
D: Butterfly Stroke Inc.
cl: VenusFort
cd+c: Masashi Taniyama
ad+d: Katsunori Aoki
art w+p: Jean-Pierre Khazem

Laforet Grand Bazar '96 Summer
D: Butterfly Stroke Inc.
cl: Laforet Harajuku
cd: Katsunori Aoki/ Ichiro Tanida/
Yasuhiko Sakura
ad+d: Katsunori Aoki
cg: Ichiro Tanida

→ Laforet Grand Bazar '96 Winter
D: Butterfly Stroke Inc.
cl: Laforet Harajuku
cd: Katsunori Aoki/
Ichiro Tanida / Yasuhiko Sakura
ad+c: Katsunori Aoki
c+cg: Ichiro Tanida

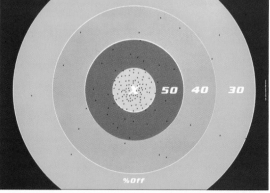

Okamoto Benetton Condom
D: Butterfly Stroke Inc.
cl: Okamoto Industries, Inc.
cd+c: Hiroshi Hasegawa
ad+d: Katsunori Aoki
p: Yoshihito Imaizumi

D: Butterfly Stroke Inc.
cl: Okamoto Industries, Inc.
cd+c: Hiroshi Hasegawa
ad+d: Katsunori Aoki
i: Bunpei Yorifuji
p: Yukihiro Onodera

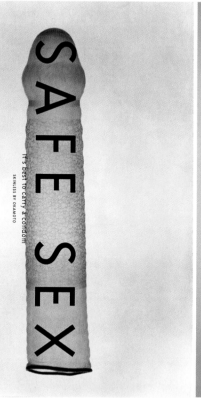

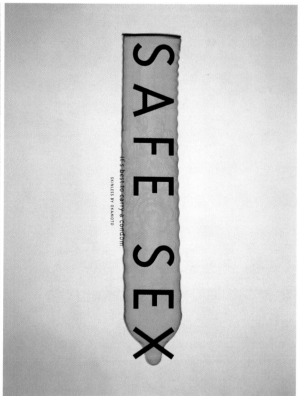

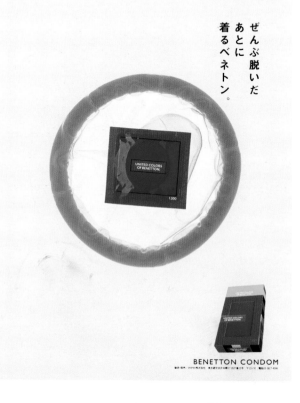

いい原料だけで
つくったから、
いいコンドームが
できた。

厳選した上質の天然ラテックス
だけでつくりました。
だから、うすくて、丈夫で、高品質。

うすさ、新鮮。
NEW SKINLESS!!

ほかのコンドームと、
比べてください。

ニュースキンレス　　　ほかのコンドーム

Q：どこがちがっているでしょう？

厳選した上質の天然ラテックス
だけでつくりました。
だから、うすくて、丈夫で、高品質。

うすさ、新鮮。
NEW SKINLESS!!

↓ Fields
Pachinco Hall Design Competition 2002
D: Butterfly Stroke Inc.
cl: Fields co.,Ltd.
cd+ad+d: Katsunori Aoki
d: Kana Takakuwa
i: Bunpei Yorifuji

→ Nike Total Performance Leadership '98
D: Butterfly Stroke Inc.
cl: Nike Japan
cd: Larry Fry
ad+d: Katsunori Aoki
d+i: Seijiro Kubo
c: Naoki Morita
p: Kouichi Ikegame   pr: Dan Odagiri

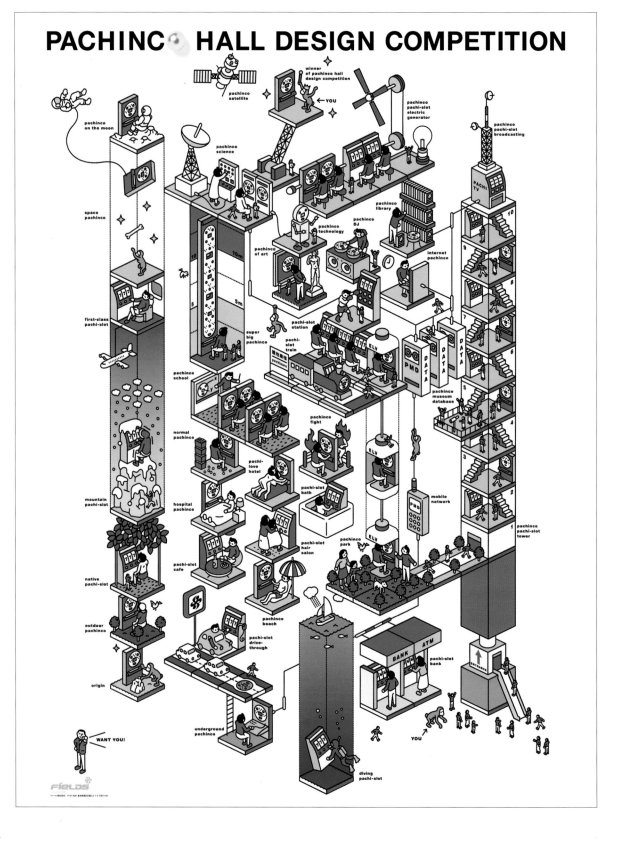

↓ Enjoy 100%, AIWA
→ D: Butterfly Stroke Inc.
cl: Sony Marketing inc.
cd+ad+d: Katsunori Aoki
cd: Masao Oshima
c: Kensho Yoshitani
i: Seijiro Kubo

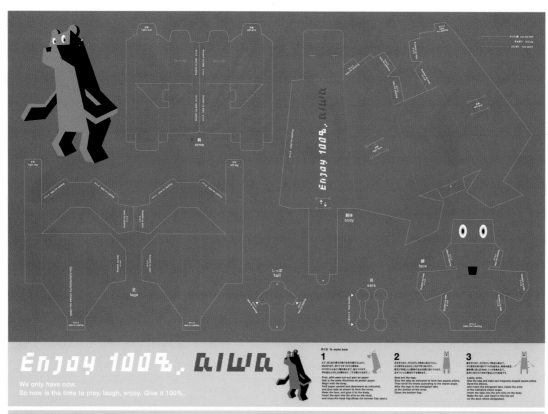

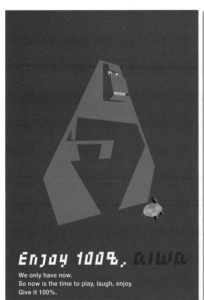

Enjoy 100%. AIWA

We only have now.
So now is the time to play, laugh, enjoy.
Give it 100%.

Enjoy 100%. AIWA

We only have now.
So now is the time to play, laugh, enjoy.
Give it 100%.

Enjoy 100%. AIWA

We only have now.
So now is the time to play, laugh, enjoy.
Give it 100%.

Enjoy 100%. AIWA

We only have now.
So now is the time to play, laugh, enjoy.
Give it 100%.

Enjoy 100%. AIWA

We only have now.
So now is the time to play, laugh, enjoy.
Give it 100%.

Enjoy 100%. AIWA

We only have now.
So now is the time to play, laugh, enjoy.
Give it 100%.

Enjoy 100%. AIWA

We only have now.
So now is the time to play, laugh, enjoy.
Give it 100%.

Enjoy 100%. AIWA

We only have now.
So now is the time to play, laugh, enjoy.
Give it 100%.

Enjoy 100%. AIWA

We only have now.
So now is the time to play, laugh, enjoy.
Give it 100%.

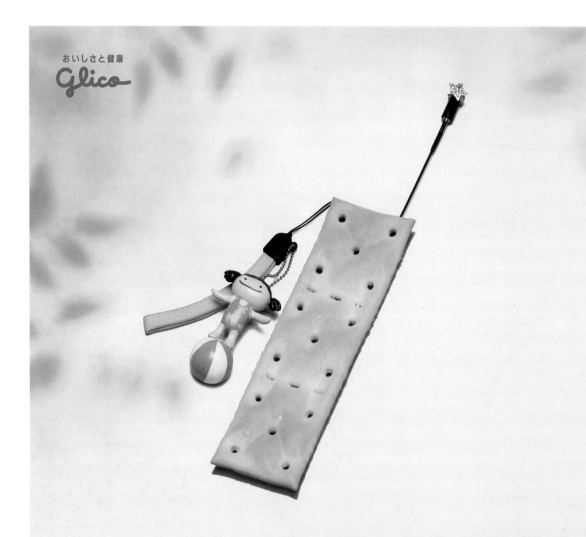

もう、手ばなせナイ モード。

新しく、スリムなったからいつでもどこでも
食事がわりにサクッとイケる。しかも、栄養バランスが
いいのにカロリーひかえ目。今どきの女の子の必需品。

カジュアルタイプになって食べやすく、携帯しやすくなった「バランスオン」は、
あっさりおいしい塩味と、香りも味わえるミックスハーブ味の2タイプ。
1箱に5種のビタミン・カルシウム・鉄分が1日に必要な量の3分の1、
バランスよく含まれています。しかも、カロリーはうれしい180kcal。
何かと忙しいけど、栄養もカロリーも気になるあなたにピッタリなのです。

[バランスオン] NEW

○カルシウム233mg（牛乳約1本分／200cc）○鉄4mg（ほうれん草約3株分）○食物繊維3.4g（レタス約1個分）※10枚当たり、当社分析値　●グリコホームページの
栄養成分ナビゲーターでは、食品の栄養成分情報の検索ができます。バランスの良い食生活づくりにお役立て下さい。　[アドレス] http://www.glico.co.jp

 江崎グリコ株式会社

ダイエットのためだけなら、食べない。

Let's おいしいコンディショニング

時間を節約するだけなら、食べない。

Let's おいしいコンディショニング!

21世木を育てます。

この広告は新潟県の森林づくりをPRし、21世紀を担う緑を、みんなで育てていこうという趣旨でつくられたものです。ここに描かれた木は、県が2001年から2100年までの100年間、毎年植樹を続けることで育っていく「21世紀の木」を表現しています。

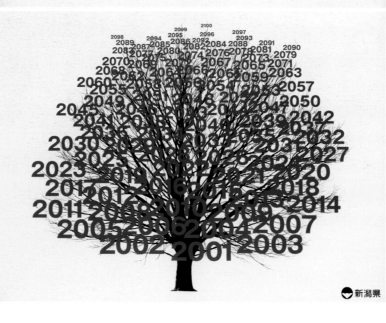

新潟県

ポスターと広告

← Nurturing the 21st CenTREE
D: Norito Shinmura
ad: Norito Shinmura
c: Masakazu Nifuji
p: Ko Hosokawa
adv: Niigata prefecture

↓ Sampling furniture 2001
D: Drawing and Manual

D&DEPARTMENT PROJECT 2001 SAMPLING FURNITURE

HONDA

photographed by Hiroshi Yoshida

↓ Art space PR poster in Narita Airport.
→ D: D-Net Co., Ltd.

220

ポスターと広告

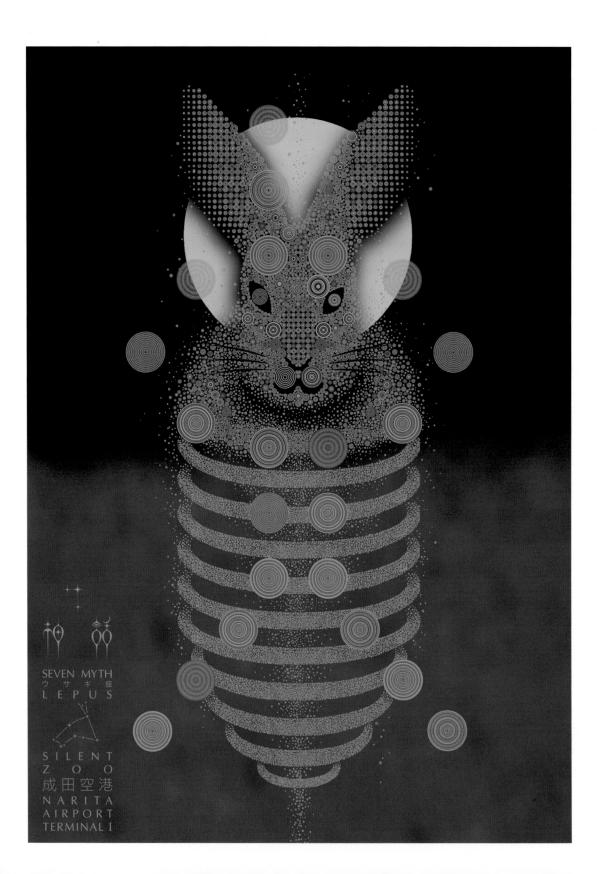

SEVEN MYTH
VULPECULA

SILENT
ZOO
成田空港
NARITA
AIRPORT
TERMINAL I

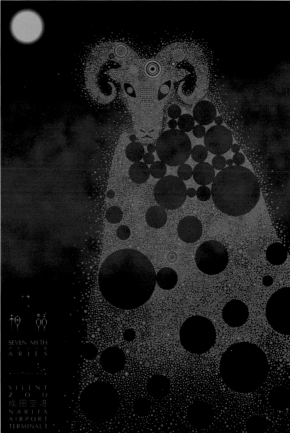

SEVEN MYTH
ARIES

SILENT
ZOO
成田空港
NARITA
AIRPORT
TERMINAL I

SEVEN MYTH
PISCES

SILENT
ZOO
成田空港
NARITA
AIRPORT
TERMINAL I

SEVEN MYTH
LEO

SILENT
ZOO
成田空港
NARITA
AIRPORT
TERMINAL I

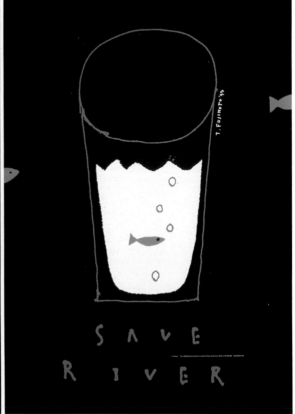

minä

← minä 2001-2002 AW Exhibition
  D: Bluemark Inc

↓ Exhibition of mina's works "Ryushi"
  D: Bluemark Inc

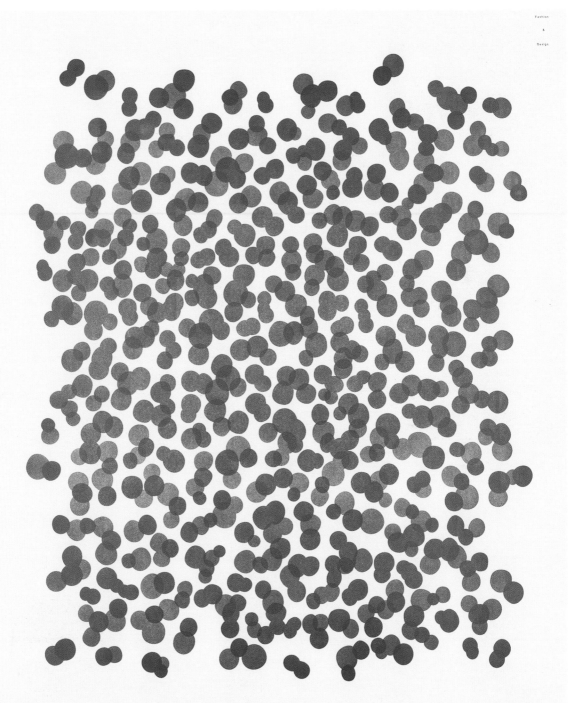

Fashion
&
Design

Exhibition of minä's works

minä

粒　子

spiral
garden.

2002 **4・23** Tue — **5・6** Mon

Open from 11:00 to 20:00   Admission : Free

Organized by : minä Ryushi Exhibition Exec. / Produced by : Atsuki Kikuchi (Bluemark) / Supported by : Bunka Gakuen "SO-EN", Bunka Publishing Bureau
Sponsored by : MINÄ Co.,Ltd. / Venue Offered by : Wacoal Art Center Co., Ltd.
In cooperation with : ART BY XEROX, Kimura Senko,Ltd., Kanagawa Lace Co.,Ltd., Hideo Ohara Textile Factory, Wago Keori Co.,Ltd., Sai Santo, Hironori Itabashi, INFAS.com

Awa Dance 2002
D: Takaaki Fujimoto
p: Akira Yonezu

Staff Service
D: Creative Power Unit

Kazumasa Ohhira Exhibition series
D: Takaaki Fujimoto
p: Akira Yonezu

人材派遣会社にも、
いい人材は必要だ。

人材が動くと、
時代が動く。

↓ Japan
D: Wataru Hasegawa

→ We love NY
D: Wataru Hasegawa

228

ポスターと広告

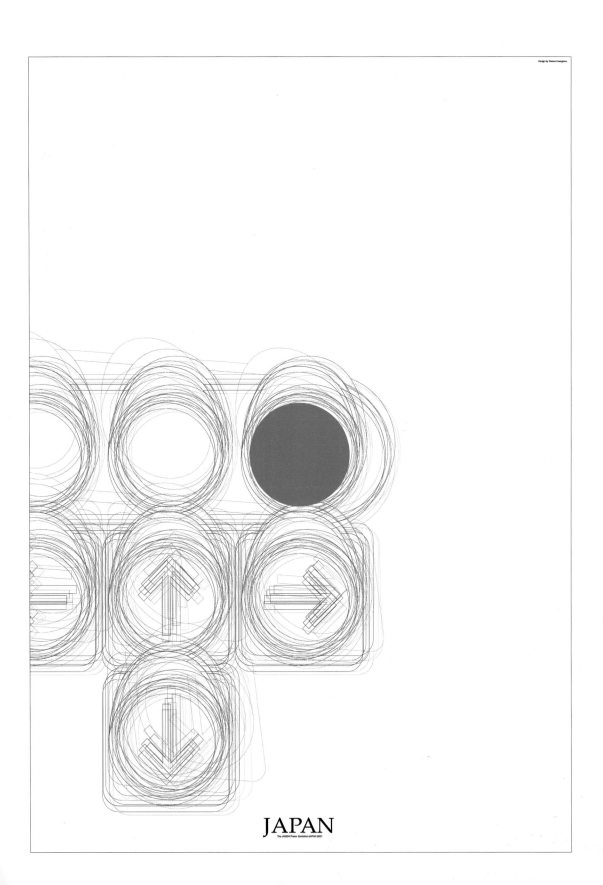

We love NY.

We love NY.

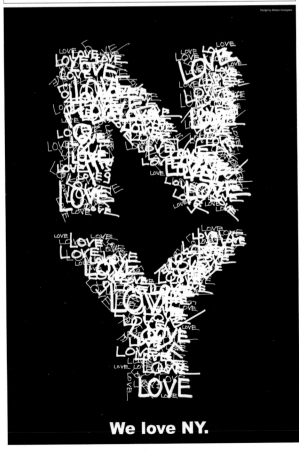

We love NY.

We love NY.

↓ The Tosei
D: Hiroshige Fukuhara

→ The Tosei
D: Hiroshige Fukuhara

ポスターと広告

230

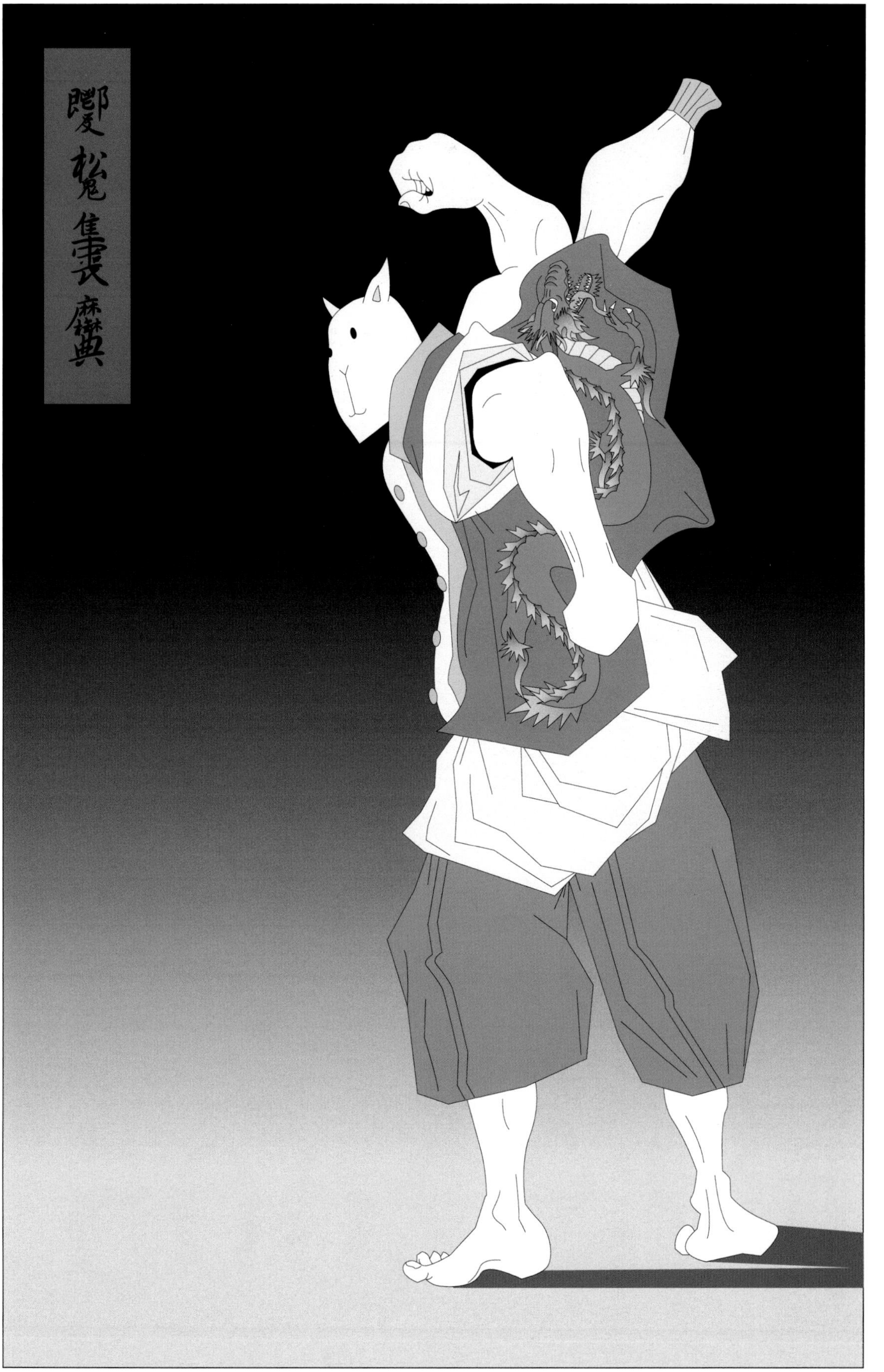

Poster for the Expo 2005 Aichi
D: Kenya Hara
ad+d: Kenya Hara
i: Shunzan Takagi / Takashi Ohno

EXPO 2005
JAPAN

2005年日本国際博覧会　新しい地球創造：自然の叡智
THE 2005 WORLD EXPOSITION, JAPAN　BEYOND DEVELOPMENT: REDISCOVERING NATURE'S WISDOM

XPO 2005
APAN

2005年日本国際博覧会　新しい地球創造：自然の叡智
S WORLD EXPOSITION, JAPAN　BEYOND DEVELOPMENT: REDISCOVERING NATURE'S WISDOM

Kazumasa Ohhira Exhibition series
D: Takaaki Fujimoto
p: Akira Yonezu

J-PHONE J-N03II
D: Creative Power Unit

234

ポスターと広告

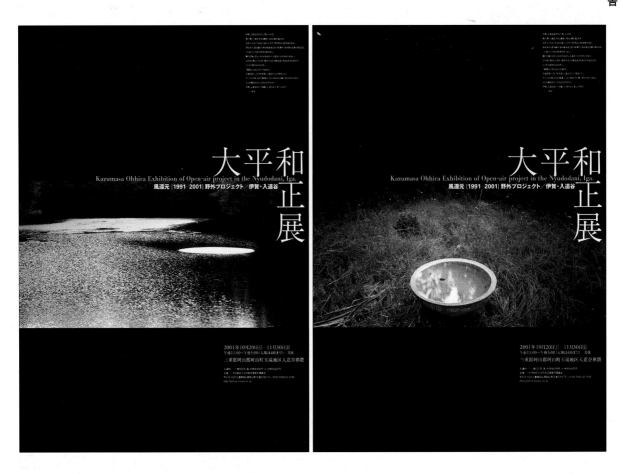

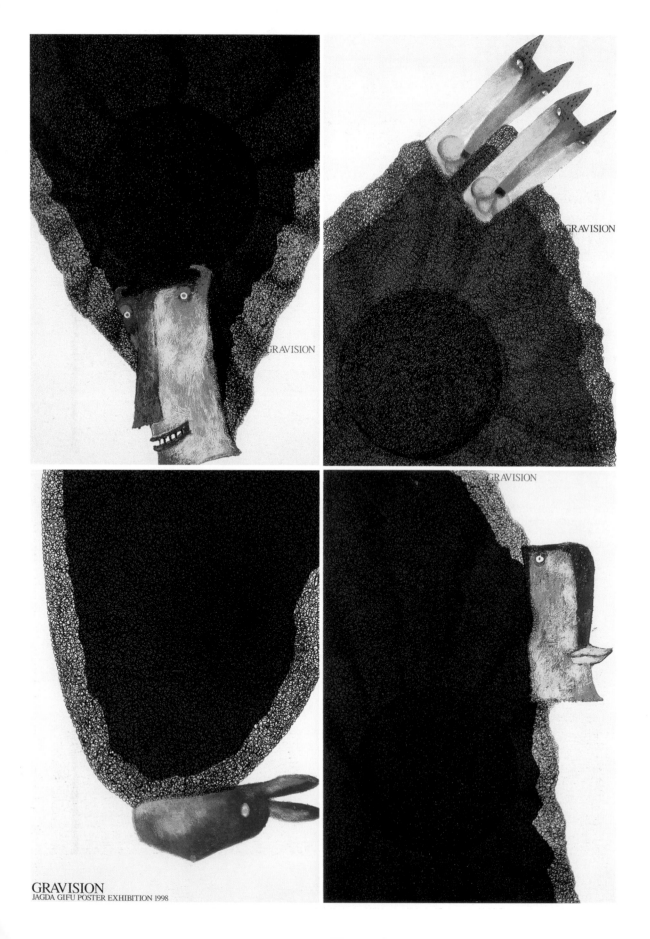

GRAVISION

GRAVISION

GRAVISION

GRAVISION

GRAVISION
JAGDA GIFU POSTER EXHIBITION 1998

← Graphic + Vision
D: D-Net Co., Ltd.

↓ "im product"
D: Kenya Hara
ad+d: Kenya Hara
p: Tamotsu Fujii

↓ MUJI
D: Kenya Hara
ad+d: Shinnoske sugisaki Hara
d: Yukie Inoue / Izumi Suge
p: Tamotsu Fujii

→ MUJI
D: Kenya Hara
ad+d: Kenya Hara
d: Yukie Inoue / Izumi Suge
p: Tamotsu Fujii

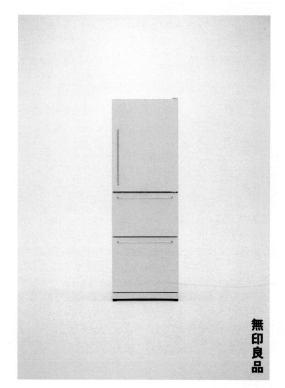

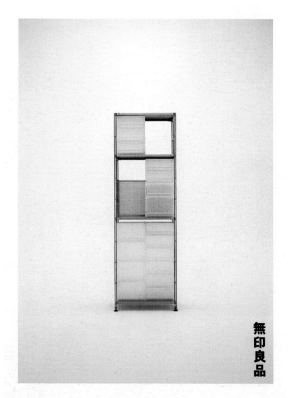

↓ Maruya
D: Noriaki Hayashi

→ Kao Creation
D: Noriaki Hayashi

ポスターと広告

240

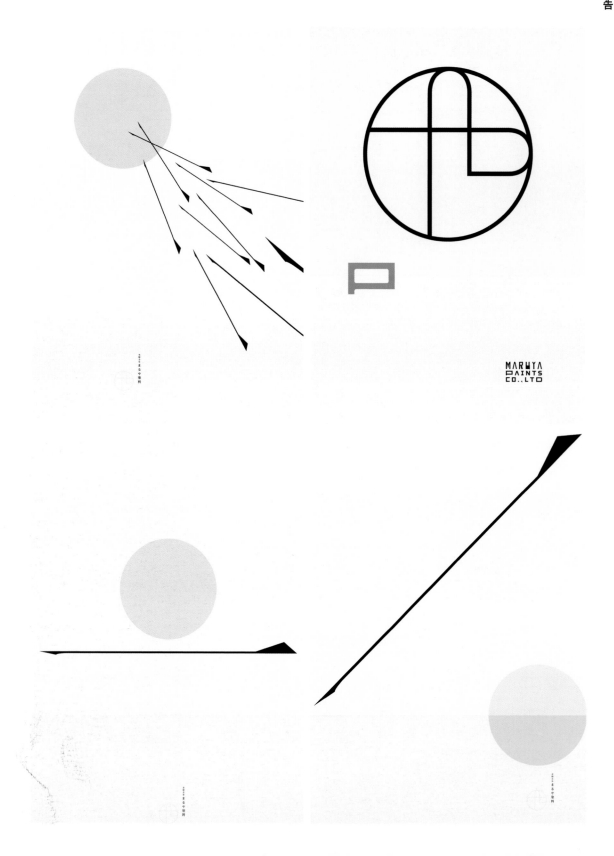

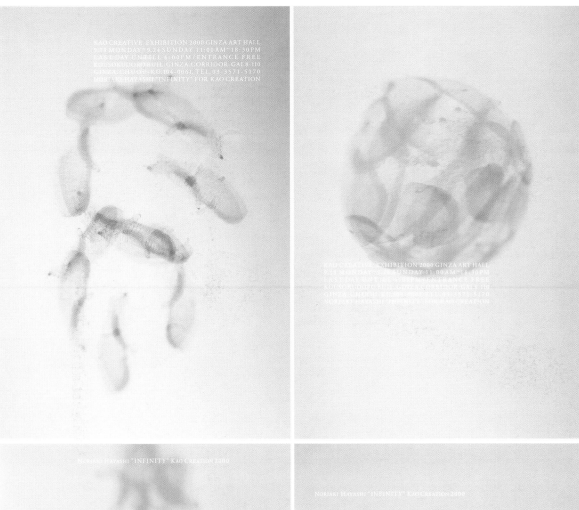

KAO CREATIVE EXHIBITION 2000 GINZA ART HALL
9.18 MONDAY~9.24 SUNDAY 11:00 AM~18:30 PM
LAST DAY UNTILL 4:00 PM / ENTRANCE FREE
ETUSOKUDORI BUIL. GINZA CORRIDOR. GAL 8-110
GINZA. CHUOU-KU 104-0061 TEL. 03-3571-5170
NORIAKI HAYASHI "INFINITY" FOR KAO CREATION

KAO CREATIVE EXHIBITION 2000 GINZA ART HALL
9.18 MONDAY~9.24 SUNDAY 11:00 AM~18:30 PM
LAST DAY UNTILL 4:00 PM / ENTRANCE FREE
ETUSOKUDORI BUIL. GINZA CORRIDOR. GAL 8-110
GINZA. CHUOU-KU 104-0061 TEL. 03-3571-5170
NORIAKI HAYASHI "INFINITY" FOR KAO CREATION

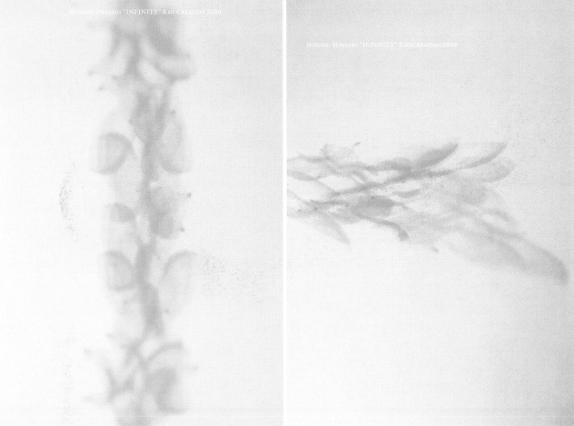

NORIAKI HAYASHI "INFINITY" KAO CREATION 2000

NORIAKI HAYASHI "INFINITY" KAO CREATION 2000

TSUKASA
construction
Co.,Ltd

TSUKASA
construction
Co.,Ltd

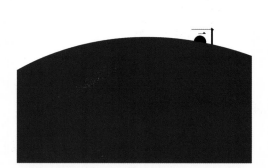

TSUKASA
construction
Co.,Ltd

TSUKASA
construction
Co.,Ltd

ポスターと広告

↓ Tsucasa
D: Noriaki Hayashi

9.11 Poster
D: Noriaki Hayashi

The JAGDA Poster Exhibition JAPAN 2001

↓ Recycle factory
D: Hiroyuki Matsuishi

→ Recycle robot
D: Hiroyuki Matsuishi

246

ポスターと広告

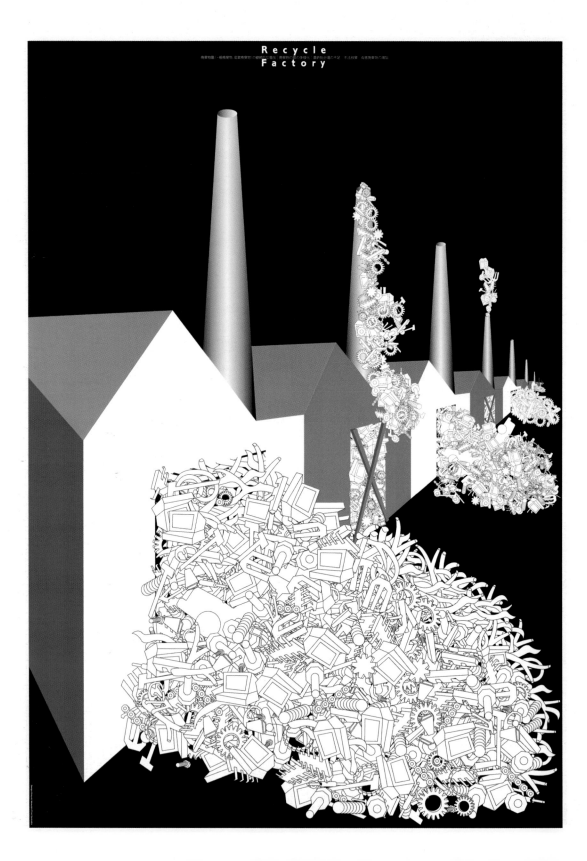

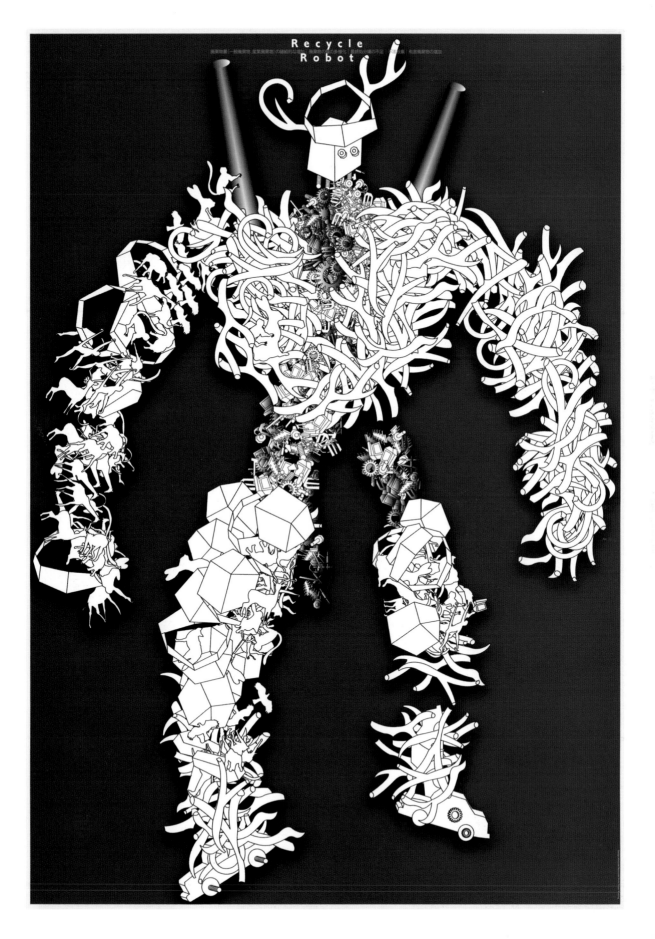

Recycle
Robot

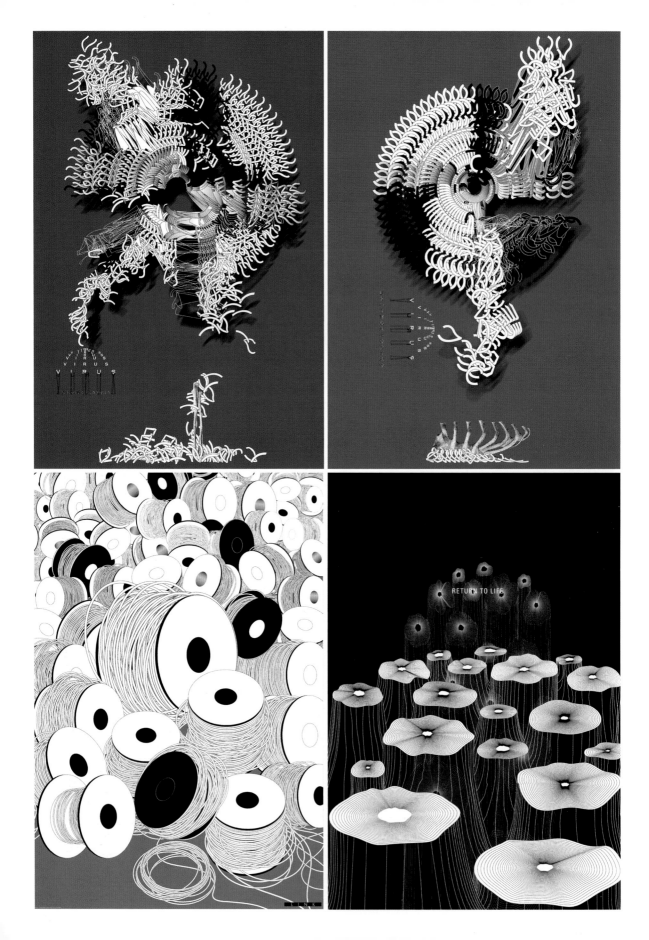

← Virus-1
D: Hiroyuki Matsuishi

Virus-2
D: Hiroyuki Matsuishi

↓ Universal Design
D: Hiroyuki Matsuishi

Link
D: Hiroyuki Matsuishi

Return to life
D: Hiroyuki Matsuishi

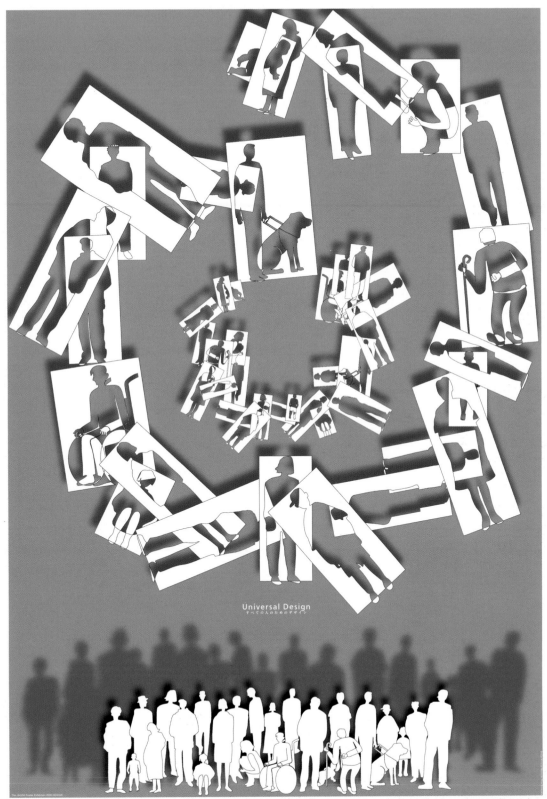

↓ Youseki Miki Exhibition
D: Hiroyuki Matsuishi

→ Hiromichi Nakano
D: Butterfly Stroke Inc.
cl: Hiromichi Nakano Design Office
Company Limited.
cd: Hiromichi Nakano
ad+d: Katsunori Aoki
i: Seijiro Kubo

250 ポスターと広告

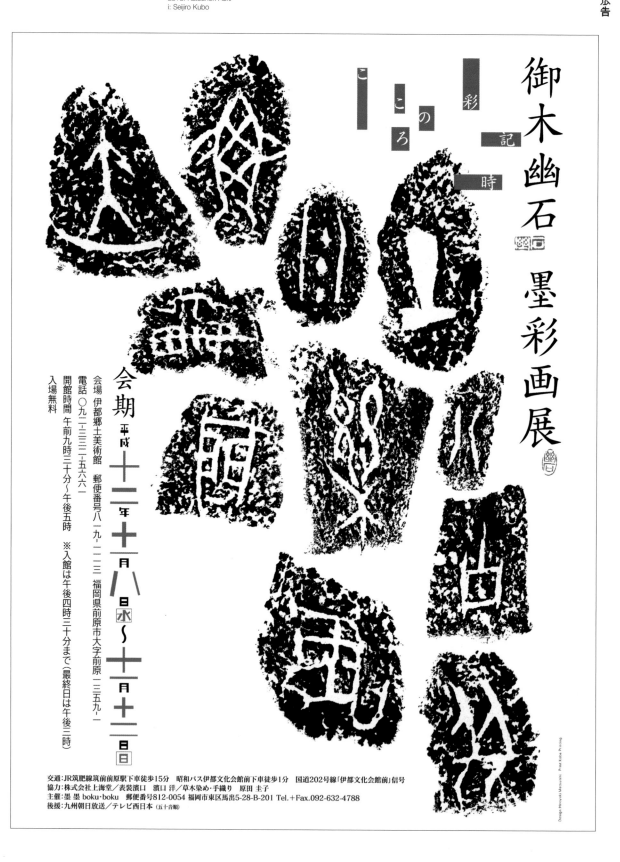

INSECT COLLECTING, *hiromichi* BY HIROMICHI NAKANO

Osaka Aquarium Ring Of Fire
Striped Beakperch
D: Itakura Design Institute Inc.

Osaka Aquarium Ring Of Fire
Green Seaturtle
D: Itakura Design Institute Inc.

Osaka Aquarium Ring Of Fire
Longhorn Cowfish
D: Itakura Design Institute Inc.

Osaka Aquarium Ring Of Fire
Rockhopper Penguin
D: Itakura Design Institute Inc.

Osaka Aquarium Ring Of Fire
Jellyfish
D: Itakura Design Institute Inc.

「磯の王様」と呼ばれるくらい、磯釣りではなかなか釣れない魚の代表格。
イシダイは何故か幼魚の時にははっきりとした7本の縞があり、シマダイとも呼ばれています。
成長につれてこの縞は徐々に薄くなり老成魚では無くなります。ところで、この縞模様は縦縞と思いますか?
それとも横縞? 一般的には縦縞に思えるのですが、魚の世界では横縞と呼んでいます。
頭を上にして縞模様を見るからなのです。それはよこしまな?と言わないでくださいね。
少しだまし絵風ですが、何に見えますか。皆さんで想像してくださいね。

  海遊館

地下鉄中央線 大阪港駅下車徒歩5分 大阪市港区海岸通1-1-10 TEL06-6576-5500-5501

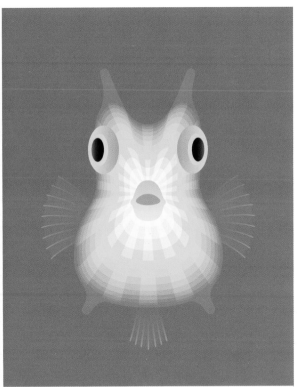

↓ Mix Nuts [CD poster]
D: Minato Ishikawa

→ 3D Poster [Display]: Nissan Elgrand
D: Minato Ishikawa

254

ポスターと広告

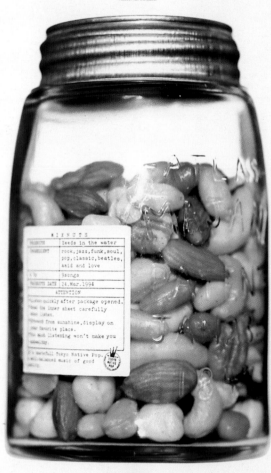

EXPLORATION

NATURE DYNAMISM

STRONG DADDY

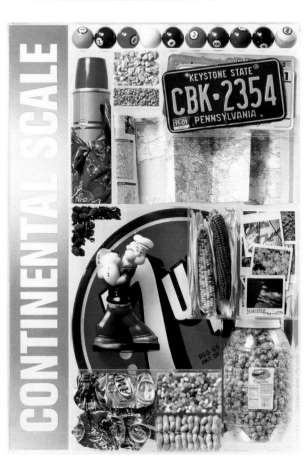

CONTINENTAL SCALE

↓ Toyobo
D: Katachi

→ Toyobo
D: Katachi

ポスターと広告

258

↓ Toyobo
D: Katachi

→ Toyobo
D: Katachi

ポスターと広告

260

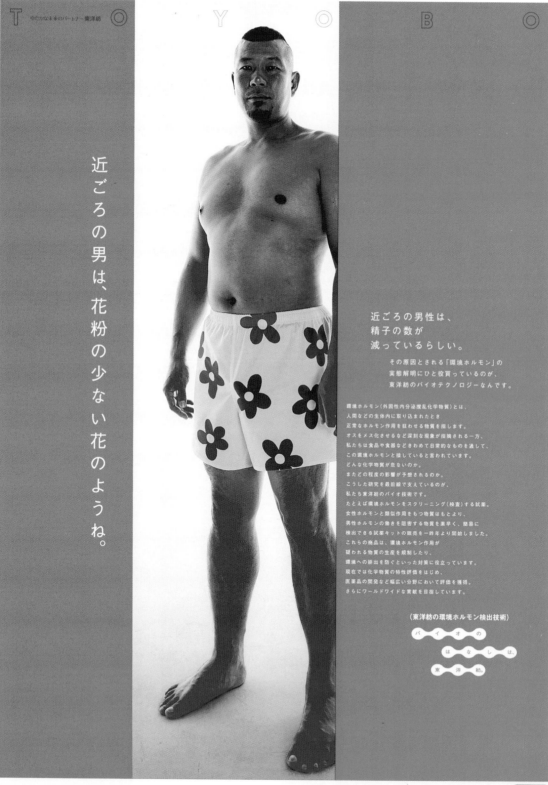

近ごろの男は、花粉の少ない花のようね。

近ごろの男性は、
精子の数が
減っているらしい。

その原因とされる「環境ホルモン」の
実態解明にひと役買っているのが、
東洋紡のバイオテクノロジーなんです。

環境ホルモン（外因性内分泌攪乱化学物質）とは、
人間などの生体内に取り込まれたとき
正常なホルモン作用を狂わせる物質を指します。
オスをメス化させるなど深刻な現象が指摘される一方、
私たちは食品や食器などきわめて日常的なものを通して、
この環境ホルモンと接していると言われています。
どんな化学物質が危ないのか。
またどの程度の影響が予想されるのか。
こうした研究を最前線で支えているのが、
私たち東洋紡のバイオ技術です。
たとえば環境ホルモンをスクリーニング（検査）する試薬。
女性ホルモンと類似作用をもつ物質はもとより、
男性ホルモンの働きを阻害する物質を素早く、簡易に
検出できる試薬キットの販売を一昨年より開始しました。
これらの商品は、環境ホルモン作用が
疑われる物質の生産を規制したり、
環境への排出を防ぐといった対策に役立っています。
現在では化学物質の特性評価をはじめ、
医薬品の開発など幅広い分野において評価を獲得。
さらにワールドワイドな貢献を目指しています。

（東洋紡の環境ホルモン検出技術）

バイオの
はなしは、
東洋紡。

www.toyobo.co.jp TOYOBO

近ごろの男は、
花粉の少ない花のようね。

男性の精子の数が減っているらしい。その原因とされる
「環境ホルモン」の実態解明にひと役買っているのが、東洋紡の技術なんです。

オスをメス化させるなど深刻かつ複雑が指摘されている環境ホルモン。私たちは食品や食品などとりわけ日常的なものを通して、
この環境ホルモンと接していると言われています。どんな化学物質が出ているのか、この程度の影響が予想されるのか。
こうした研究を最前線で支えているのが、東洋紡のバイオ技術です。例えば環境ホルモンをスクリーニング（検査）する試薬。
女性ホルモン様作用を示すつの環境ホルモンのほどより、男性ホルモンの働きを阻害する物質を測定し、簡易に検出する試薬キットの販売を通じて、
環境ホルモン作用が疑われる物質の生産を抑制したり、環境への被害を防ぐといった対策に役立っています。
現在では化学物質の総合評価をはじめ、医薬品の開発など幅広い分野において評価を推進し、さらにワールドワイドな展開を目指しています。
○環境ホルモン検出キット専用ホームページ www.e-hormone-kit.com/
（このホームページは伊藤忠商事株式会社御薬支社御機電化学品部と共同運営しています。）
○お問合せ先：東洋紡績株式会社バイオ事業本部TEL06-6348-3760 広報部TEL06-6348-3443

（ 東洋紡の環境ホルモン検出技術 ）

TOYOBO www.toyobo.co.jp

東洋紡とオーダーメイド。
ただし、ファッションの話ではない。

体形にフィットした服を仕立てるように、
体質にぴったり合った治療をおこなう
夢の「オーダーメイド医療」。その実現のために
ひと役買っているのが、東洋紡の技術なんです。

自分のカラダをもっと深く知ることができます。
将来かかりそうな病気を予防したり、自分に合った副作用の
少ない薬を作ってもらえるかもしれない。結果として医療費って
安く済むになるかもしれない。そんな夢の医療が、遺伝子の解析によって
現実のものになろうとしています。誰もどのゲノム、全遺伝子中に
数十万から数百万個ある、一人ひとりの体質を決定づけている
「SNPs（スニップス）」という遺伝情報、病気の可能性や
薬の効き具合に関わるSNPsの特定は、オーダーメイド医療への
近道とされています。東洋紡では、こうした解析に必要な試薬や
技術を世界中の研究室に提供し、高い評価を獲得しているのです。
最先端の研究成果を、一日も早くあなたを夢の医療が現代へ。
東洋紡のバイオテクノロジーは、その原動力でありたいと願っています。
○お問合せ先：株式会社東洋紡ジーンアナリシス TEL.0770-22-7688

（ 東洋紡の遺伝子解析技術 ）

TOYOBO www.toyobo.co.jp

↓ No quiet poster
D: Katachi

→ National Toilet no himitsu
D: Katachi

ポスターと広告

262

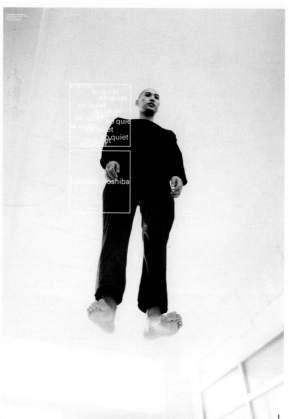

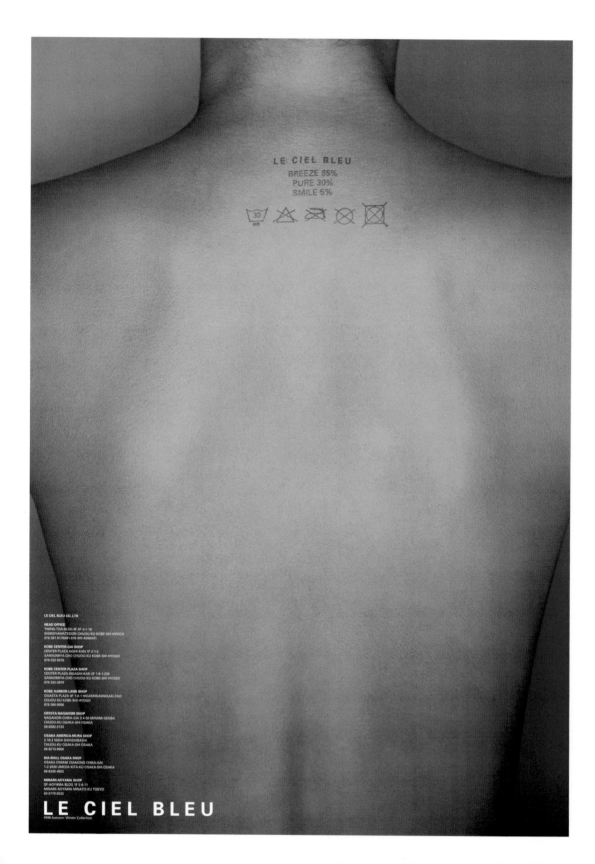

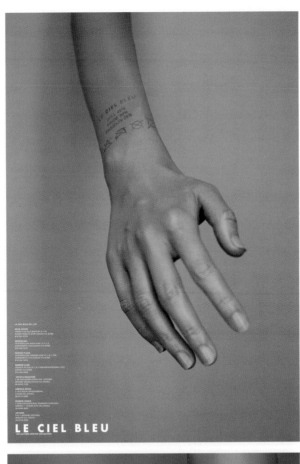

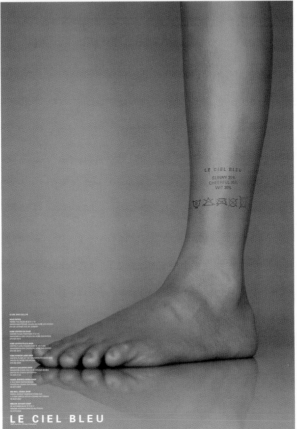

↓ Royal Shoes Appartment
D: Katachi

→ Wacoal Shimashima Shaper
D: Katachi

266

ポスターと広告

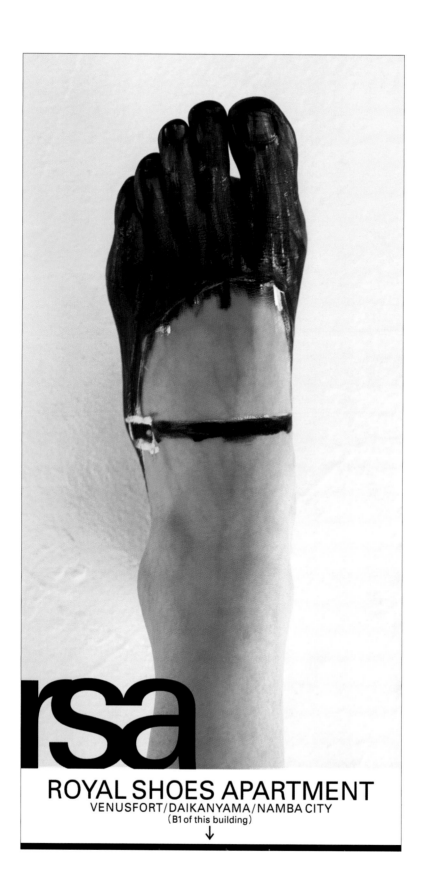

rsa

ROYAL SHOES APARTMENT
VENUSFORT/DAIKANYAMA/NAMBA CITY
(B1 of this building)
↓

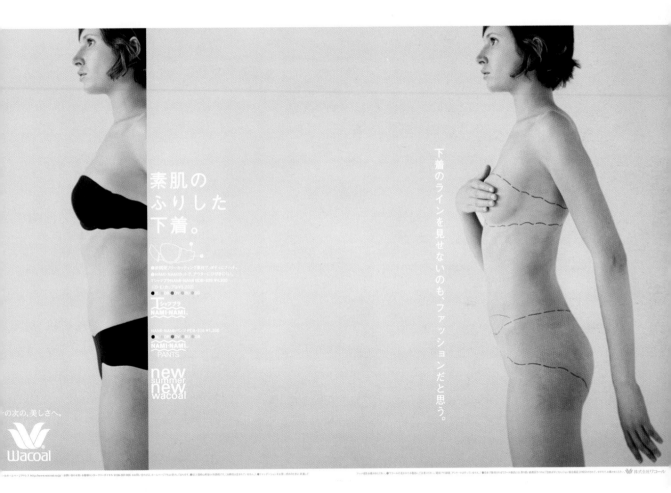

↓ Gekkeikan
D: Katachi

→ Wakayama Sightseeing Association
D: Katachi

ポスターと広告

268

お酒は20歳になってから。お酒はおいしく適量を。

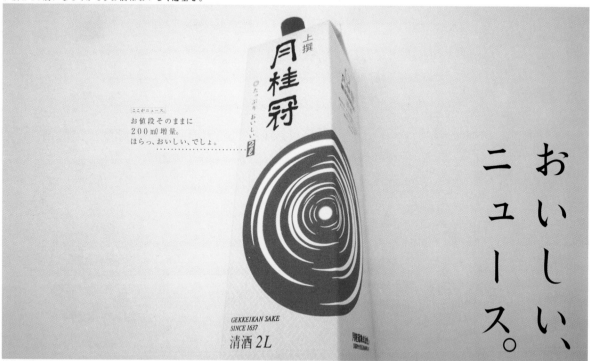

月桂冠上撰さけパック20誕生。 月桂冠上撰さけパック20 1,816円 ※価格はメーカー希望小売価格(消費税別) ○お問い合わせは、お客様相談室 TEL.075-623-2040(9:00～17:00平日のみ) ○インターネットホームページアドレス http://www.gekkeikan.co.jp/ 月桂冠株式会社

お酒は20歳になってから。お酒はおいしく適量を。

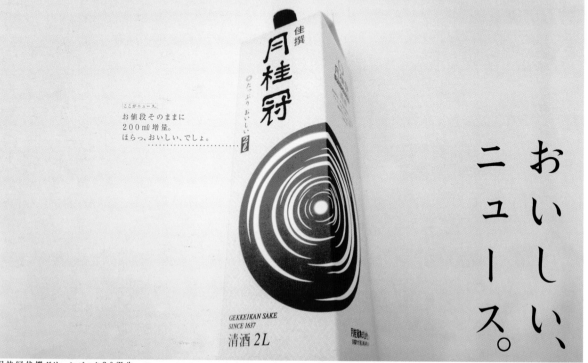

月桂冠佳撰グリーンパック20誕生。 月桂冠佳撰グリーンパック20 1,573円 ※価格はメーカー希望小売価格(消費税別) ○お問い合わせは、お客様相談室 TEL.075-623-2040(9:00～17:00平日のみ) ○インターネットホームページアドレス http://www.gekkeikan.co.jp/ 月桂冠株式会社

原始熊野。

あこがれの熊野へ、男は、千年前、都の人々は憧れの行列のように熊野を訪れた。そこには結界浄土があった。いまも熊野に立てば、彼らにとって熊野は地球の果て、過去に守られているような、不思議な感覚になる。熊野は遺伝子で幸せを感じるところなのだ。

心 情 和 歌 山

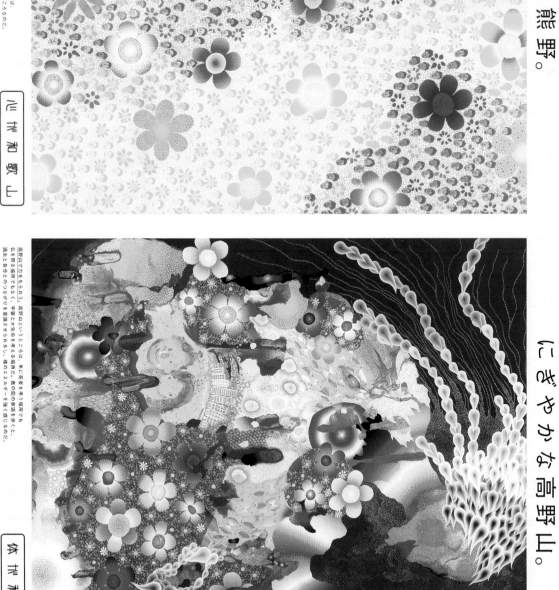

にぎやかな高野山。

高野山で死をもらおう。高野山というところは、特に死者を弔う場所でも仏を祭る場所でもなく、宇宙から生命を考える場所だ。男の股の感覚を歩くと、過去と自分とのつながりを認識させられるし、魂のエネルギーを強く感じるのだ。

体 情 和 歌 山

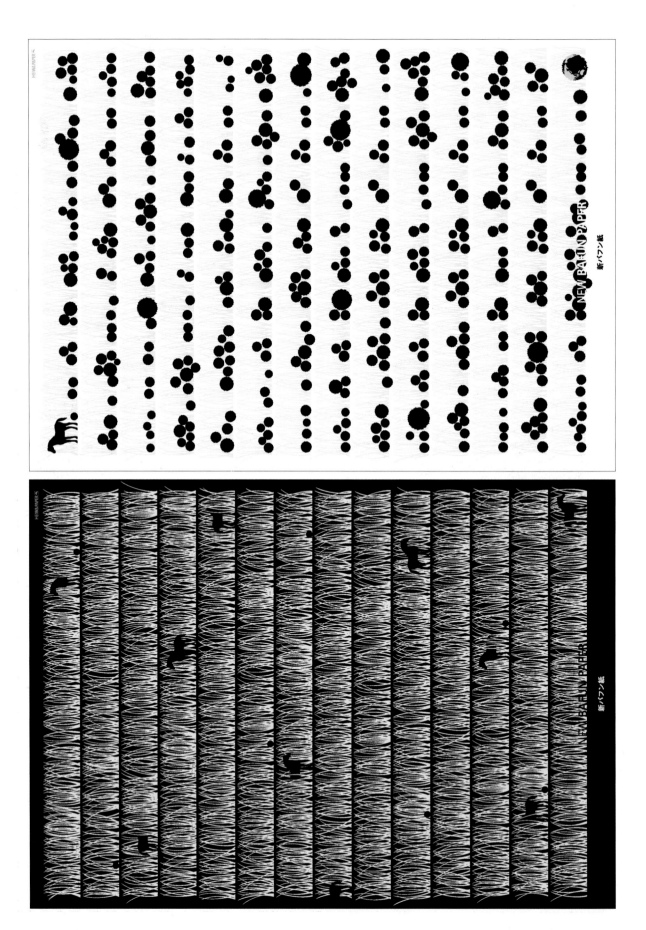

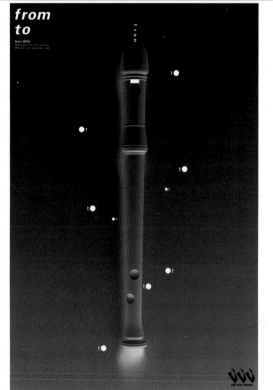

↓ Heiwa's Peace
D: Ken Miki & Associates

→ Heiwa's Peace
D: Ken Miki & Associates

ポスターと広告

272

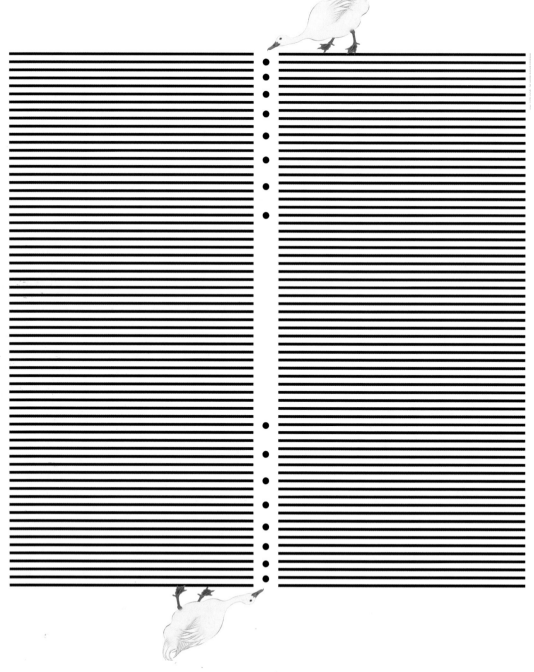

へいわ→わたし→しあわせ→せかい。これ、伝達の公式。

平和紙業株式会社

HEIWA's PEACE

ココロ×ココロ＋ゆめ＝笑顔。これ、創造の方程式。　　　　平和紙業株式会社

HEIWA's PEACE

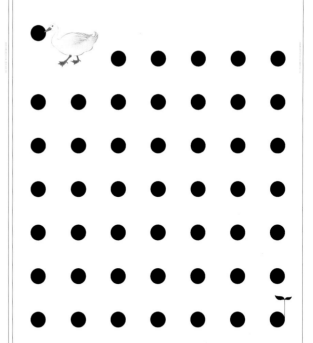

いのちのリレー。これ、再生の法則。　　　　平和紙業株式会社

HEIWA's PEACE

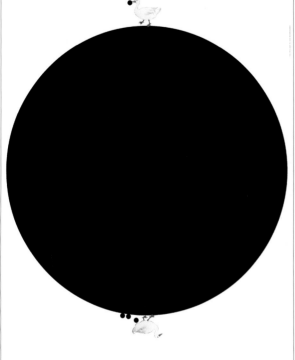

食べたら還す。これ、循環の原理。　　　　平和紙業株式会社

HEIWA's PEACE

見えないカタチを見つめる→↓←↑。これ、表現の真理。　　　　平和紙業株式会社

↓ Two Tops
    D: Ken Miki & Associates

→ Two Tops
    D: Ken Miki & Associates

274

ポスターと広告

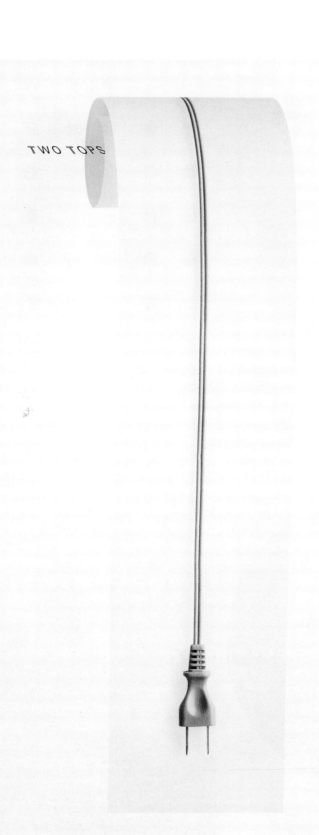

Arjo Wiggins
fine papers - papiers fins

TWO TOPS

Arjo Wiggins
fine papers - papiers fins

Arjo Wiggins
fine papers - papiers fins

Arjo Wiggins
fine papers - papiers fins

Arjo Wiggins
fine papers - papiers fins

TWO TOPS

TWO TOPS

↓ Suntory Collection
D: Ken Miki & Associates

→ Suntory Collection
D: Ken Miki & Associates

ポスターと広告

276

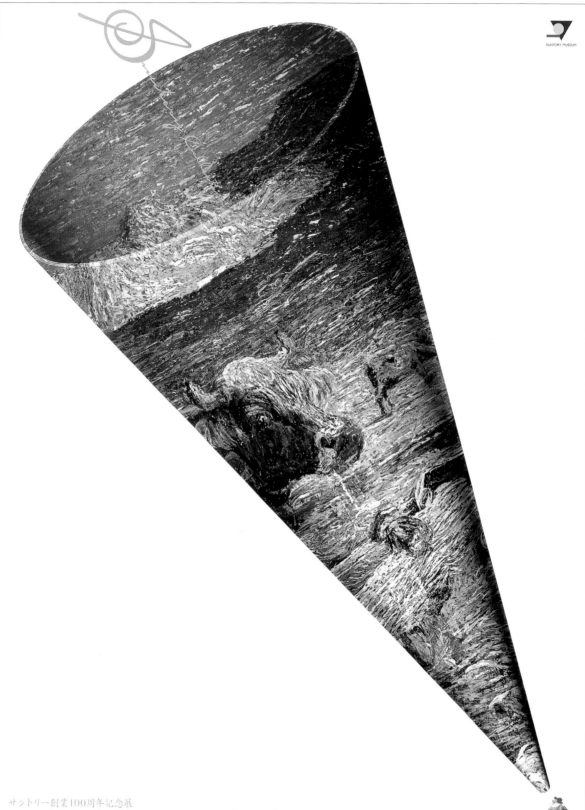

サントリー創業100周年記念展

サントリーコレクション—夢回廊

LIFE AND BEAUTY FROM JAPAN AND THE WEST
日本の生活美と西洋絵画・印象派から現代まで

会期／1999年11月20日(土)—2000年1月16日(日)　会場／サントリーミュージアム［天保山］ギャラリー

開催時間　10:30-19:30(最終入場は19:00まで)　入場料　大人1000円(900円)　高・大学生700円(630円)　小・中学生400円(360円)　(　)は前売入場券です。チケットぴあ、ローソンチケット、CNプレイガイドで発売しております。

休館日　毎週月曜日及び12月31日(11月22日、2000年1月3日・10日は開館いたします)　主催　サントリーミュージアム［天保山］、サントリー美術館　〒552-0022 大阪市港区海岸通1-5-10 Telephone 06-6577-0001 http://www.suntory.co.jp/culture/smt/

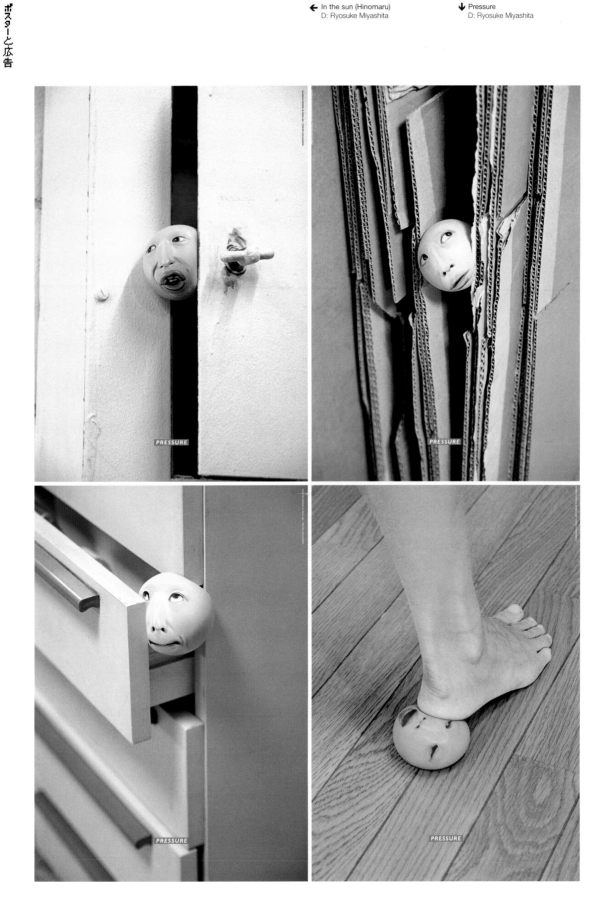

ISSEY MIYAKE

ポスターと広告

VIA BUS STOP

VIA BUS STOP

ISSEY MIYAKE MEN

ISSEY MIYAKE

ISSEY MIYAKE

↓ S/N
D: Hideki Nakajima

→ I Love Japan
D: MooN Project

ポスターと広告

284

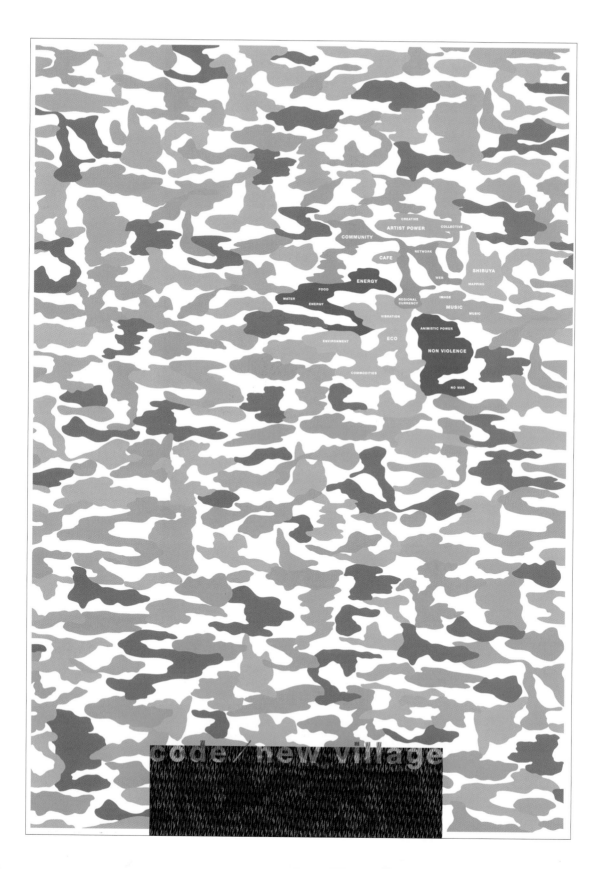

↓ I am walking
D: Hideki Nakajima

→ S/N
D: Hideki Nakajima

S/N
D: Hideki Nakajima

ポスターと広告

286

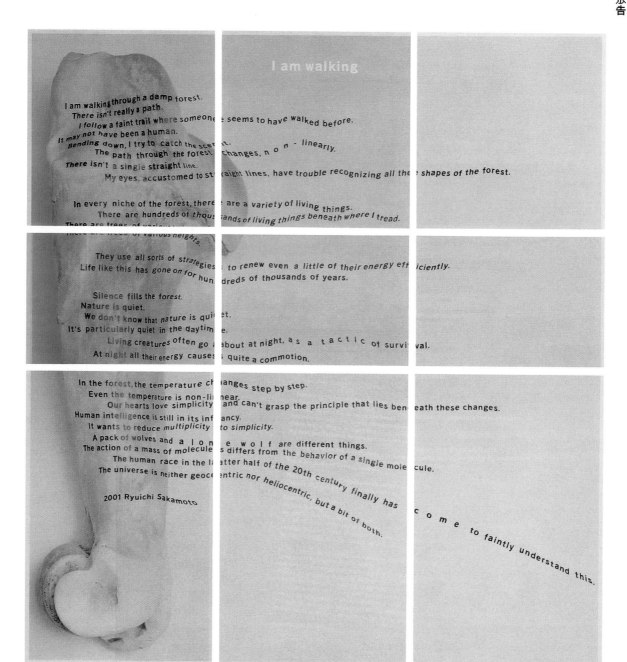

I am walking

I am walking through a damp forest.
There isn't really a path.
I follow a faint trail where someone seems to have walked before.
It may not have been a human.
Bending down, I try to catch the scent.
The path through the forest changes, n o n - linearly.
There isn't a single straight line.
My eyes, accustomed to straight lines, have trouble recognizing all the shapes of the forest.

In every niche of the forest, there are a variety of living things.
There are hundreds of thousands of living things beneath where I tread.
There are trees of various heights.
They use all sorts of strategies to renew even a little of their energy efficiently.
Life like this has gone on for hundreds of thousands of years.

Silence fills the forest.
Nature is quiet.
We don't know that nature is quiet.
It's particularly quiet in the daytime.
Living creatures often go about at night, as a t a c t i c of survival.
At night all their energy causes quite a commotion.

In the forest, the temperature changes step by step.
Even the temperature is non-linear.
Our hearts love simplicity and can't grasp the principle that lies beneath these changes.
Human intelligence is still in its infancy.
It wants to reduce multiplicity to simplicity.
A pack of wolves and a l o n e w o l f are different things.
The action of a mass of molecules differs from the behavior of a single molecule.
The human race in the latter half of the 20th century finally has come to faintly understand this.
The universe is neither geocentric nor heliocentric, but a bit of both.

2001 Ryuichi Sakamoto

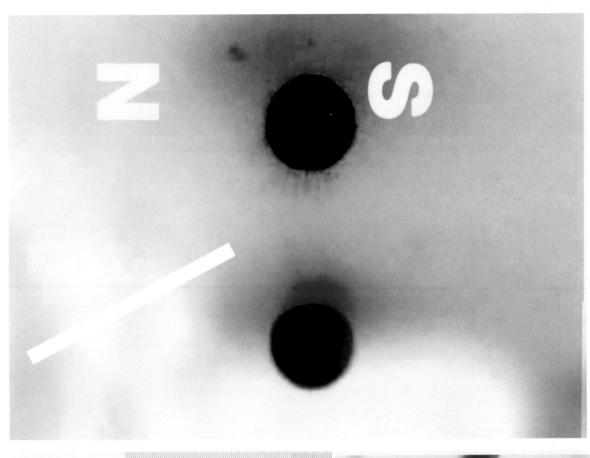

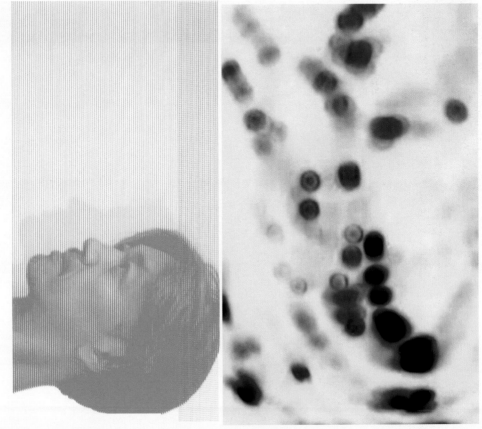

↓ Silent force
D: Ryosuke Miyashita

→ Kenny A Inc. Public Relations
D: Kenny A Inc.

Azumino Art Line
D: Kenny A Inc.

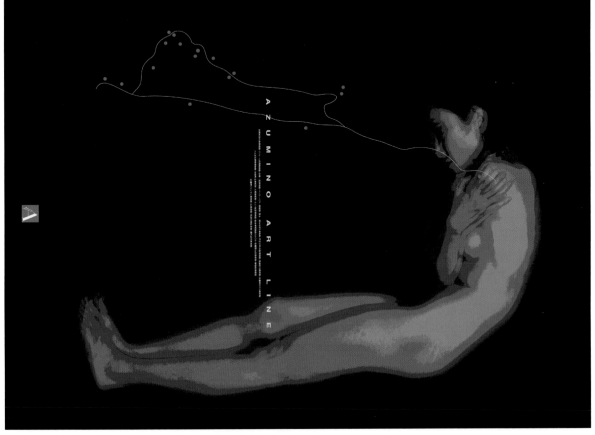

↓ Sony Music Art Audition
Sony Music Entertainment Inc.
D: Norio Nakamura

→ Close-Up of Japan in São Paulo
D: Norio Nakamura

Toy "Pootiki"
Cube Co., Ltd (c)anchovy2000
D: Norio Nakamura

ポスターと広告

290

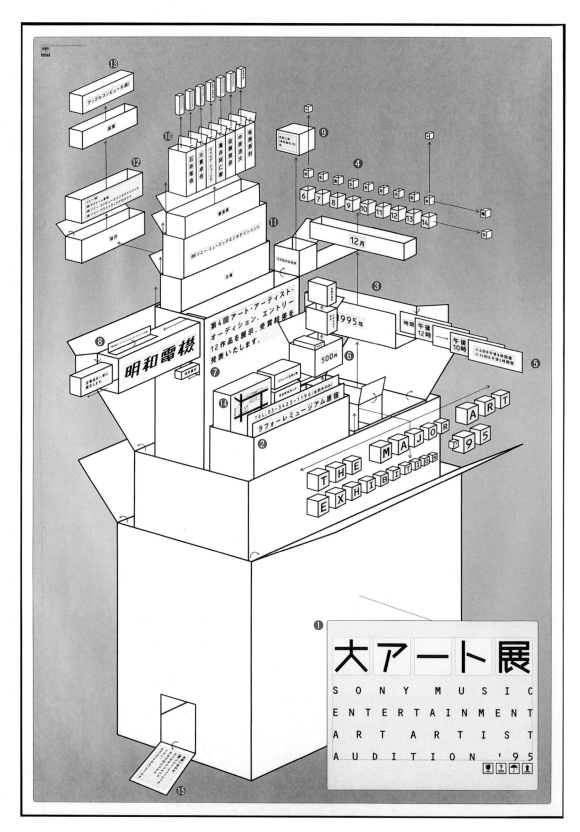

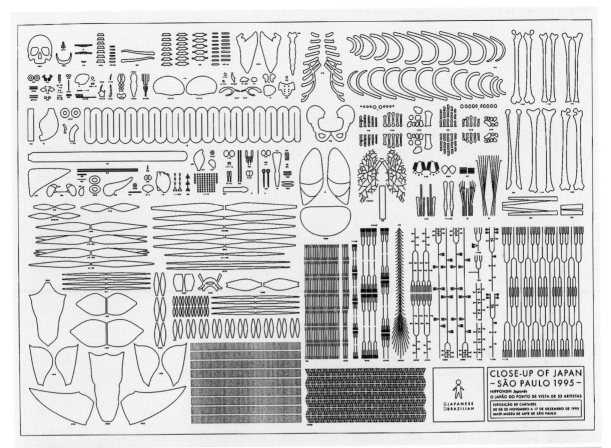

CLOSE-UP OF JAPAN
— SÃO PAULO 1995 —

NIPPONJIN *Japonês*
O JAPÃO DO PONTO DE VISTA DE 23 ARTISTAS
EXPOSIÇÃO DE CARTAZES
DE 08 DE NOVEMBRO A 17 DE DEZEMBRO DE 1995
MASP-MUSEU DE ARTE DE SÃO PAULO

☐ JAPANESE
☐ BRAZILIAN

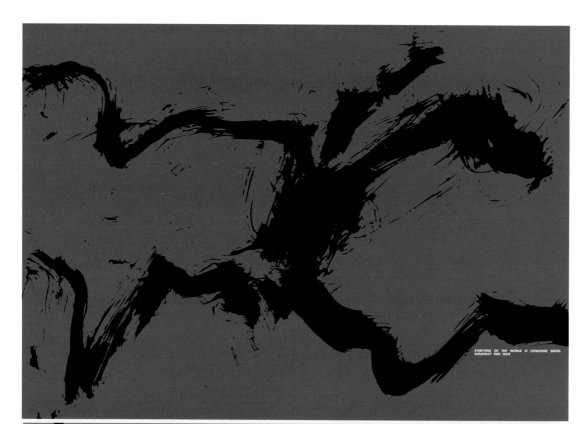

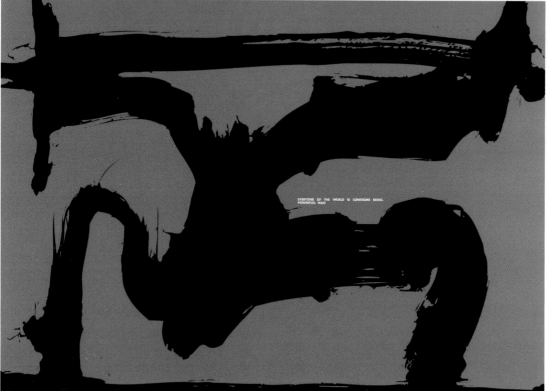

HELP vol.1
D: Koshi Ogawa

HELP vol.2
D: Koshi Ogawa

Why!
D: Koshi Ogawa

Is that the earth where you are?
D: Koshi Ogawa

294

ポスターと広告

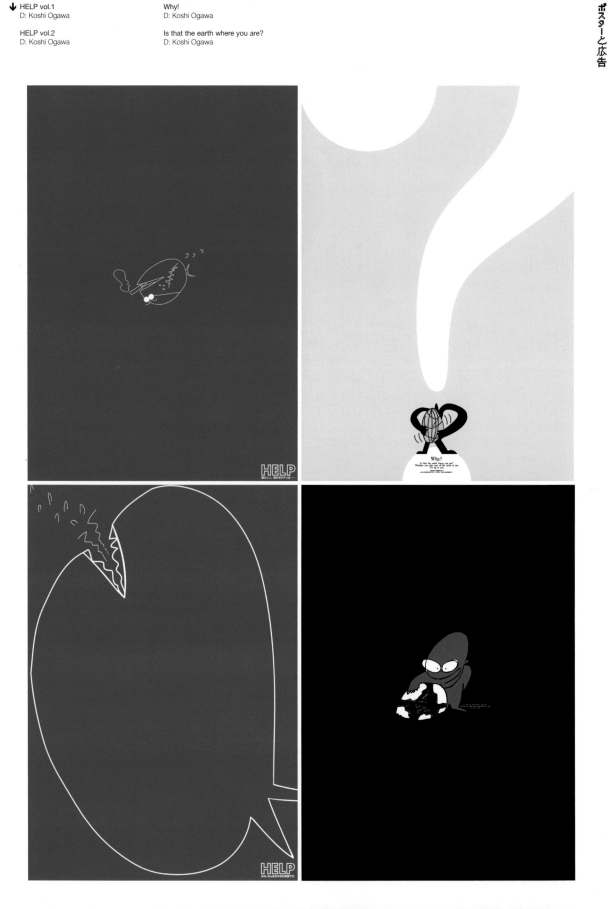

↓ The 3th Enshu Yokosuka-kaido
Cultural Exhibition
D: Koshi Ogawa

Froid
D: Koshi Ogawa

Kyizin butik UN vol.2
D: Koshi Ogawa

Kyizin butik UN vol.1
D: Koshi Ogawa

The 3th Enshu Yokosuka-kaido Cultural Exhibition
2001.10/26Fri/27sat/28sun

Open at 5pm. We warmly welcome you, serving excellent SAKE and original dishes.
walk up! walk up!

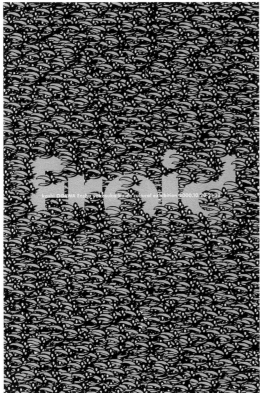

Just a drink, slight drink…
…Another drink! さあ、呑みましょう!

↓ Human Intellect
D: Akio Okumura

➜ XI'An Image [Serenity]
XI'An Image [Vivacity]
D: Akio Okumura

ポスターと広告

296

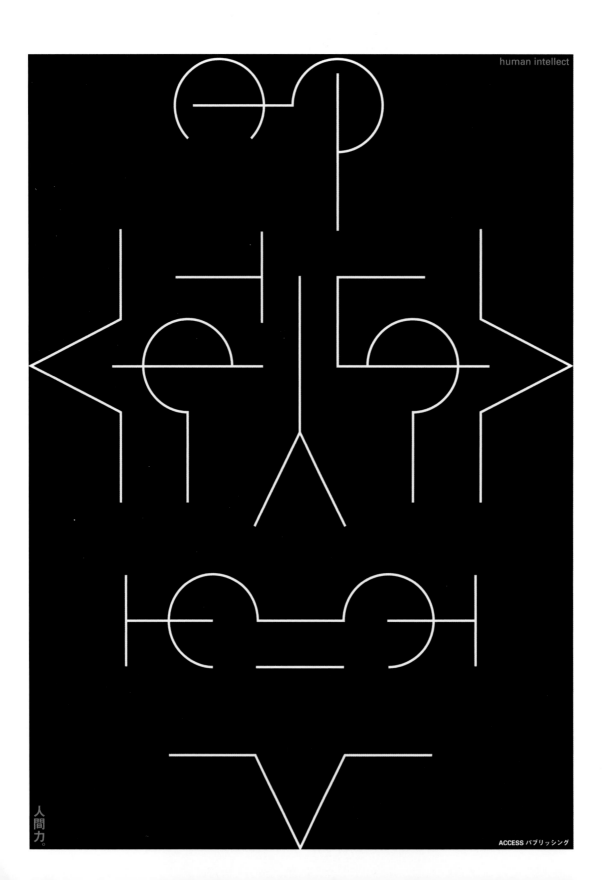

human intellect

人間力。

ACCESS パブリッシング

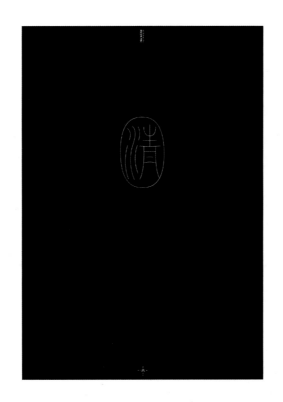

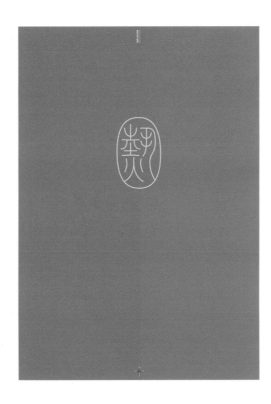

ポスターと広告

↓ Okumura Akio Match
D: Akio Okumura

Kyoto University Of Art
D: Akio Okumura

Oji Paper Gallery Ginza
D: Akio Okumura

Kyoto University Of Art
D: Akio Okumura

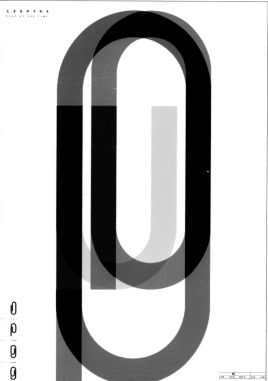

↓ Make yourself comfortable
D: Rocketdesign

→ Rain Boys
D: Rocketdesign

Manmanman
D: Rocketdesign

300

ポスターと広告

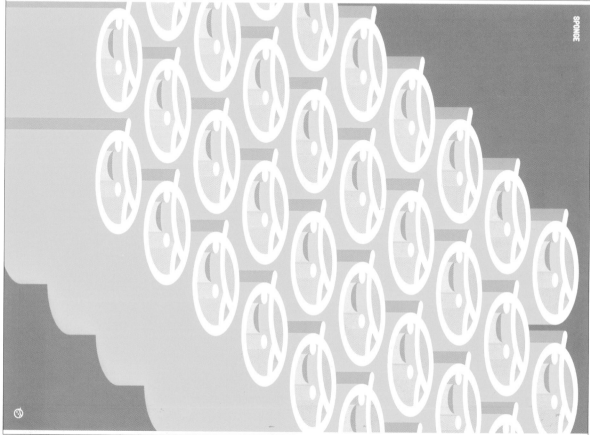

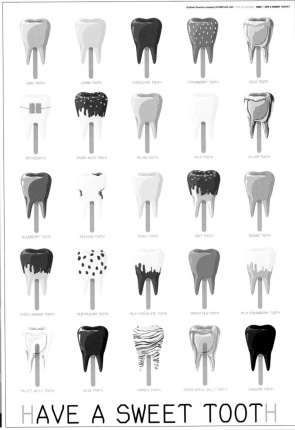

HAVE A SWEET TOOTH

YELLOW by OutSide Directors company limited

← Poster O / Poster P / Poster H / Poster Y
D: Osamu Sato /
Outside Directors Company Ltd.
ad+d: Osamu Sato
d: Shintaro Minami
cg: Noboru Iizuka
c: Hiroko Nishikawa

↓ Poster for Tokyo Academy
of Hairdressing and Beauty
D: Osamu Sato /
Outside Directors Company Ltd.
ad+d: Osamu Sato
d: Shintaro Minami
cg: Noboru Iizukac and Hiroko Nishikawa

学 校 法 人
田中芸術学園　東京美容専門学校 **TOKYO ACADEMY OF HAIRDRESSING & BEAUTY**

〒161-8557　東京都新宿区下落合1-2-4　☎ 0120-344276　http://www.tahb.ac.jp/

Lexmark X5150
D: Romando Co., Ltd.

Ellesse concept visual
D: Romando Co., Ltd.

304

ポスターと広告

隠したくなるプリンタは、悪だ。

世界のレックスマークから、日本へ。史上最もスマートな複合機、X5150登場。

Smart DESIGN
Smart FUNCTION
Smart PRICE

プリンタは、もはや周辺機器ではない。それは、知的インテリアに進化すべきである。
磨き抜かれたデザインと、真に求められる機能。そして"Printing"を身近にする理想価格。
プリンタ、スキャナ、コピーを最も"Smart"に凝縮したLexmark X5150 オールインワン・ステーション。
プリンタのグローバルブランド、レックスマークからの新提案を、いま日本へ、そしてあなたへ。

Printing Smart LEXMARK

www.lexmark.co.jp/x5150

驚きのスマートプライスは、店頭で。

○PRINTER:解像度4800×1200dpi ○SCANNER:解像度600×2400dpi, CCDスキャナ搭載 ○COPY:原体使用可, 拡大縮小倍率 25～400% ○W469×H240×D395mm 対応OS:
Win 98,Me,2000,XP/Mac OS 9.2.2, OS X10.1.5 ○X5150のサービス, サポートには, 1年間無償保証に加え, 故障が発生した場合に交換製品を発送する"LexExpress""が含まれます。

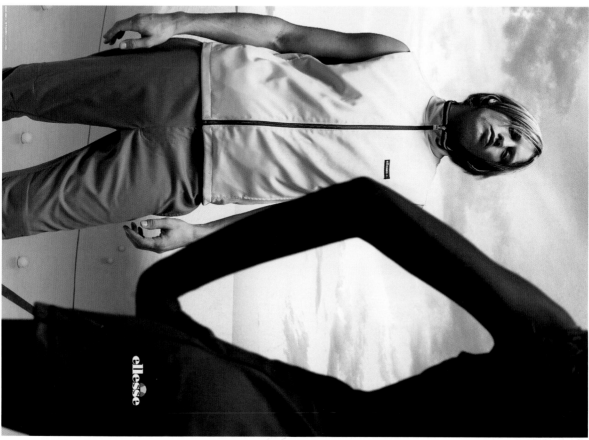

Honda HR-V
  D: Butterfly Stroke Inc.
  cl: Honda Motor Co., Ltd.
  cd: Hidenobu Ni-zuma
  ad+d: Katsunori Aoki
  i: Enlightenment

Honda Motor's Step Wgn "Star Chart"
  D: Samurai

ポスターと広告

306

Honda Motor's Step Wgn Whitee! "Dinosaur"

Honda Motor's Step Wgn Whitee! "Fish"

Honda Motor's Step Wgn Deluxee! "Robot"
D: Samurai

Honda Motor's Step Wgn Launching Champaign "Where shall we go with the kids?"

Honda Motor's Step Wgn "Woolen Yarn"
D: Samurai

↓ Fishing Net
D: Norito Shinmura
ad: Norito Shinmura
c: Kazutaka Sato a: Masashi Shinmura
p: Kogo Inoue adv: Shinmura Fisheries

Island's Spring
ad: Norito Shinmura
c: K. Sato adv: Shinmura Fisheries

Fishing Net "Ray"
D: Norito Shinmura
ad: Norito Shinmura
c: Kazutaka Sato a: Masashi Shinmura
p: Kogo Inoue adv: Shinmura Fisheries

Island's Summer
ad: Norito Shinmura
c: K. Sato adv: Shinmura Fisheries

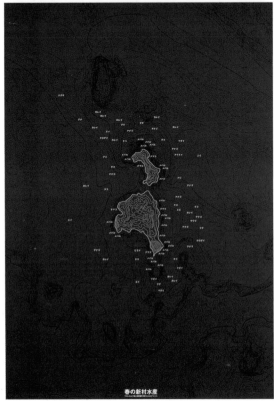

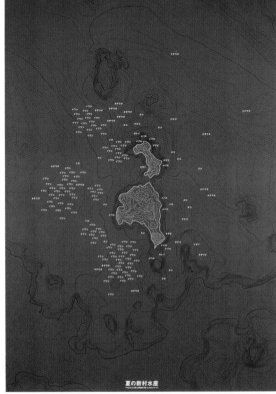

↓ Strategy is Freshness "sardine"
D: Norito Shinmura
ad: Norito Shinmura
c: Kazutaka Sato p: Ko Hosokawa
adv: Shinmura Fisheries

Waterdrops "octopus"
ad: Norito Shinmura
c: Kazutaka Sato p: Kiyofusa Nozu
adv: Shinmura Fisheries

Strategy is Freshness "octopus"
D: Norito Shinmura
ad: Norito Shinmura
c: Kazutaka Sato p: Ko Hosokawa
adv: Shinmura Fisheries

Waterdrops "horse mackarels"
ad: Norito Shinmura
c: Kazutaka Sato p: Kiyofusa Nozu
adv: Shinmura Fisheries

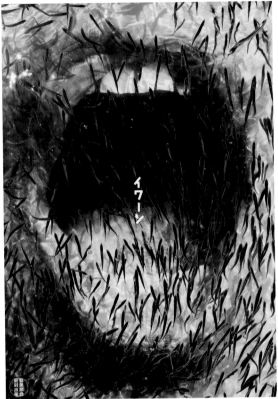

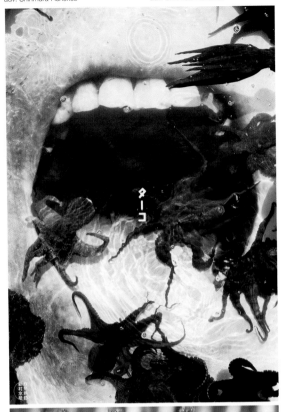

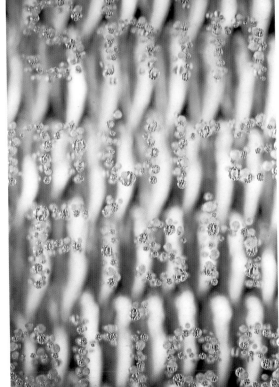

海の魚は、森に育てられる。

藻は、海の果である。

魚の子孫までが、獲られている。

きれいにする洗剤が、海を汚している。

← Sea Fishes are nurtured by the forest
D: Norito Shinmura
ad: Norito Shinmura c: Motoharu Sakata
p: Teiichi Ogata adv: Yamaguchi Fisheries Cooperative
Associations

Catching fishes even their posterity
ad: Norito Shinmura
c: Masakazu Nifuji p: Ko Hosokawa
adv: Yamaguchi Fisheries Cooperative Associations

The seaweed is a nest of the sea
D: Norito Shinmura
ad: Norito Shinmura
c: Masakazu Nifuji p: Ko Hosokawa
adv: Yamaguchi Fisheries Cooperative Associations

The cleanser which makes things clean pollutes the sea
ad: Norito Shinmura
c: Masakazu Nifuji p: Ko Hosokawa
adv: Yamaguchi Fisheries Cooperative Associations

↓ Japan for Ecology
D: Norito Shinmura
ad: Norito Shinmura
c: Hiroshi Uehara
p: Kogo Inoue
adv: JAGDA

The JAGDA Poster Exhibition: JAPAN 2001

Japan
for
Ecology

↓ Be a Happy Camper
D: Norito Shinmura
ad: Norito Shinmura
c: Hiroyuki Nakazaki
p: Masahiro Soga
cl: MUJI

仲間を集めてキャンプへ行こう。

↓ Be a Happy Camper
D: Norito Shinmura
ad: Norito Shinmura
c: Hiroyuki Nakazaki
p: Kogo Inoue
cl: MUJI

自然の笑顔に逢いに行こう。

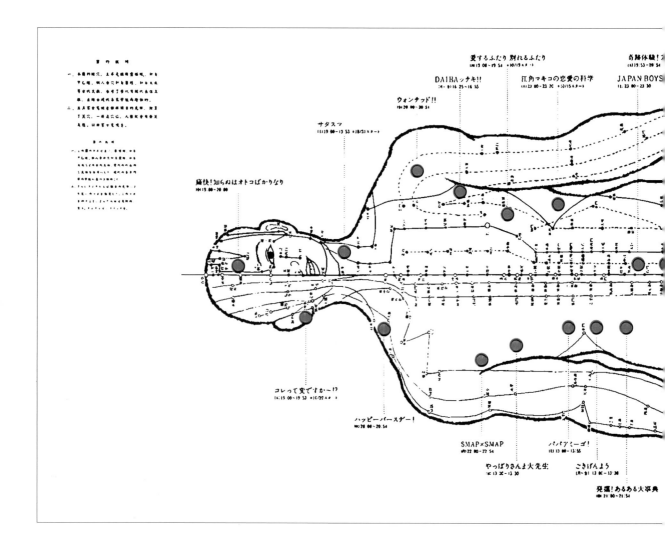

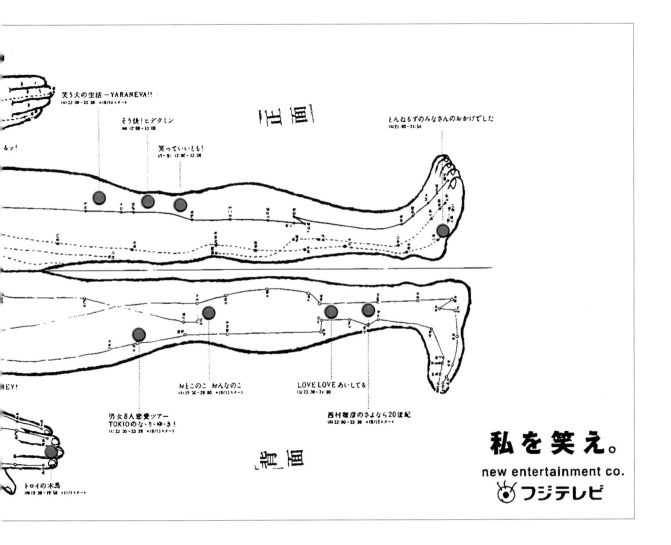

私を笑え。

new entertainment co.

フジテレビ

新幹線が
ひと肌脱ぎます。

新庄
shinjo

TSUBASA

♨ 温泉新幹線 12月

《お得なきっぷのご案内》 ◎東京庄内2WAY回数券 ◎つばさ回数券（6枚

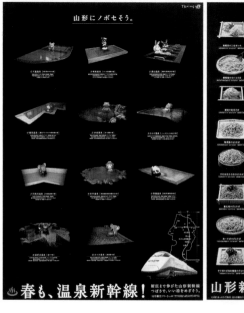

山形にノボセそう。

春も、温泉新幹線！

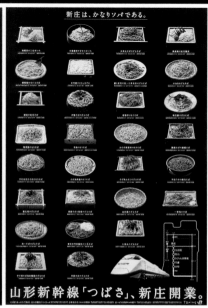

新庄は、かなりソバである。

山形新幹線「つばさ」、新庄開業。

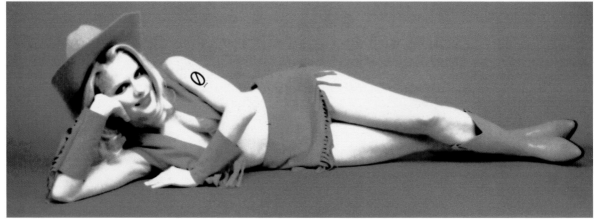

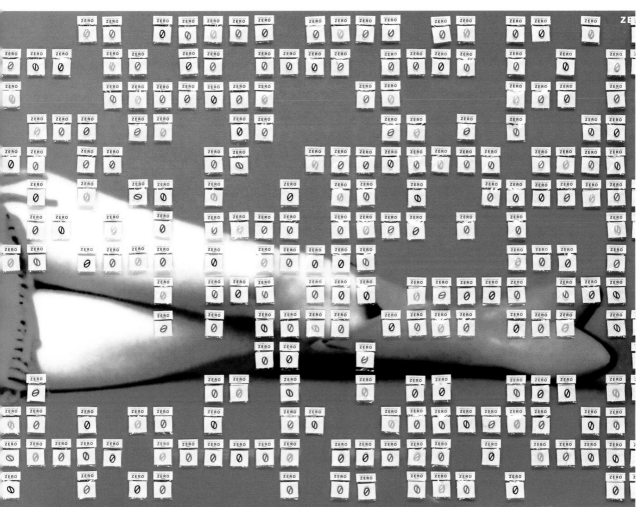

↓ Sega ch@b
D: TUGBOAT

→ JR East JR Snow
D: TUGBOAT

ポスターと広告

326

未公開KAB. 発表。>ALL ソングラをホネまでチャぶろう。5/5 渋谷ちゃぶ台（代々木第2体育館 横）で、待つ。 www.isao.net

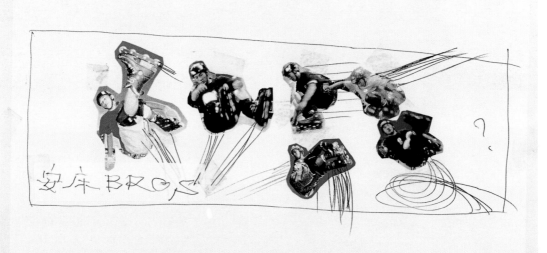

兄）エイトの1080フラットスピン 弟）タケシのマックツイスト900 インライン世界Champをホネまでチャぶろう。5/4・5 渋谷ちゃぶ台（代々木第2体育館 横）で、待つ。 www.isao.net

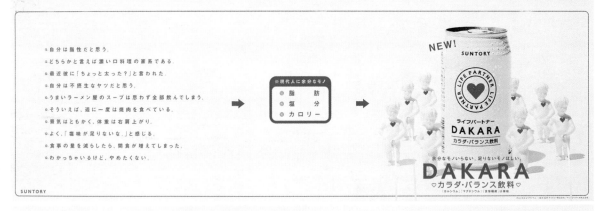

わたしたちの食堂は、24h 開いている。

↓ Sega Dreamcast
D: TUGBOAT

→ Global warming
AD: Norito Shinmura
C: Hiroyuki Koyama
P: Ko Hosokawa
ADV: Mainichi News paper

334

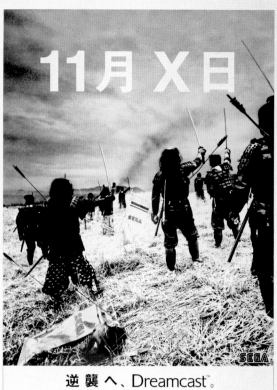

今ほどの豊かさが本当に必要なのでしょうか？ 地球温暖化がこのまま進むと、海水の膨張や氷河の融解により、21世紀末には海面が15〜95cm上昇します。日本では、海面以下の地域が2.7倍にひろがり、人口4□□万人が危険にさらされ

。

↓ Hot Pepper
D: Creative Power Unit

→ Bals Corporation Franc franc Design
D: TUGBOAT

336

ポスターと広告

Franc franc Xmas

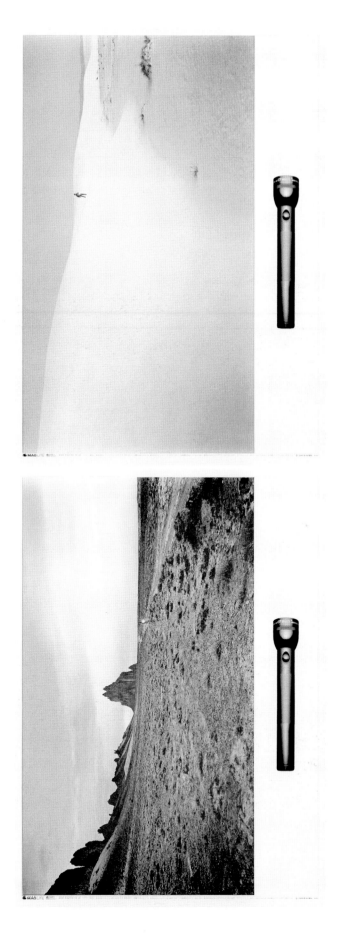

Franc franc DESIGN

人 生 楽 し も う 。 と 、思 え る ポ ジ テ ィ ブ デ ザ イ ン が 欲 し い 。　　w w w . f r a n c f r a n c . c o m

Franc franc DESIGN

The 10th anniversary presentation

一瞬でも自由になれた気がするリラックスデザインが欲しい。 www.francfranc.com

Franc franc DESIGN

バカンスなんかに行かなくても楽しめるリゾートデザインが欲しい。 www.francfranc.com

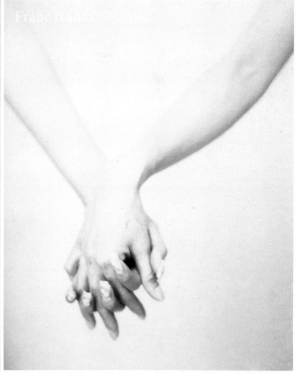

Franc franc DESIGN

もはや性別をも超越したブライダルデザインが欲しい。 www.francfranc.com

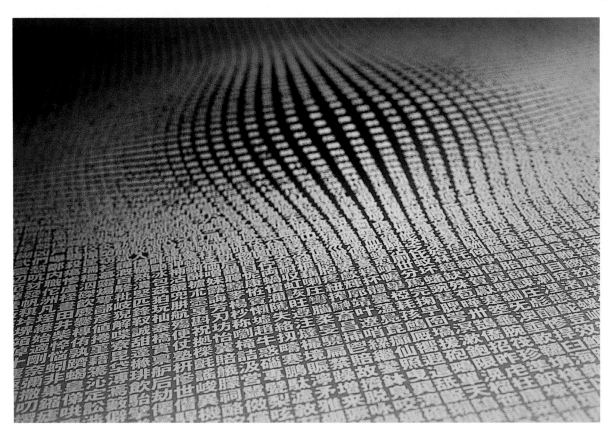

↓ Elementism, Multiple Square
D: Shinnoske Sugisaki

→ Elementism Crop Circle
D: Shinnoske Sugisaki

<<<98
D: Shinnoske Sugisaki

344   ポスターと広告

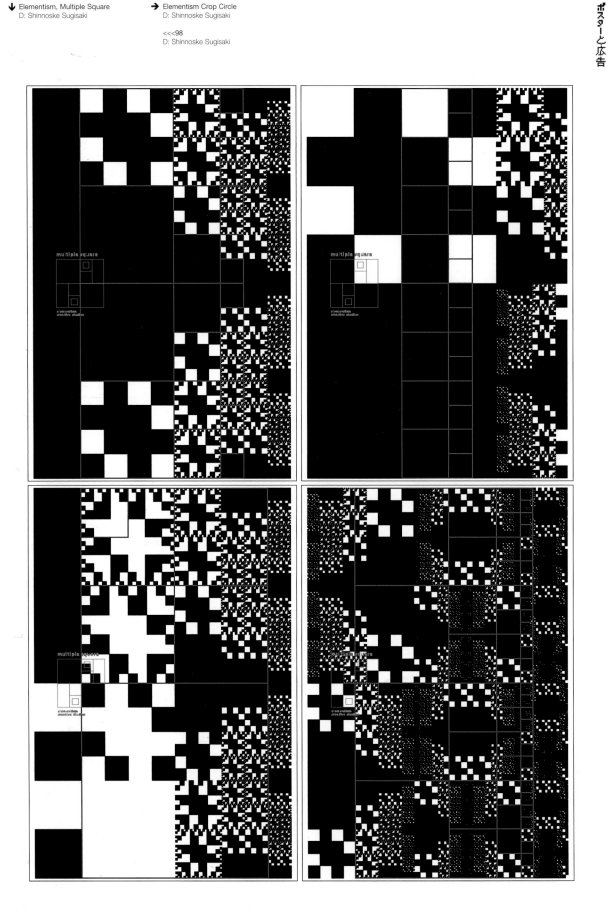

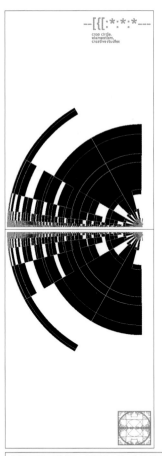
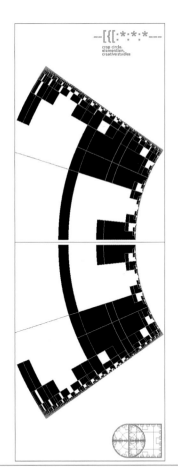
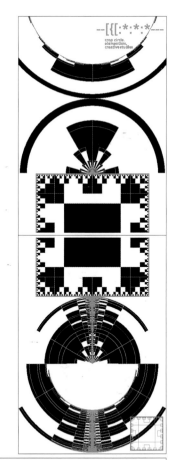
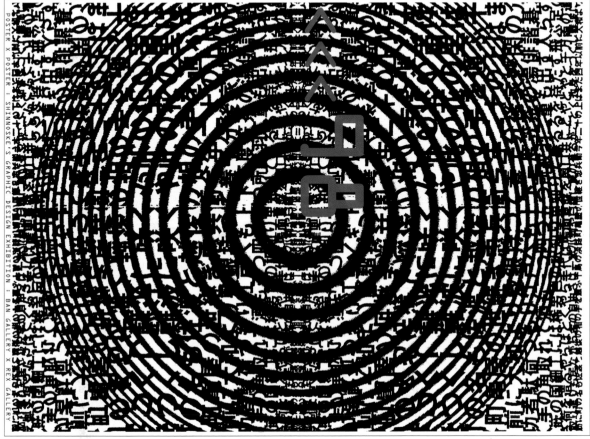

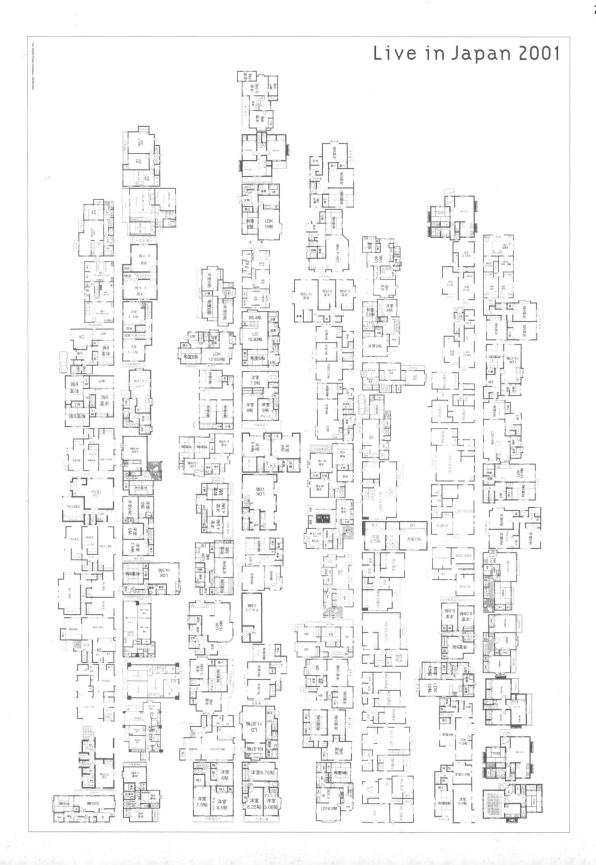

Live in Japan 2001

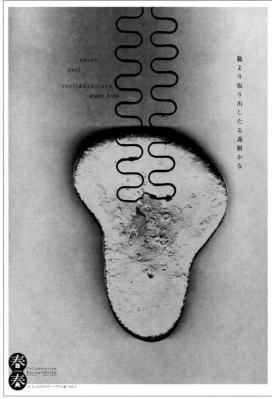

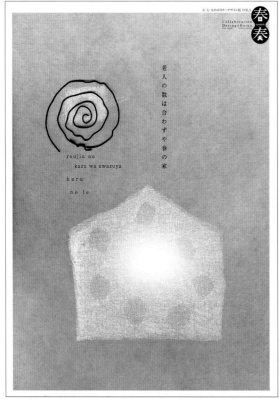

↓ Haiku (Japanese 17-syllabled poem)
Syukyo
D: Hiroyuki Ueno

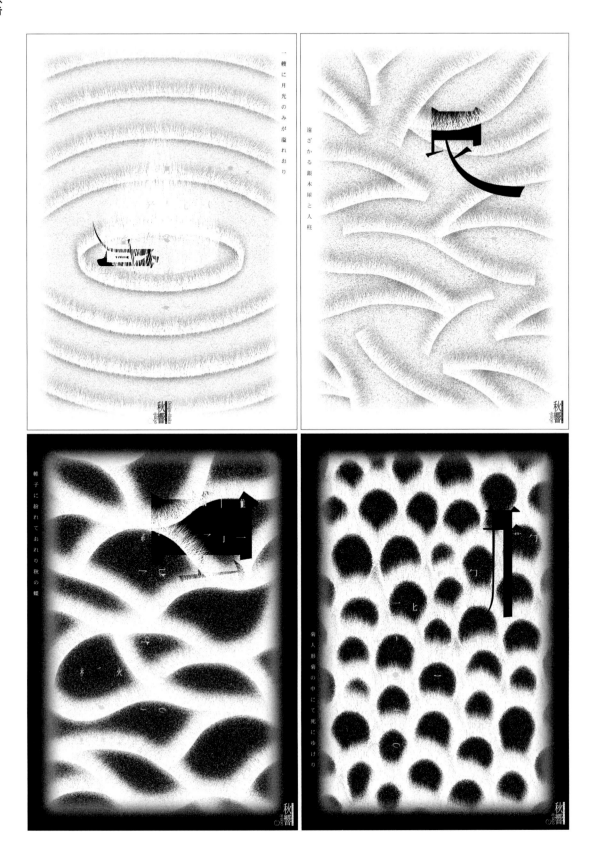

きょうはうさぎ
あしたはきりん

TAMALA2010
a punk cat in space

CATTY&CO.

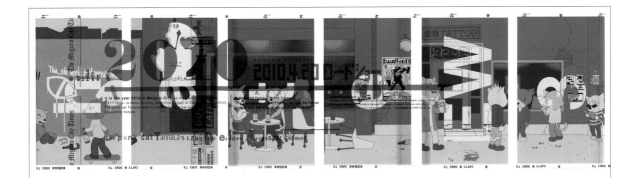

TAMALA 2010 A PUNK CAT IN SPACE

NEKO EARTH MEGURO CITY   supported by むねこちゃん and

TAMALA2010
a punk cat in space

↓ Poster for competition
D: Toshihiro Watanabe

→ Save energy
D: U.G.Sato

Japanese Sake "Ippin"
D: U.G.Sato

Where can Japan go?
D: U.G.Sato

Visual communication
D: U.G.Sato

354

ポスターと広告

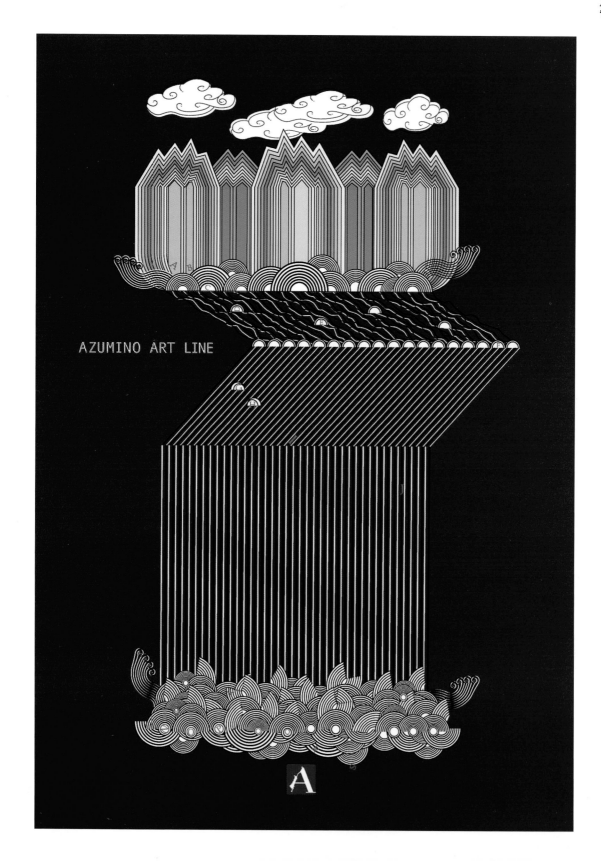

S A V E   E N E R G Y

Where can Japan go ?

V I S U A L   C O M M U N I C A T I O N

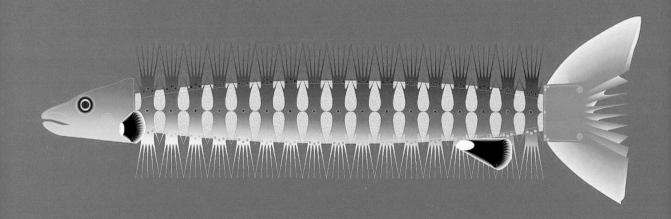

← Fish001

Fish005
D: Toshihiro Watanabe

↓ Jellyfish
D: Toshihiro Watanabe

Catfish
D: Toshihiro Watanabe

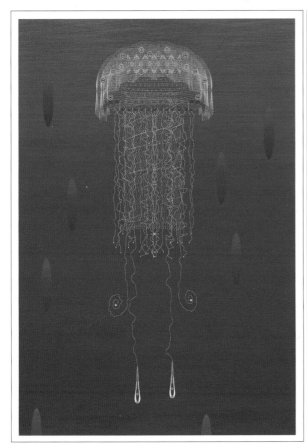

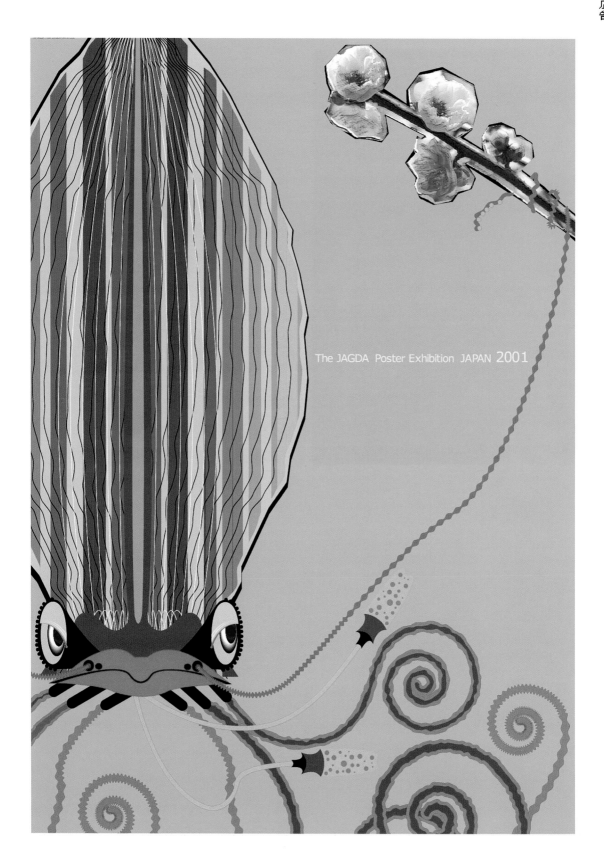

↓ JAGDA poster for exhibition
D: Toshihiro Watanabe

→ Octopus
D: Toshihiro Watanabe

358

ポスターと広告

The JAGDA Poster Exhibition JAPAN 2001

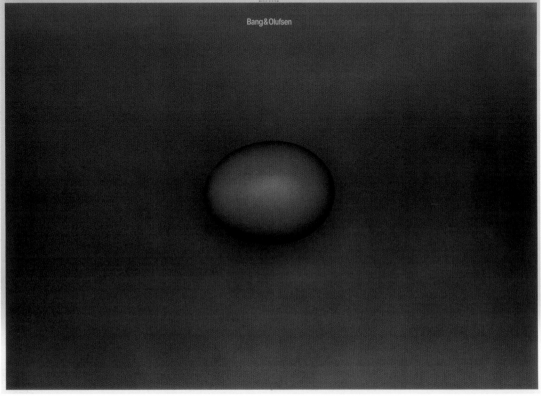

ポスターと広告

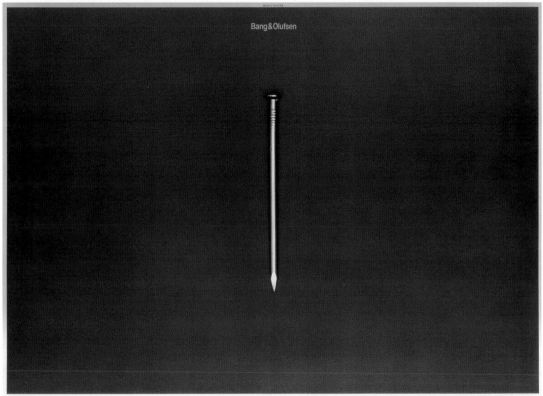

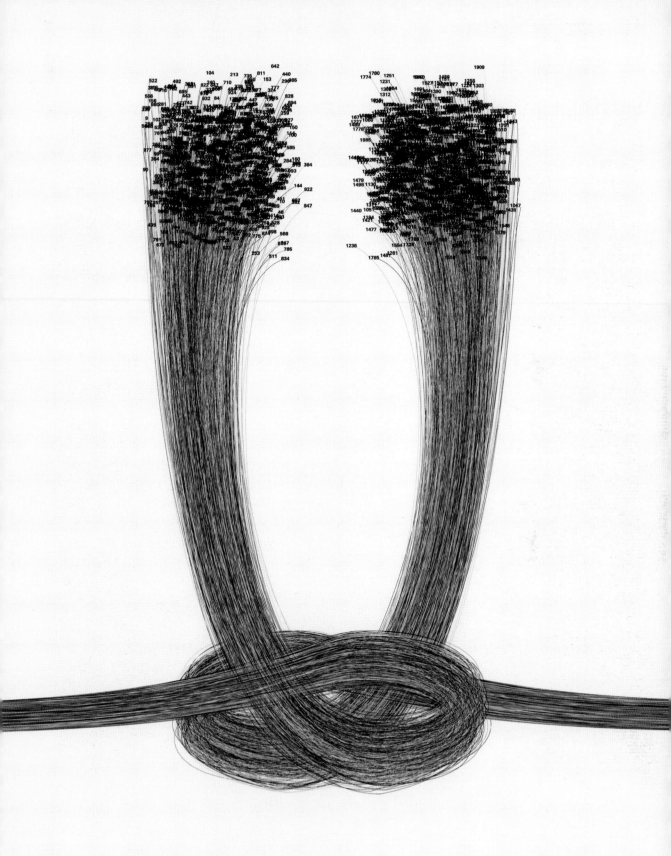

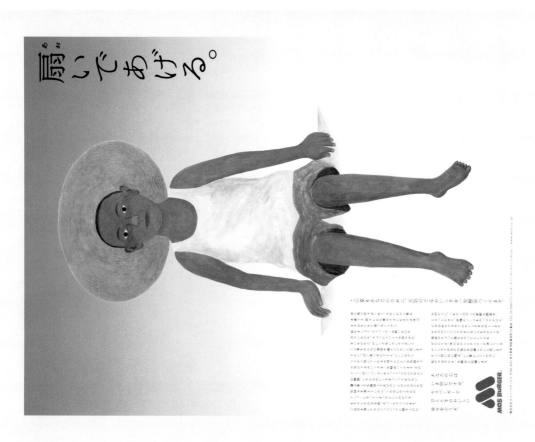

← Mos Burger Summer NP
D: Yoshie Watanabe

Mos Burger Summer NP
D: Yoshie Watanabe

↓ Caslon Quoits
D: Yoshie Watanabe

Caslon Bamboo dragonfly
D: Yoshie Watanabe

虬　虹　虻　蚓　蚣　蚋
蚊　蚌　蛆　蛇　蛙　蛞
蛟　蛤　蛭　蛛　蛾　蜆
蛻　蛸　蜂　蛹　蜊　蜷
蜩　蜻　蝦　蝸　蝌　蝎
蝗　蝍　蝶　蝮　蝙　蟒
蟆　螭　螺　蟻　蟬　蟫
蟻　蠍　蟾　蠅　蠖　蠟

創業昭和六年

渋谷宮益坂上

志賀昆蟲普及社

創業昭和六年

渋谷宮益坂上

志賀昆蟲普及社

↓ Poster of Shiga Insect
D: Taku Satoh

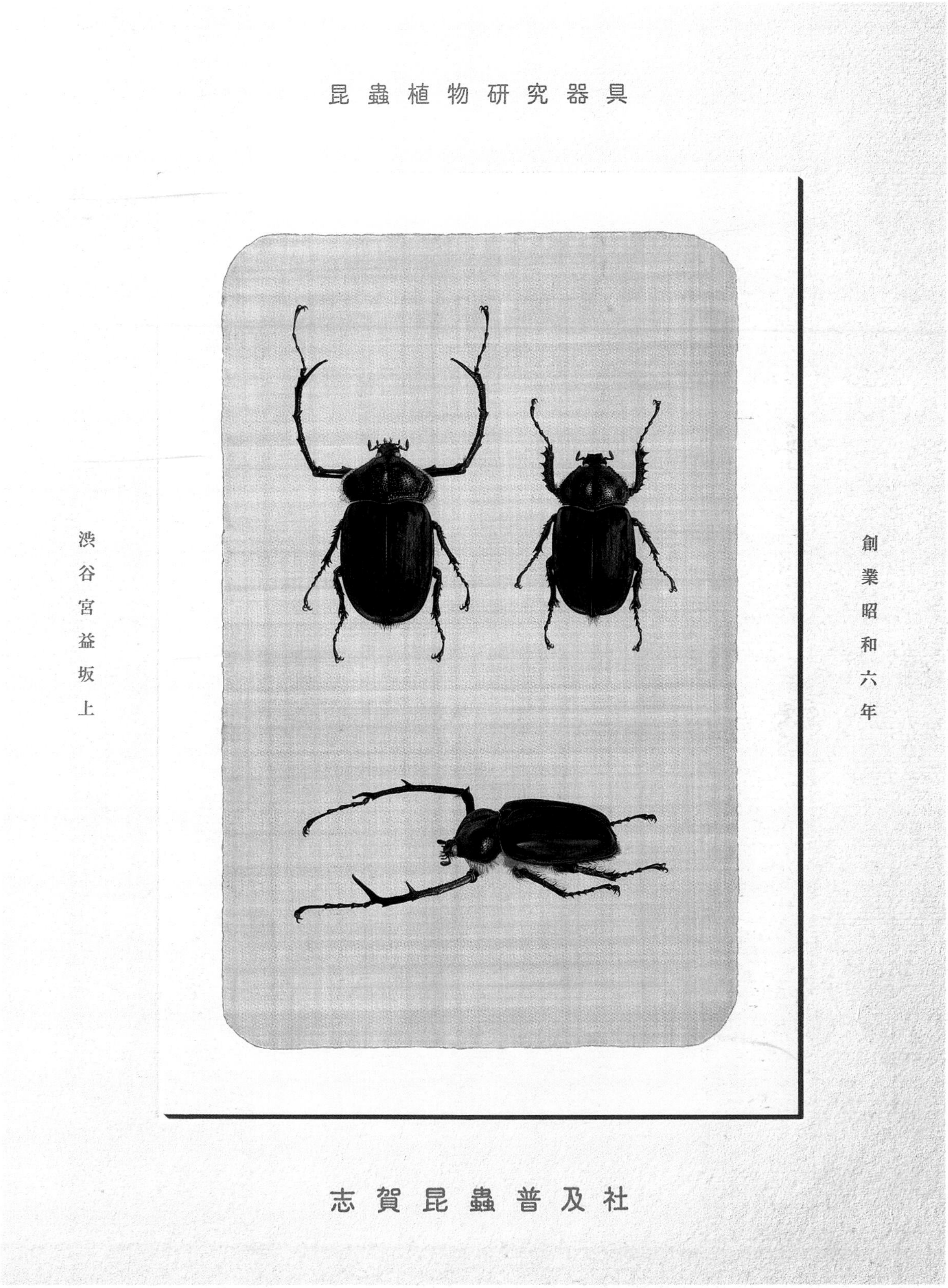

昆 蟲 植 物 研 究 器 具

渋 谷 宮 益 坂 上

創 業 昭 和 六 年

志 賀 昆 蟲 普 及 社

↓ Poster of Design-02
D: Taku Satoh

→ Analysis of the Massproduct Design=
Fujifilm (UTSURUNDESU)
D: Taku Satoh

368

ポスターと広告

Analysis of the Massproduct Design

デザインの解剖②＝フジフイルム・写ルンです

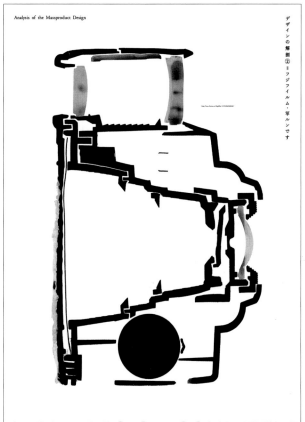

Body Frame Section of Fujifilm "UTSURUNDESU"

JAPAN DESIGN COMMITTEE

Analysis of the Massproduct Design

デザインの解剖②＝フジフイルム・写ルンです

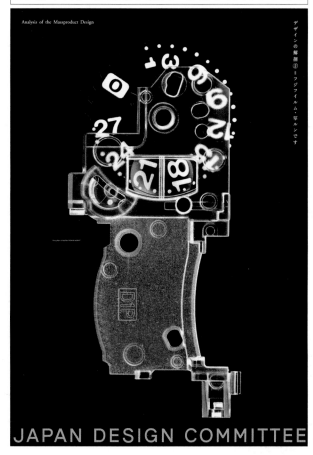

Wrong Part of Fujifilm "UTSURUNDESU"

JAPAN DESIGN COMMITTEE

DATE

October 17th (Thu)
— December 14th (Sat), 2002

PLACE

The Japan Foundation Toronto
131 Bloor Street West, Suite 213
The 2nd floor of The Colonnade Building

ADMISSION

Free

HOURS

Monday to Friday 11:30 A.M. — 4:30 P.M.
Thursdays   11:30 A.M. — 7:00 P.M.
Saturdays   NOON — 5:00 P.M.

INQUIRIES

416-966-1600, ext.229
taoyagi@jftor.org
www.japanfoundationcanada.org

CLOSED

Sundays
(Monday November 11th Remembrance Day)

CO-PRESENTED BY

The Japan Design Committee
& The Japan Foundation Toronto
The Japan Foundation

INVISIBLE DESIGNER

Interrelation of Product & Environment in Design by Taku Satoh

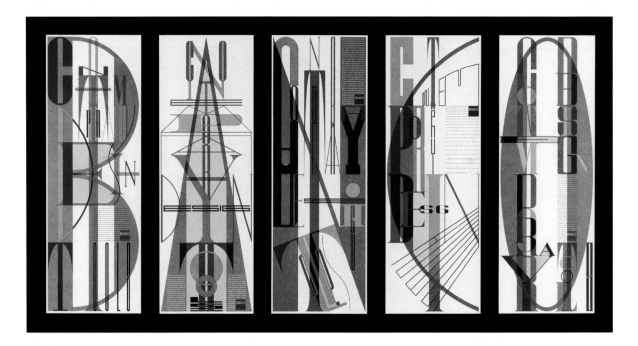

↓ Poster of Banco
D: Taku Satoh

→ Rebuild
D: Taku Satoh

372

ポスターと広告

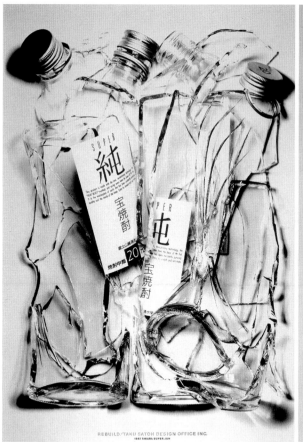

REBUILD/TAKU SATOH DESIGN OFFICE INC.
1992 TAKARA SUPER JUN

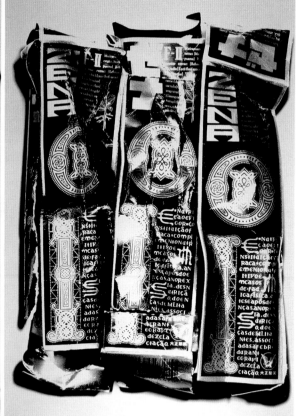

REBUILD/TAKU SATOH DESIGN OFFICE INC.
1993 TAISHO PHARM ZENA

REBUILD/TAKU SATOH DESIGN OFFICE INC.
1993 TAKARA SUPER CANCHUHI

REBUILD/TAKU SATOH DESIGN OFFICE INC.
1993 CALPIS

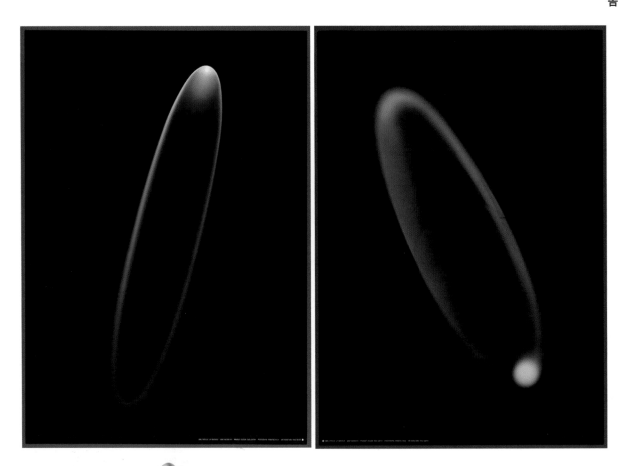

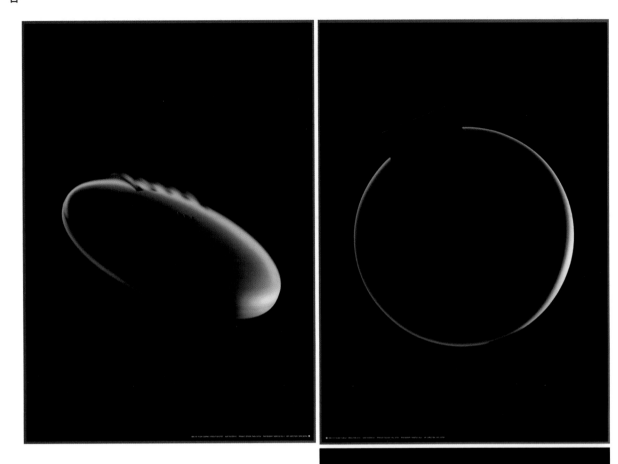

Dog Run

Cat Laugh
D: Hakuhodo Inc.
cl: Five Foxes Co., Ltd.

Dog Fight

Cat Run
D: Hakuhodo Inc.
cl: Five Foxes Co., Ltd.

Comme Ca Du Mode "Planets"
D: Hakuhodo Inc.
cl: Five Foxes Co., Ltd.

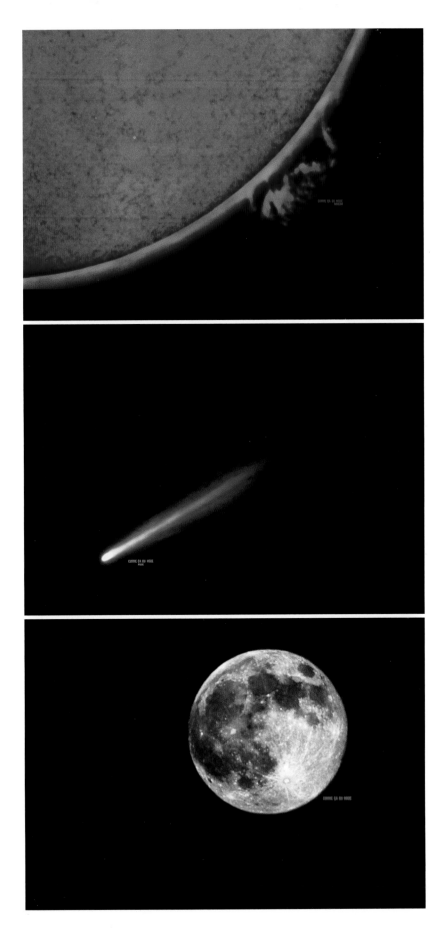

↓ Yo, Sinful Sushi

Act Now
D: Hakuhodo Inc.
cl: World Wide Fund for Nature Japan

ポスターと広告

378

↓ Let's go to Toshimaen

Toshimaen Pool
D: Hakuhodo Inc.
cl: Toshimaen Co., Ltd

ポスターと広告

← Cross Cloths
D: Hakuhodo Inc.

↓ Man
D: Hakuhodo Inc.
cl: Japan Rugby Football Union

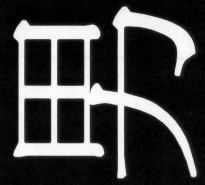

RUGBY FOOTBALL
2001 SEASON OPENING MATCH.
JAPAN ✕ PRESIDENT'S XV
09.07 FRI. 2001 19:00 KICK OFF   AT 国立競技場

主催：(財)日本ラグビーフットボール協会　主管：関東ラグビーフットボール協会　後援：読売新聞社　TV放送：Jスカイスポーツ
入場料金：A自由席 2,000円　B自由席 1,000円 *消費税込み　高校生以下入場無料（要生徒証提示）　入場券発売所：チケットぴあ 03-5237-9977 /
ファミリーマート / ローソンチケットガイド 03-5537 9999 / CNプレイガイド 03-5802 9999 / 協会指定プレイガイド 03-3401-3290　*5日あめ0
問い合わせ先：(財)日本ラグビーフットボール協会事務局　03-3401 3290　www.rugby-japan.or.jp

↓ Insight (the economical car)
D: Hakuhodo Inc.
cl: Honda Motor Co., Ltd.

382
ポスターと広告

スピードはひかえめに、シートベルトをしめて安全運転。

HONDA

人と、地球に「夢・発見・ドラマ」を。

35km!/ℓ

世 界 記 録 を 、 世 界 発 売 。

personal hybrid *insight*

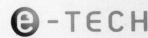

パ ー ソ ナ ル ハ イ ブ リ ッ ド ［ イ ン サ イ ト ］ 新 発 売

インサイトは、量産ガソリン車で世界一の低燃費リッター35kmを達成（10・15モード、5速MT車）。アメリカ、ヨーロッパ、アジアでも順次発売。

ECOLOGY CONSCIOUS TECHNOLOGY **HONDA ⊖-TECH**

もっともっとたのしむために。ホンダの環境技術。

↓ Let's Make a Baby, Now
  D: Hakuhodo Inc.
  cl: Takarajimasha Inc.

→ Ballon (Light Weight)

  Breast (Safety)
  D: Hakuhodo Inc.
  cl: Japan Glass Bottle Association

384

ポスターと広告

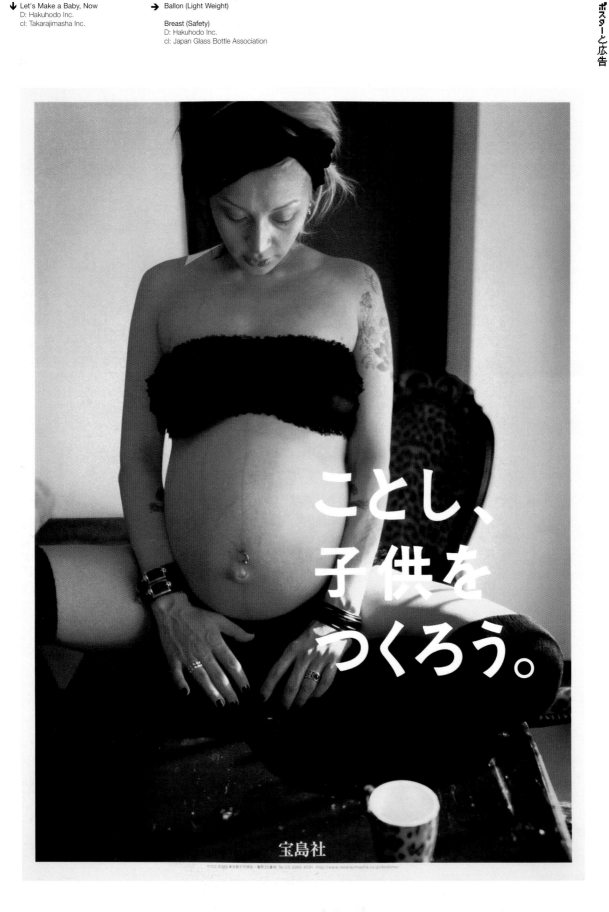

スシリを、フワリにかえました。超軽量びん
日本ガラスびん協会

赤ちゃんに、脇をはってのませられるもの。
日本ガラスびん協会

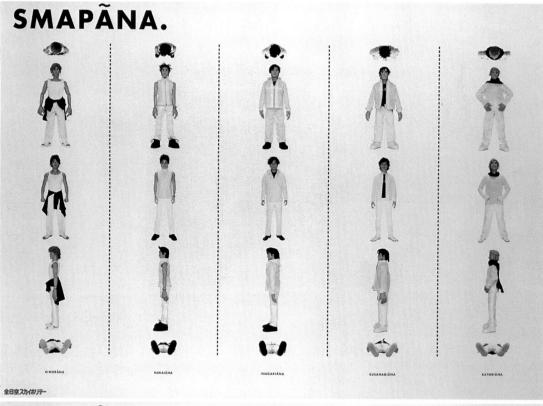

↳ Suntory "Malts"
D: Soeda Design Factory

➜ Nike Sandlot Baseball
Magazine Advertising
D: Soeda Design Factory

390

ポスターと広告

メジャーって、つまり、
すごい草野球みたいな
ものだよな。

「草」とは「ヘタ」ではない。
「草」とは「愛」だ。

ゴルファーという名のアスリートへ。
Nike Tour Forged Titanium 350 Driver X Version
Nike Tour Forged Titanium 275 Driver

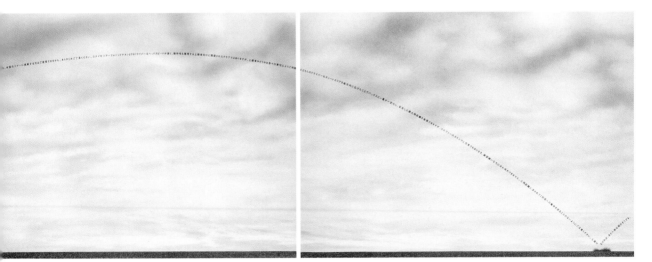

一本、筋を通したウイスキー。

山崎のモルト原酒だけでつくる。
きっぱりとした個性がある。
それは山崎で生まれ山崎で育った。純血である。
ただ一つの自分をぐいと主張する。長い年月を重ね
すべてを受けとめる懐の大きさ。向かい合うと背筋を
すっと伸ばしたくなる。清々しい緊張感がある。
サントリーピュアモルトウイスキー山崎

飲酒は20歳を過ぎてから

↓ Zero Halliburton P-series

Zero Halliburton Black
D: Masaki Negishi

→ Hitachi maxell [ZD3]
D: Masaki Negishi

ポスターと広告

396

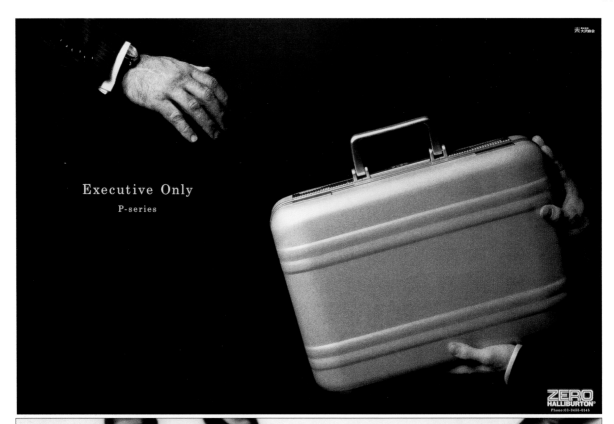

maxell
COMPACT DIGITAL CAMERA ZD3
DESIGNED BY ZERO HALLIBURTON
share the wonder
http://www.maxell.co.jp

↓ My Exhibition of Fireworks
D: Masaki Negishi

→ Yu-yu daidokutsu

Summer Image

Squirt Gun
D: Masaki Negishi

ポスターと広告

398

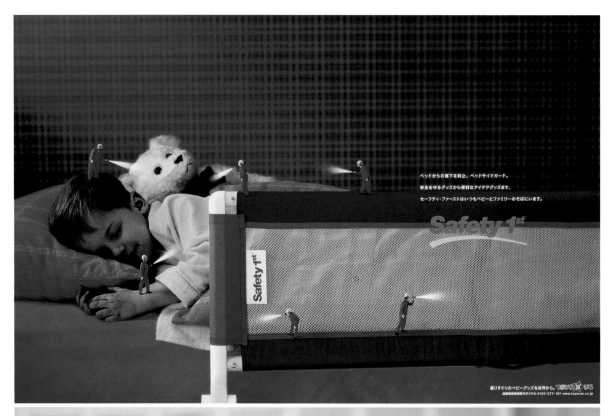

ベビーを感電から守る、コンセント・ガード。

安全を守るグッズから便利な アイデア・スキ。

セーフティ・ファーストはいつもベビーとファミリーのそばにいます。

Safety 1st

食べるために。眠るために。遊ぶために。生きるために。

real love

ジョン・レノンのアートから生まれたブランドです

Graco [Snow Board]
D: Masaki Negishi

Graco [Spa]
D: Masaki Negishi

402

ポスターと広告

ベビーカーが楽しいと、お出かけが楽しい。

アメリカNo.1赤ちゃんブランド お出かけ便利機能いっぱいで、¥25,800

GRACO®
The No.1 American Baby Brand

ポスターと広告

← Murata vegetables and fruits
Egg plant

Tomato

Cabbage
D: Masaki Negishi

↓ Murata vegetables and fruits
Petit Tomato

Banana
D: Masaki Negishi

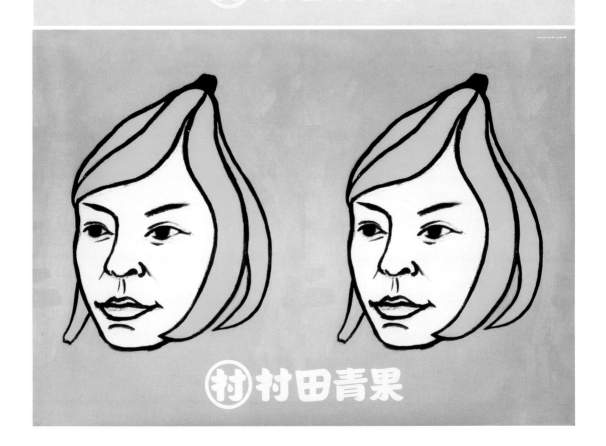

↓ Save nature
  D: Kazumasa Nagai

→ Life 2002
  D: Kazumasa Nagai

Life 2002
D: Kazumasa Nagai

Life 2001
D: Kazumasa Nagai

Life 2001
D: Kazumasa Nagai

ポスターと広告

406

save nature

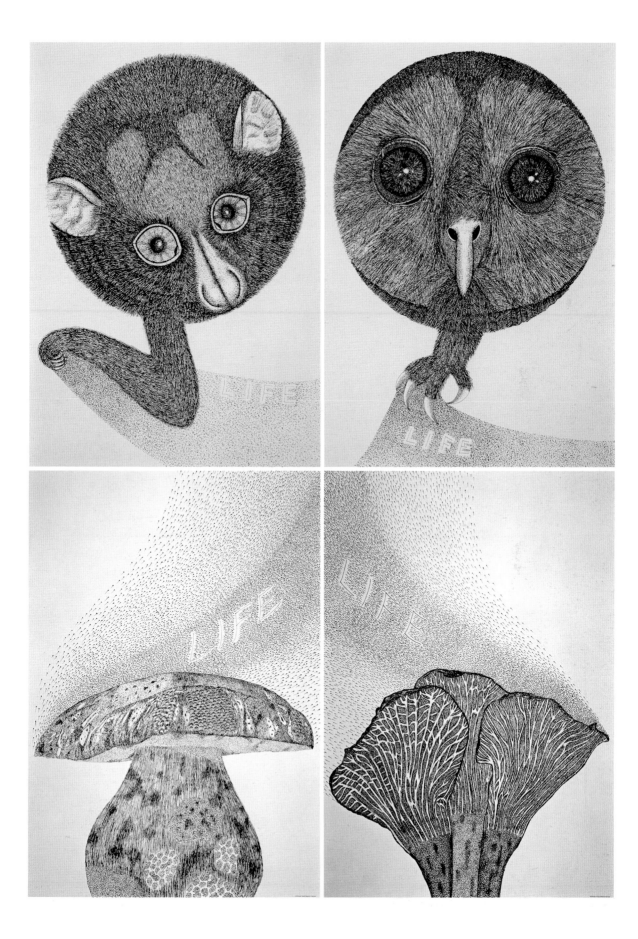

Life 2001
D: Kazumasa Nagai

Life 2000
D: Kazumasa Nagai

Life to share
D: Kazumasa Nagai

Life to share
D: Kazumasa Nagai

Life 2000
D: Kazumasa Nagai

408

ポスターと広告

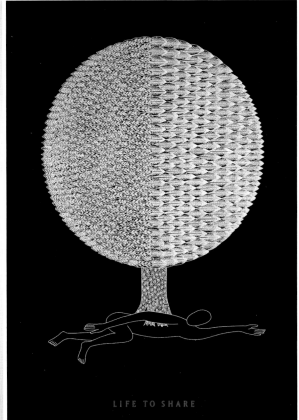

LIFE TO SHARE

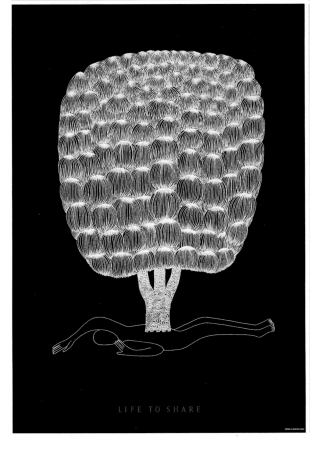

LIFE TO SHARE

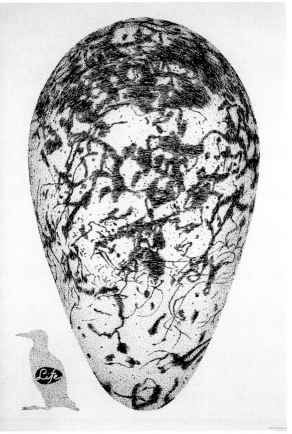

↓ Coexist (Help)
D: Kazumasa Nagai

Coexist (Coexist)
D: Kazumasa Nagai

Coexist (Save)
D: Kazumasa Nagai

ポスターと広告

410

↓ Save
D: Kazumasa Nagai

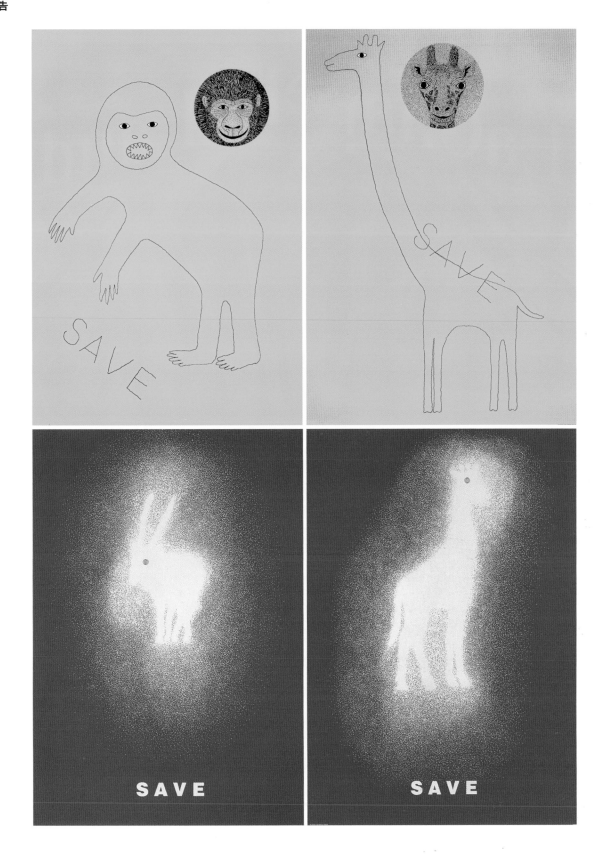

↓ Poster LaChapelle Land
  Tadanori Yokoo
  D: Callaway Edition Inc.

→ Brutus Magazine Cover
  art w: Tadanori Yokoo
  cl: Magazine House Ltd.

412

ポスターと広告

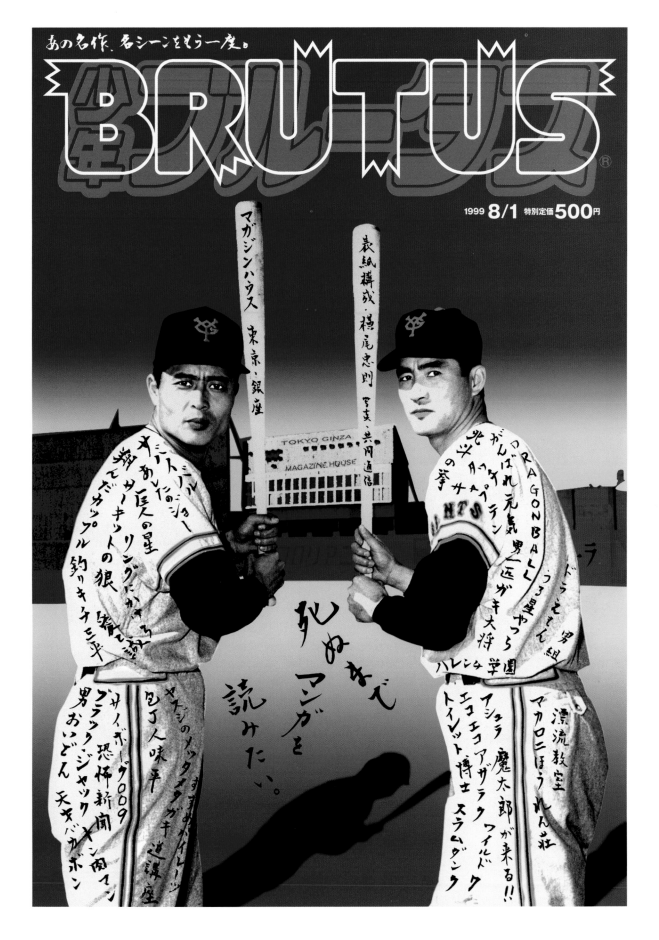

↓ Issey Miyake Body Works
D: Tadanori Yokoo
cl: Miyake Design Studio

→ Glay Expo`99 Survival
D: Tadanori Yokoo
cl: Unlimited Records Inc.

Gohatto
D: Tadanori Yokoo
cl: Shochiku Co., Ltd.

414

ポスターと広告

GLAY

御法度
GOHATTO

↓ Shinkansen in Spring
East Japan Railway Co. poster

Sleepingcar in Autumn East Japan
Railway Co. poster
D: Kuzunari Hattori
cl: JR East

→ Kewpie Half poster
D: Kuzunari Hattori
cl: Kewpie

416

ポスターと広告

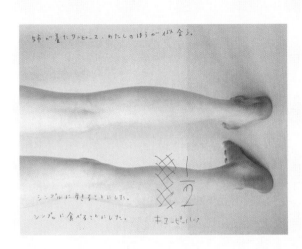

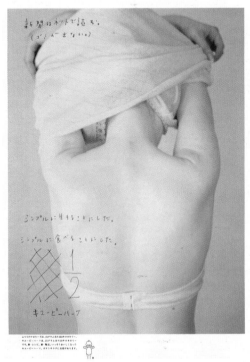

Print

www.kanpai.lager.com

www.kanpai.lager.com

カンパイ!! ラガー

2002 March 03

monday	tuesday	wednesday	thursday	friday	saturday
2/25	2/26	2/27	2/28	1	2
4	5	6	7	8	9
11	12	13	14	15	16
18	19	20		22	23
25	26	27	28	29	30

www.kanpai.lager.com

カンパイ!! ラガー

2002 June 06

monday	tuesday	wednesday	thursday	friday	saturday
5/27	5/28	5/29	5/30	5/31	1
3	4	5	6	7	8
10	11	12	13	14	15
17	18	19	20	21	22
24	25	26	27	28	29

プリント

← Kirin Lager Beer Calendar 2002
D: Butterfly Stroke Inc.
cl: Kirin Brewery Co., Ltd.
cd+ad+d: Katsunori Aoki
cd+c: Hidenori Azuma
d: Kana Takakuwa
i: Bunpei Yorifuji

↓ Lager Beer Logo mark
D: Butterfly Stroke Inc.
cl: Kirin Brewery Co., Ltd.
cd+ad+d: Katsunori Aoki
i: Bunpei Yorifuji

↓ Shinmachi Atrium 1st
D: Takaaki Fujimoto

→ Brochure for Beniya "Mukayu"1995
D: Kenya Hara
ad+d: Kenya Hara
d: Rie Shimoda

プリント

424

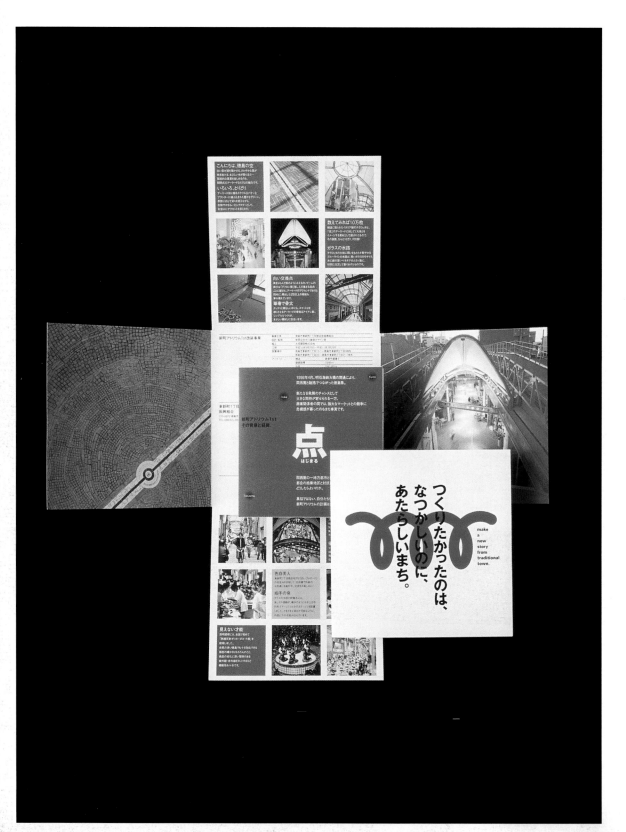

余白のような時間——ゆかゆう

無门有

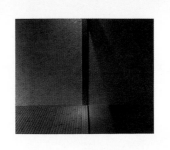

↓ Olympic Winter Games, Nagano 1998
→ Opening Ceremony Program
D: Kenya Hara
ad+d: Kenya Hara
d: Chihiro Murakami / Yukie Inoue
i: Hiroki Taniguchi

プリント

426

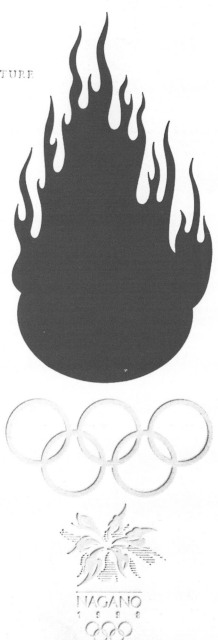

PROGRAMME DE LA
CÉRÉMONIE D'OUVERTURE

OPENING CEREMONY
PROGRAMME

開会式プログラム

7 FÉVRIER 1998

7 FEBRUARY 1998

1998年2月7日

NAGANO
1 9 9 8

Section 1

L'érection des *Onbashira* va
transformer le stade en espace sacré.

御柱

建御柱
聖なる空間の創造

Raising of the *Onbashira*
to Consecrate 'Sacred Ground'

Le chœur entonne un chant sacré
alors que des milliers
d'habitants de la région de
Nagano s'apprêtent à ériger huit
arbres géants de plus de dix
mètres, les *onbashira*.
Il s'agit d'une
coutume ancestrale de Suwa,
une région proche de Nagano.
La croyance veut que dresser des
arbres coupés dans la forêt
contribue à purifier l'espace.
Ces arbres, censés abriter des
divinités, figurent les quatre
portes de l'Est, de l'Ouest
du Sud et du Nord.
À Nagano, la nature est à la fois
bienveillante et hostile.
Apôtre un hiver habituellement
rigoureux et ennuigé,
les habitants attendent avec
impatience la venue du printemps.
Dans la rudesse de cet
environnement, sont nés ces
sentiments de peur et de
respect de la Nature qui ont
inspiré ces rites et croyances.
C'est en unissant leur espoir et
leurs forces que ces hommes
parviennent à dresser des sapins
pesant chacun deux tonnes.
Ainsi, le site de l'ouverture des
Jeux s'est transformé par l'érection
du *onbashira* en un espace sacré
apte à accueillir les athlètes.

To the sound of celebratory
singing, more than 1,000 local
people make their entrance.
Eight ceremonial wooden
pillars over 10 meters tall, known
as *onbashira*, are raised in the
arena to form four gates:
north, south, east, and west.
The Onbashira Festival,
originating in the Suwa region
of Nagano Prefecture,
is a tradition handed down from
ancient times.
According to ancient Japanese
beliefs, gods reside in the wood
of these pillars.
People in the Suwa region have
long believed that the way to
purify a place is by erecting pillars
cut from mountain forests.
Year after year, Nagano residents
endure long, snow-blanketed
winters, while eagerly anticipating
the first breath of spring.
These conditions have engendered
an awe of nature and an abiding
respect for the environment.
This wish to coexist in harmony
with nature manifests itself
in folk festivals passed down
over the ages.
The raising of the *onbashira*
transforms the Olympic Stadium
into a sacred arena,
ready to welcome the athletes.

La fête de Suwa

La région de Suwa est située
au centre-est de
la région de Nagano.
Tous les sept ans, se déroule la
plus importante des rituels,
relié des pêlerin sacrés.
On érige des sapins géants à
chaque coin des quatre bâtiments
du temple dévonaire de Suwa
afin de séparer le sacré
du profane et de purifier l'espace.
Des milliers de personnes importent
les arbres au son d'une chanson
traditionnelle.
Ces arbres, censés abriter des
divinités qu'il génère.
La palerone entre
au temple dans l'eau
(Kisuméi), puis
par l'autre gangil
le précurseur *naquiuméi*
accompagné d'un porteur
de sabre cérémonial.

The *Onbashira* Festival, which takes
place every seven years, is the biggest
folk festival in the Suwa area of
central Nagano Prefecture.
In this festival,   the people
raise huge   logs at
each of the   four
corners of the   four shrines
within the Suwa   Taisha
precincts. This separates the dwelling
place of the gods from the secular world
and purifies the sacred ground.
The logs, cut from the mountain forests
around Suwa, are borne aloft by
several thousand people, singing a special
log-carrying song as they go.
Highlights include *Kiotoshi* (sliding the
giant logs down a mountainside) and
kawagoe (carrying them across a river).
Many people consider
the Onbashira Festival one of Japan's
most unique folk festivals.

八
8

九
9

Section 2

土俵入

La cérémonie *Dohyo-iri*:
Les lutteurs de Sumo consacrent l'arène

力士入場・土俵入り
関取・横綱が勝負の場を清める

The *Dohyo-iri* Ceremony:
Sumo Wrestlers Consecrate the Arena

Les lutteurs de Sumo vêtus
de leur tablier de cérémonie *keho-
mawashi*, pénètrent dans l'arène.
L'arrivée dans cette arène
dohyo-iri constitue un véritable
cérémonial au cours
duquel les concurrents prêtent un
serment d'équité.
Le Sumo est un art militaire
consacré aux divinités.
En ce sens, il rejoint les Jeux
Olympiques dédiés aux divinités
de l'Antiquité.
Le Sumo est porteur d'une
importance charge spirituelle
pour un Japonais.
Le champion poheoranu, fait son
entrée dans l'arène.
Il chasse les forces néfariques
maléfiques et purifie le lieu destiné
à recevoir les athlètes.
Chacun de ses pas est salué
par un *Yoshé! - aovte de hale
japonaise - scandé par
les cinquante mille spectateurs.

Sumo wrestlers wearing their
ceremonial *keho-mawashi* aprons
gird themselves for the *dohyo-iri*,
the ring-entering ceremony.
The ceremony reaches its climax
when the *yokozuna* grand
champion wrestler enters the
dohyo and stamps his feet to drive
away evil spirits and purify the
ground for the athletes.
The audience of 50,000 calls out
the traditional shout, "*Yoshé!*".
Like the ancient Olympic Games,
sumo matches are dedicated to the
gods. Sumo is a sport that not only
incorporates both strength
and technique,
but also embodies the Japanese
spirit in every one of its rituals.

Sumo

L'origine du Sumo
nommnuvt à la préhistoire.
C'était un rite destiné à la
divinité pour lui demander une
récolte abondante et pour
la consacrer de sa protection.
Les lutteurs disparaient
du macerats per un,
le grade le plus haut
étant celui du poheoranu.
Son saut est compensé à
celui de la couronne
qu'il génère. Le poheoranu entre
au temple dans l'eau (kisméi), guidé
par l'autre gangil et
le précurseur *naqutimeé*
accompagné d'un porteur
de sabre cérémonial.

Sumo

Sumo dates back to before
the beginning of recorded history,
and has spawned a myriad of
myths and traditions.
Traditionally, sumo matches were
held as an offering to the gods
— as a means of praying for a good
harvest and thanking the gods
for their protection.
Sumo is now the Japanese
national sport, and reverentness
are held six times a year.
The top rank in sumo wrestling is
yokozuna; this was the
original name for the ceremonial
straw rope that grand champions
wore around their waists.
The *yokozuna*, led by a *yayi* (usher)
and a *taperkai* (herald) and
accompanied by a *tachimochi*
(swordbearer), enters the ring to
perform the *dohyo-iri* ceremony.

十
10

十一
11

Section 3

Allumage de la Flamme olympique,
serments de l'athlète et de l'arbitre

Lighting of the Olympic Flame;
Oaths by Athlete and Judge

聖火点火
選手宣誓・審判員宣誓

聖火

Allumée à Olympie le 19
décembre 1997 et expédiée
par avion au Japon, la Flamme
olympique a été
relayée par des milliers de
coureurs sur le territoire
japonais avant de parvenir
dans l'arène olympique.

Le Baron Pierre de Coubertin,
père des Jeux Olympiques
modernes a déclaré:
"Toi qui veux te dépasser,
forge ton corps et ton âme
pour découvrir le meilleur
de toi-même,
vise toujours un degré
au-dessus de celui que tu t'es
fixé; Plus vite, plus haut,
plus fort."
'Citius, Altius, Fortius'
Au nom de tous les athlètes
des Jeux de Nagano,
leur représentant prête le
serment de se conformer
à l'esprit des Jeux Olympiques.
Une fois le serment
des solteros prononcé,
des milliers de ballons se
forme de colonnes sont lâchés.
Ces ballons portent
des messages
de paix écrits par
les enfants de Nagano à
destination du monde entier.

The Nagano Olympic flame was
kindled in Olympia, Greece,
on December 19, 1997
and flown to Japan.
It was then hand-carried by
several thousand runners
throughout the country in a torch
relay to the Olympic Stadium.

Baron Pierre de Coubertin,
father of the modern Olympics,
said: 'You who wish to excel,
forge your body and soul to
discover the best in yourself,
always aim one degree
higher than the goal
you have set for yourself: faster,
higher, stronger.'
His words live on as the
Olympic motto: '*Citius, Altius,
Fortius*.' On behalf of all the
athletes gathered here, an athlete
stands before the world
and so diligently raised for the
Nagano Olympics, and
athlete represents to uphold
the spirit of the Olympics.
A judge's representative
then swears an oath on behalf
of the judges. Next, thousands of
helium balloons shaped like
doves are released.
The balloons carry written
messages of peace and friendship
from the children of Nagano.

La Flamme olympique

La Flamme olympique a été
transportée depuis le palais de Héra
vers le Japon par avion.
Le courou de relais commencée
le 6 janvier 1998,
a respecté tous intéressions
différents qui couvrent tous les
départements japonais.
Lorsque les différentes torches ont pris
comme sur le stade japonais
des minutes son arrivée Nagano,
celles-ci ont fusionné en une seule.
Ce qui s'est à allumer la Flamme
olympique du stade.
Cette coutume de la source
de relais de la Flamme olympique
a été instituée aux Jeux de
Berlin en 1936 et s'est perpétuée en
s'adaptant aux us et costumes de
chacun des pays libres.

The Olympic Flame

The Olympic torch was kindled in Olympia
and flown to Japan, where the torch relay
began on January 6, 1998. The relay covered
all the different prefectures, consisting of all of Japan's
prefectures, ran simultaneously.
The torches used on the three routes were lit
from their original flame. When the torches
reached Nagano, they were reunited into a
single flame, which has been carried to
the Opening Ceremony venue
and used to light the Olympic
Flame. The Olympic relay torch
has reintroduced Japanese pieces
ceremonial Japanese piece torch, while
the flames never resembles a signal flare.
With its beginning at the 1936 Berlin
Olympics, the torch relay
has grown into a tradition, which
each host country carries out in a manner
reflecting their own unique culture.

十八
18

十九
19

↓ Disco Free food / bionic rockers
For Silent Propaganda Recordings
CD jacket
D: Artless Inc.
ad+d: Shun Kawakami
p: Ikuma Yamada

→ Like sound collection
CD jacket
D: Rocketdesign

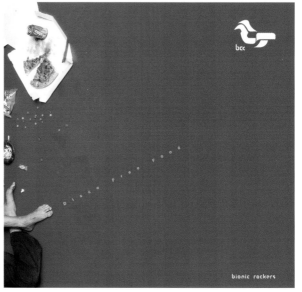

LIKE
SOUND
COLLECTION

www.clubking.com

CLUBKING CD-R Selection ♣
© CLUBKING CO.,
© rocketdesign/Shingo Kikuchi

LIKE
SOUND
COLLECTION

CLUBKING CO., ♣ www.clubking.com

function Conveniently designed inside space —

書類などビジネス用途に使用する空間と

衣類などを入れる

プライベートな空間を分けるなど

you can part and pack your belongings according to the purpose : documents are into the business room and clothes the private.

収納するものの用途や大きさに応じて

スペースの大きさ・種類・使用を目的別に考え

より使い易さを追求しました

9·1·394   9·1·415   9·1·393   9·1·416   9·1·408   9·1·399   9·1·453   9·1·391   9·1·419   9·1·418

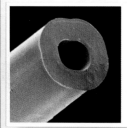

material Ultra-lightness and hyper-durability —— both

ケミカル素材のなかでも

水に浮くほどの軽さと撥水性を

合わせ持った画期的な新素材

realized a miracle chemical fiber, "Polyester Hollow Fiber (Aerocapsule)".

ポリエステル中空糸

(エアロカプセル)を使用

軽量でしかも耐久性に優れています

ORGANIZER BRIEF 9·1·390	OVERNIGHT BRIEF 9·1·392	OVERNIGHT BRIEF 9·1·393	SLIM ATTACHE 9·1·394	SLIM ATTACHE 9·1·415	SOFT ATTACHE 9·1·416
ファスナーが大きく開き 整理に便利な仕切切付き	衣類と書類に分けた2重構造 機能的が出来る内蔵式装備	衣類と書類に分けた2重構造 機能的が出来る内蔵式装備	軽量なハニカムフレーム構造 内側のフラップ付きでより分割収納可能	軽量なハニカムフレーム構造 内側のフラップ付きでより分割収納可能	軽量なハニカムフレーム構造 レイアウトしやすいフルオープンファスナー
○素材 840デニール ポリエステル軽量中空糸 ○仕様 超撥水加工 ○金具 牛革ソフト ○ショルダーベルト付 ○¥25,000	○素材 840デニール ポリエステル軽量中空糸 ○仕様 超撥水加工 ○金具 牛革ソフト ○ショルダーベルト付 ○¥30,000	○素材 840デニール ポリエステル軽量中空糸 ○仕様 超撥水加工 ○金具 牛革ソフト ○ショルダーベルト付 ○¥36,000	○素材 840デニール ポリエステル軽量中空糸 ○仕様 超撥水加工 ○金具 牛革ソフト ○¥30,000	○素材 840デニール ポリエステル軽量中空糸 ○仕様 超撥水加工 ○金具 牛革ソフト ○¥33,000	○素材 840デニール ポリエステル軽量中空糸 ○仕様 超撥水加工 ○金具 牛革ソフト ○¥35,000

← im product MOVE
Catalog
D: Taku Satoh

↓ Smap goods
D: Samurai

Ura Smap goods
D: Samurai

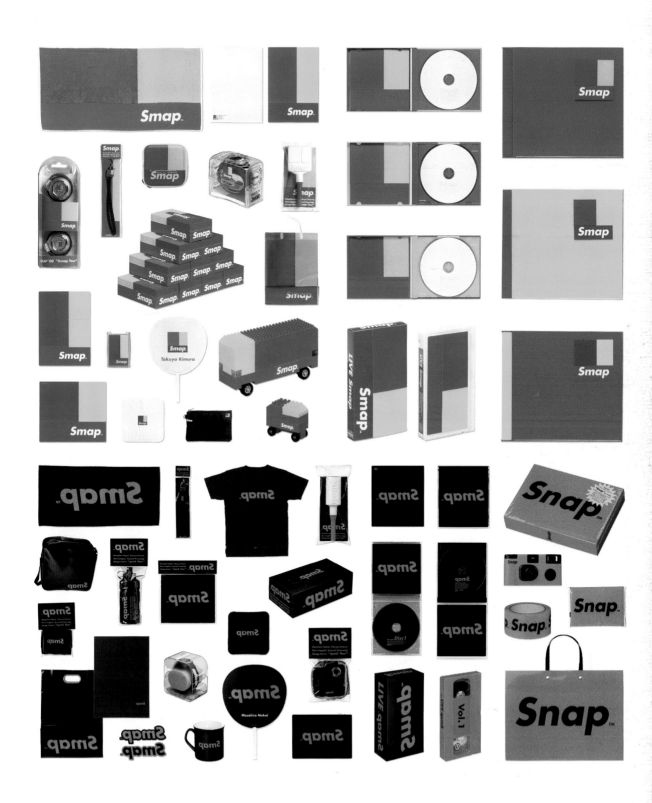

↓ Dress-up
　Direct Mail
　D: Yoshie Watanabe

→ Greeting card
　D: Yoshie Watanabe

　Greeting card
　D: Yoshie Watanabe

プリント

432

Playing the Orchestra 1997, Ryuichi Sakamoto
CD jacket
D: Hideki Nakajima

1996, Ryuichi Sakamoto
CD jacket
D: Hideki Nakajima

El Mar Mediterrani, Ryuichi Sakamoto
CD jacket
D: Hideki Nakajima

Kinjito, Kazuyoshi Nakamura
CD jacket
D: Hideki Nakajima

Crescent Moon
CD jacket
D: Hiroyuki Matsuishi

Kitakyushu Media Dome
CD jacket
D: Hiroyuki Matsuishi

crescentmoon I

SPORTS
CONVENTION
CONCERT
MULTI MEDIA CULTURE EVENT
EXHIBITION

Kitakyushu Media Dome

北九州メディアドーム

PROMOTION VIDEO CD

Shima Takada

DRIVING BAY BLUES

Shima Takada
DRIVING BAY BLUES

Shima Takada
DRIVING BAY BLUES

←Shima Takada, Driving Bay Blues
CD jacket
D: Alfa Eyes Design Inc.
p: Akitada Hamasaki

↓NO?YES!!, Complex
CD jacket
D: Alfa Eyes design inc.
p: Hisayoshi Osawa

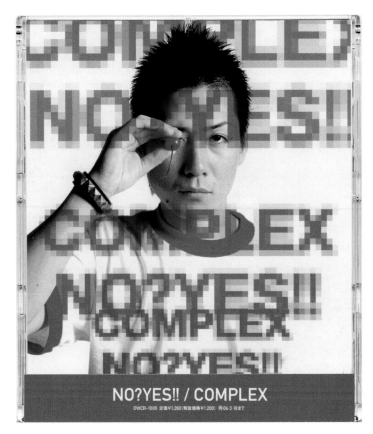

Zoophilia, Innocent
CD jacket
D: Alfa Eyes Design Inc.
p: Jin Ohashi

→ NO?YES!!, Crossroad
"tokimeki wa kimagure"
CD jacket
D: Alfa Eyes Design Inc.
p: Shigekazu Ohnuma

Illumina, "Ikuokubun no
ichi no kakuritsu"
CD jacket
D: Alfa Eyes Design Inc.
p: Hideo Kanno

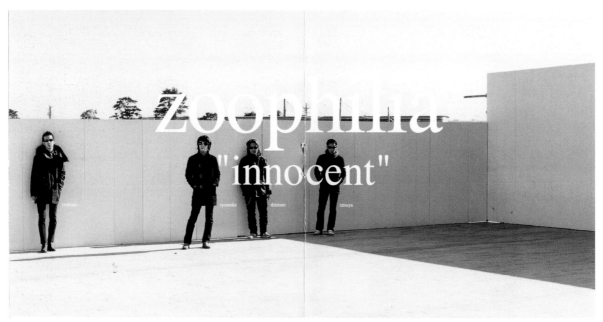

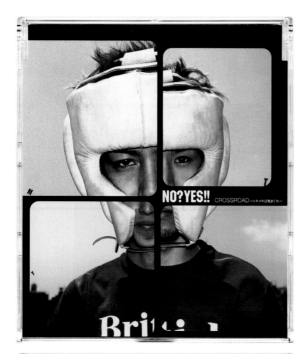

NO?YES!! CROSSROAD ~トキメキは気まぐれ~

幾億分の一の確率 ILLUMINA

ILLUMINA

1. CROSSROAD ~トキメキは気まぐれ~ 4:14
2. きらめきの花 4:10
3. とこも風の強い春の日に 4:26
4. CROSSROAD ~トキメキは気まぐれ~ [Instrumental] 4:14

bass ● TAKA   guitar ● TAR   vocal & guitar ● Nao   drums ● SATOM (L→R)

ILLUMINA ◆ new maxi single
未来 Akira Nishihira produce
WOWOW ◆ MUSIC FACTORY hyper 2000
Opening Theme ◆ SAT. 0:00〜0:30 NON SCRAMBLE
4songs and CD-EXTRA included!! PCCAX-00016

← Illumina, Mirai
CD jacket
D: Alfa Eyes Design Inc.
p: Hideo Kanno

↓ Bamboo Shigeru, engawa<->ucyu
CD jacket
D: Alfa Eyes Design Inc.
p: Hisayoshi Osawa

SHINJI TANIMURA

PCCA-01251

← Shinji Tanimura, Raban
CD jacket
D: Alfa Eyes Design Inc.
p: Kurou Doi

↓ Screaming Poets, Radio
CD jacket
D: Alfa Eyes Design Inc.
p: Kenji Kubo

Bionic rockers
D: Artless Inc.

Wina Co.,Ltd
D: Artless Inc.

Sawayakatoiki
D: Creative Power Unit

3rd Designer's Gallery
D: Creative Power Unit

Mate Sha Inc.
D: Butterfly Stroke Inc.
ad+d: Katsunori Aoki

Mate Sha Inc.
D: Butterfly Stroke Inc.
i: Bunpei Yorifuji / Takuya Shibata

さわやか吐息

↓ Hiromichi Nakano Baby Logo mark
D: Butterfly Stroke Inc.
cl: Hiromichi Nakano Design
Office Company Limited
cd: Hiromichi Nakano
ad+d: Katsunori Aoki
i: Seijiro Kubo

Miyagawa Pharmacy
Inagaki co.,ltd
Shinmachi Atrium 1st
D: Takaaki Fujimoto

Deguchi Insurance Office
Noguchi Architect & Associates
Ichikawa-cho Cultural Center
D: Takaaki Fujimoto

446

トシント

**DEGUCHI
INSURANCE
OFFICE**

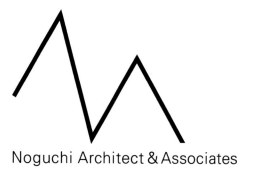

Noguchi Architect & Associates

Shinm**achi**
ATRIUM1st

市川町文化センター
Ichikawa-Cho Cultural Center

↓ WonderBorg
D: Devilrobots Inc.

Futureshot logo
D: Yoshihito kawata

ABE Survey
D: Ken Miki & Associates

Tram
D: Devilrobots Inc.

Futureshot logo&mark
D: Yoshihito kawata

Paper Studio
D: Ken Miki & Associates

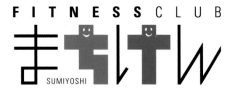

Isshin

Kikuya

Cuisine Kanya
D: Takaaki Fujimoto

Cuisine Kanya

Fujimoto Noodle

Cuisine Kanya
D: Takaaki Fujimoto

↓ Benribon

You-ple
D: Takaaki Fujimoto

Manpuku-King

You-ple
D: Takaaki Fujimoto

プリント

450

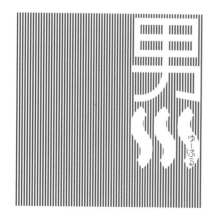

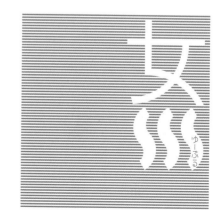

↓ TV DoNightShow
D: Takaaki Fujimoto

POOL
プール

COACHINGROOM
コーチルーム

SHOWER
シャワー

WARMINGROOM
採暖室

POWDERROOM
パウダールーム

STUDIO1
スタジオ 1

STUDIO2
スタジオ 2

TRAININGGYM
トレーニングジム

MEN'SLOCKER
ロッカールーム

NURSERY
託児室

GIRLSLOCKER
おんなの子のロッカー

KIDS POOL
こどもプール

ATELIER
アトリエ

MAN
おとこ

LADY
おんな

↓ Cuoca.com
D: Takaaki Fujimoto

shop

kitchen

café

casher

office

school

working room

meeting room

dressing room

male rest room

female rest room

mother and daughter rest room

male rest room

multipurpose rest room

staff rest room

Tsukasa Logo
D: Noriaki Hayashi

Appare Sanuki [Noodle Shop]

OZ Entertainment Inc.
D: Minato Ishikawa

Maruya Logo
D: Noriaki Hayashi

Umehati Co., Ltd. [Pickled Ume Shop]

Kenso Co., Ltd. [Constructor]
D: Minato Ishikawa

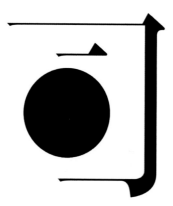

↓ Sumikawa Orthopedic Clinic

Arjo Wiggins Paper Collection

Heiwa
D: Ken Miki & Associates

Abilit

Futuristic Pulse

Ecology paper
D: Ken Miki & Associates

↓ Hokusetsu

Paper studio

KSC Kamoike Bild.
D: Ken Miki & Associates

Kagawa Education Institute of Nutrition

World Environment Day'99

2001 Wine
D: Ken Miki & Associates

プリント

456

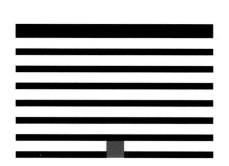

↓ Fontic, Logomark

Kawasaki Electronics, Logomark

Sumire Clinic, Logomark
D: Hiroyuki Matsuishi

Hako Cafe, Symbolmark

Hakoshiki, Logomark

Sanwagiken, Symbolmark
D: Hiroyuki Matsuishi

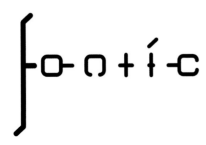

HAKOCAFE

KAWADEN

HAKOSHIKI

↓ Tsukitei Happo

02

Sasaya
D: Koshi Ogawa

Kokoro

Swimming

Car
D: Koshi Ogawa

プリント

458

↓ Port/End

Akio Okumura

Wind
D: Akio Okumura

Glico

Web-Database-Logistics

Interface Humanities
D: Akio Okumura

port/end

IM-LAB

物流工作

Interface Humanities

Iwate Nature School
D: Norito Shinmura
cl: Seiyu

Renkonya
D: Norito Shinmura

Crawl X Crawl
D: Norito Shinmura
ad+d: Norito Shinmura

Gradog
D: Norito Shinmura

Tachibana
D: Norito Shinmura
cl: Tachibana Town

Potter's pot
D: Norito Shinmura
ad+d: Norito Shinmura

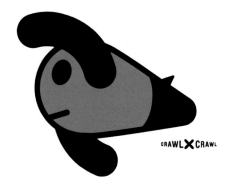

Oceankid

Hibiki no sato
cl: Oyama town

Green Smile
D: Norito Shinmura
cl: Shinmura Design Office
ad+d: Norito Shinmura

Kenkoukan

Wintec Wire

Watanabe Dental Clinic
D: Norito Shinmura
ad+d: Norito Shinmura

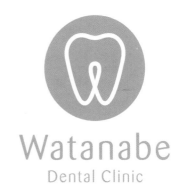

Rocketdesign
D: Rocketdesign

Core+
D: Rocketdesign

Qina
D: Rocketdesign

Numero Deux
D: Rocketdesign

Sponge
D: Rocketdesign

Okawariya
D: Ganta Uchikiba

OKAWARI-YA

↓ Keiya

Owas inc

Nandaimon
D: Ganta Uchikiba

Harunado bakery

Studio Rhythmoon

Mishima Ritsue
D: Ganta Uchikiba

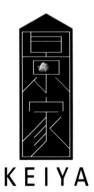

↓ Hanayoshino Country Club

Allied Material Corp.

Patio Supermarket
D: TCD

Kobayashi Pharmaceutical Co.,Ltd.

JA Izumo

Toho Co.,Ltd. A-price
D: TCD

464

プリント

花吉野カントリー倶楽部

小林製薬

ALLIED MATERIAL

IZUMO

Patio

A-PRICE

↓ Amenity Garden Shanghai "Tohohkaen"
cl: Matsushita Electric Works Housing, Ltd.

Otemae University

Koizumi Sangyo Corp.
D: TCD

Kokuyo Universal Design
cl: Kokuyo Co., Ltd.

Bukkyo University

Inada Chair
cl: Family Inada Inc.
D: TCD

ADMT (AD Museum Tokyo)
D: TUGBOAT

Flag
D: TUGBOAT

Concept
D: TUGBOAT

Medical Channel (Courtesy of Sony)
D: Masaaki Omura

Xiidea
D: Romando Co., Ltd.

Coamix
D: Romando Co., Ltd.

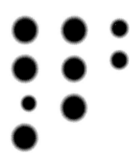

Ultrawash
D: Romando Co., Ltd.

東京都民銀行
TOKYO TOMIN BANK

↓ Japan Design Committee Logotype
D: Taku Satoh

Issey Miyake HaaT Logo
D: Sayuri Studio, Inc.

BS Asahi Logo
D: Taku Satoh

Usui
D: Katsu Kimura

Usui
D: Katsu Kimura

JAPAN DESIGN COMMITTEE

↓ Business card

Salon-de-message Business card

Katachi Business card
D: Katachi

→ Celartem Technology, Inc.
D: Shinnoske Sugisaki

474

プリント

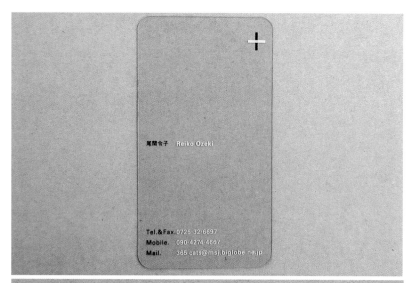

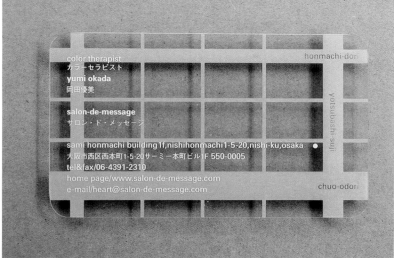

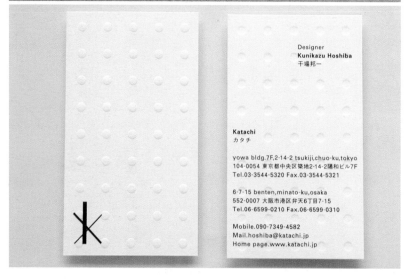

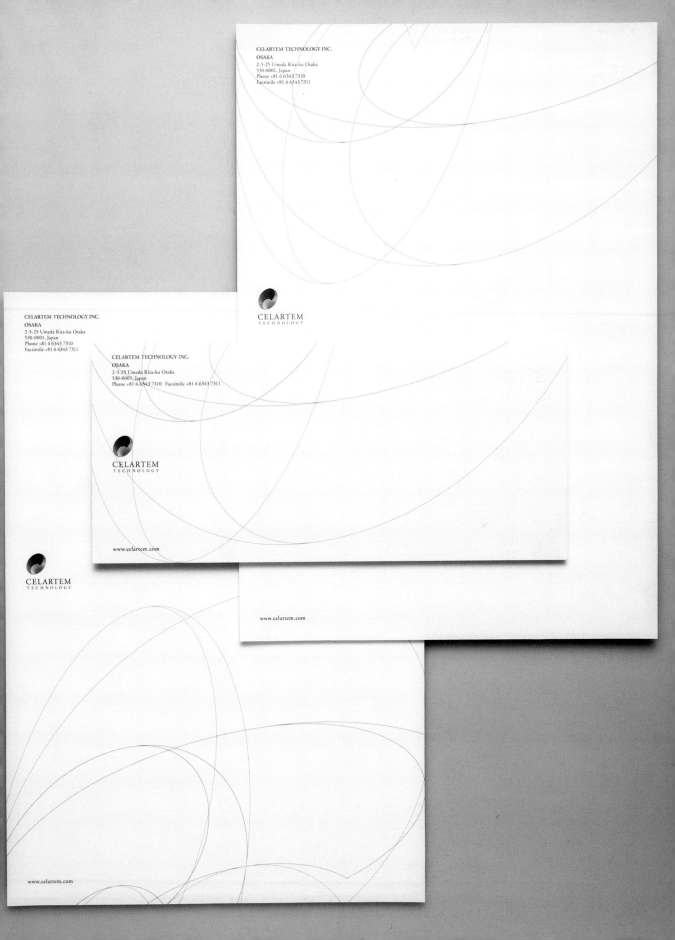

↓ BS Asahi
Stationery, CI-Manual
D: Taku Satoh

→ Japanese paper stationery
D: Mihiko Hachiuma

プリント

476

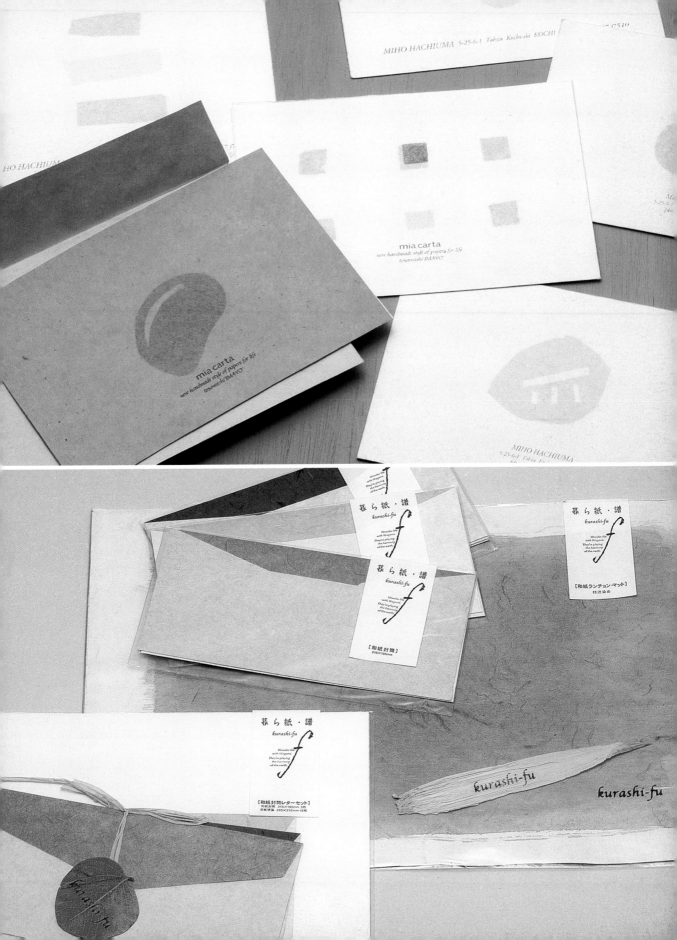

↓ Adding:blue Menu, shop card, etc.
D: Taku Satoh

478

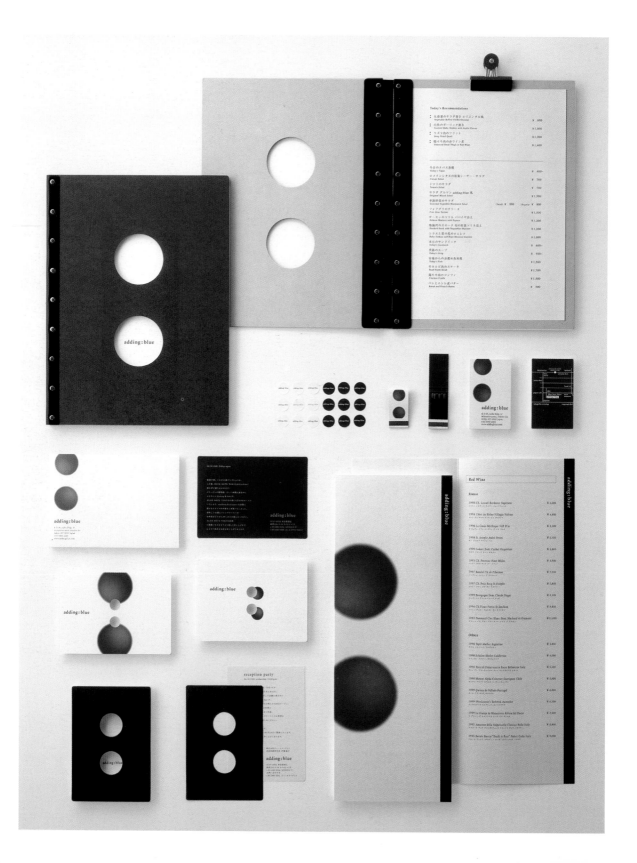

3-6-1 Ginza, Chuo-ku Tokyo 104-8130 Japan
Phone: 03-3561-2572
Facsimile: 03-3561-6038
E-mail: jdcommit@yb3.so-net.ne.jp

JAPAN DESIGN COMMITTEE

secretary general

Mariko Tsuchida

3-6-1 Ginza, Chuo-ku Tokyo 104-8130 Japan
Phone: 03-3561-2572   Facsimile: 03-3561-6038
E-mail: jdcommit@yb3.so-net.ne.jp

JAPAN DESIGN COMMITTEE

3-6-1 Ginza, Chuo-ku Tokyo 104-8130 Japan
Phone: 03-3561-2572
Facsimile: 03-3561-6038
E-mail: jdcommit@yb3.so-net.ne.jp

JAPAN DESIGN COMMITTEE

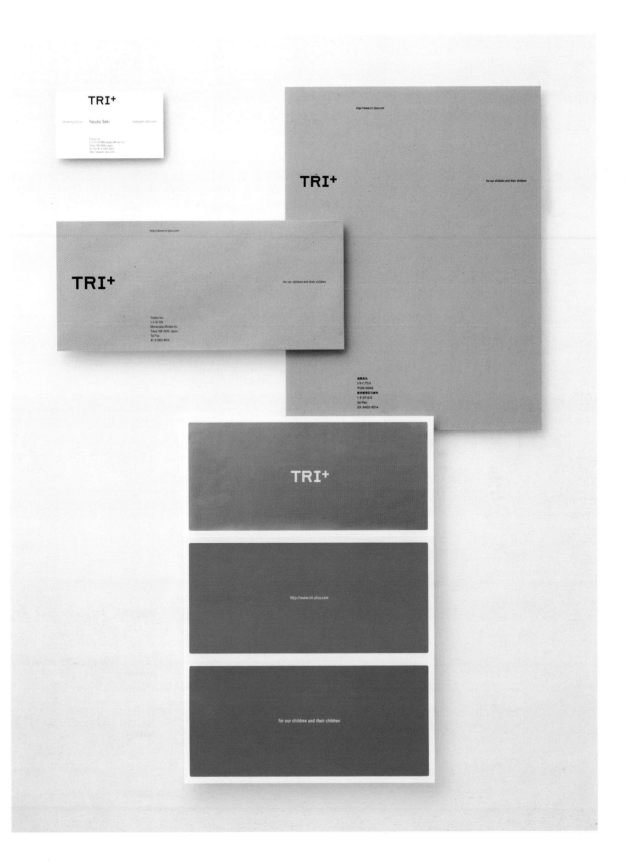

◀ Matsuya Ginza Renewal Project Facade

Matsuya Ginza Renewal Project:
Temporary Enclosure
D: Kenya Hara
ad+d: Kenya Hara
d: Maho Ike

▼ Matsuya Ginza Renewal Project Signage
D: Kenya Hara
ad+d: Kenya Hara
d: Maho Ike

Matsuya Ginza Renewal Project Shopping Bag
ad+d: Kenya Hara
d: Chihiro Murakami

↓ Signage for Katta Hospital
D: Kenya Hara
ad: Kenya Hara
d: Yuji Koisoa

プリント

484

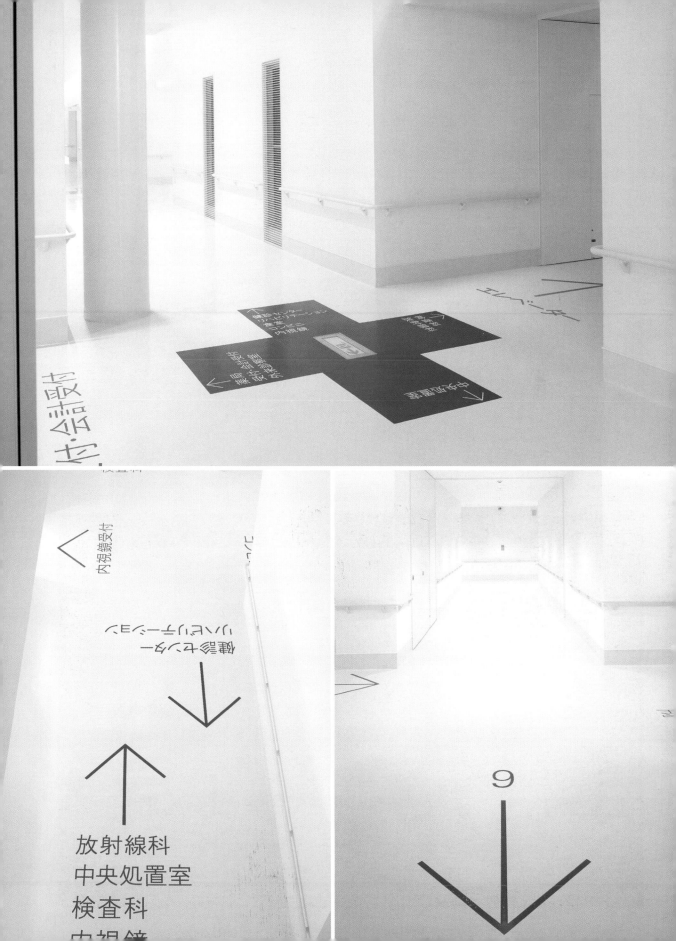

Mori Building.co., Ltd
Visual Identity Project: Application
D: Kenya Hara
ad+d: Kenya Hara
d: Rie Shimoda

Signage for Umeda Hospital
D: Kenya Hara
ad+d: Kenya Hara
d: Yukie Inoue
patternner: Masako Takeda

Ichikawa-cho Cultural Center
Visual Identity
D: Takaaki Fujimoto

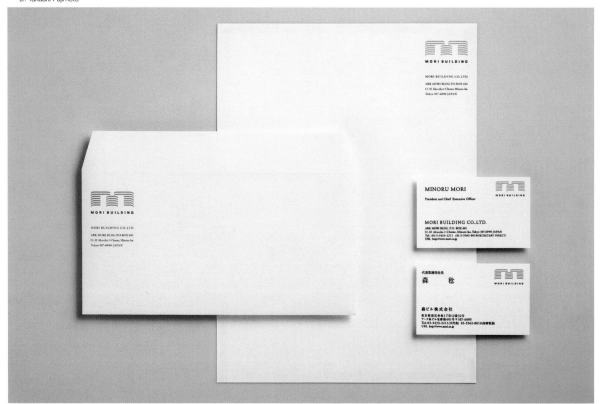

← Shiseido PN display
Display design
D: Sayuri Studio, Inc.

↓ Issey Miyake HaaT
Collateral items
D: Sayuri Studio, Inc.

PLEATS
PLEASE
ISSEY MIYAKE

7月9日(火)〜7月21日(日)
先行販売
本店3階 プリーツ プリーズ イッセイ ミヤケ

MITSUKOSHI

← Pleats Please window display
Display design
D: Sayuri Studio, Inc.

↓ Pleats Please promotional CD
D: Sayuri Studio, Inc.

www.pleatsplease.com

A.D.2000

The very first work of
butterfly stroke inc.
katsunori aoki

keiko aoki / masumi saito / yuji sakai / keisuke takizawa

A.D.2000

david duval-smith / enlightenment / groovision / hiroyoshi koyama / seijiro kubo
tomomi maeda / takashi murakami / ichiro tanida / bunpei yorifuji / masayuki yoshinaga

← A.D.2000
Cover design
D: Butterfly Stroke Inc.
ad+d: Katsunori Aoki
i: Bunpei Yorifuji / Enlightenment

↓ A.D.2000
Page design

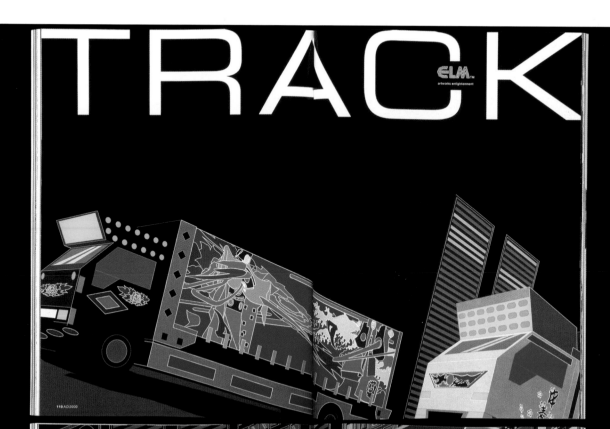

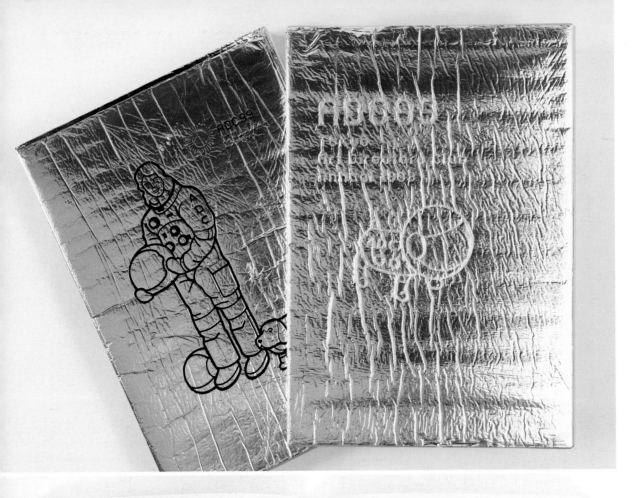

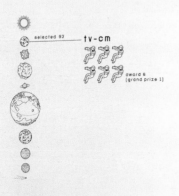

selected 93

tv-cm

award 6
[grand prize 1]

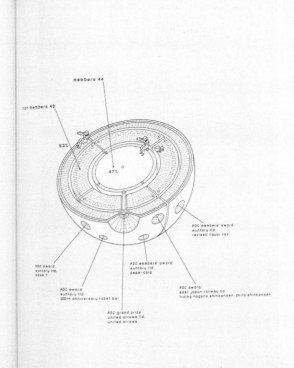

members 44

non members 49

53%

47%

ADC members' award
suntory ltd.
revised liquor tax

ADC award
suntory ltd.
boss 7

ADC members' award
suntory ltd.
pepsi cola

ADC award
suntory ltd.
100th anniversary robot bar

ADC award
east japan railway co.
train nagano shinkansen, akita shinkansen

ADC grand prize
united arrows ltd.
united arrows

◀ Tokyo Art Directors Club Annual '99
Cover and page design

Client: Tokyo Art Directors Club
D: Butterfly Stroke Inc.
cd: Kaoru Kasai
ad+d: Katsunori Aoki
i: Bunpei Yorifuji

↓ Fields The greatest leisure for all people
D: Butterfly Stroke Inc.
cl: Fields co,Ltd.
cd+ad+d: Katsunori Aoki
ad+d: Nobuo Sekiguchi
i: Bunpei Yorifuji
p: Akira Kitajima / Aya Tokunaga
Art W: Fumio Tachibana / Takeshi Sakaue

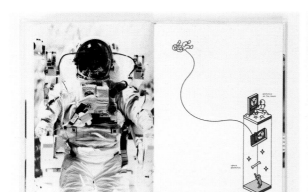

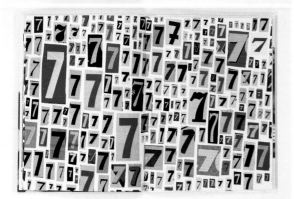

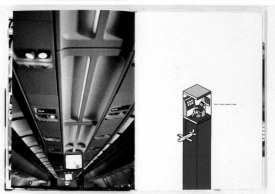

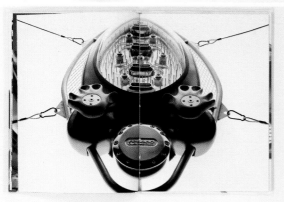

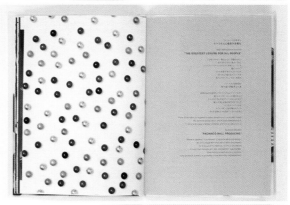

↓ Tokyo Copy Writers Club Annual '00   → Tokyo Copy Writers Club Annual '00
Page design   Cover design
D: Butterfly Stroke Inc.
cl: Reiko Kojima
ad: Katsunori Aoki
i: Enlightenment

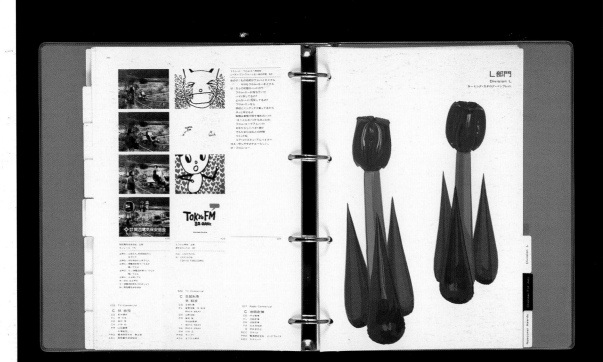

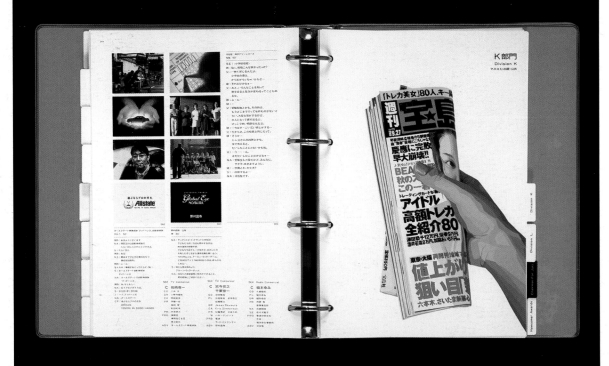

↓ +81 magazine vol.19
Editorial design
D: Artless Inc.
d: Shun Kawakami

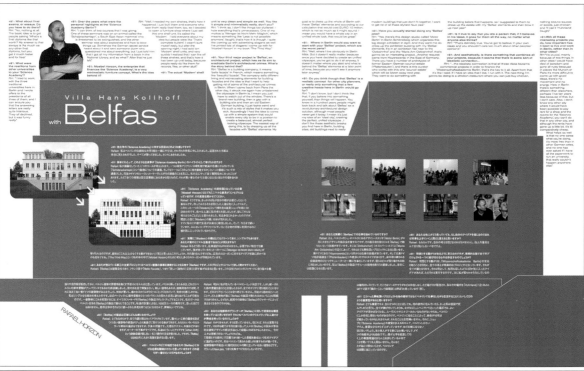

Villa Hans Kollhoff
with **Belfas**

RAFAEL HORZON

Berlin Palace
with **Belfas**

RAFAEL HORZON

MOEBEL HORZON

↓ Graphic in case
D: Artless Inc.
p+d: Shun Kawakami
Translation: Roger Lakhani

WSI products catalogue
D: Artless Inc.
ad+d: Shun Kawakami
i: Tadashi Ura
p: Ikuma Yamada
style: Miyoshi
painting: Akira Ohsawa

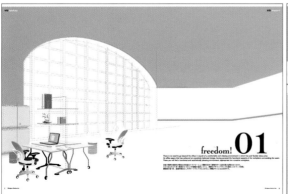

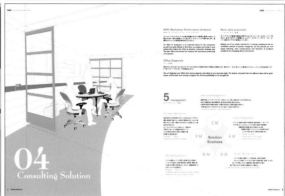

← Mina Ryushi
Book design
D: Bluemark Inc.

↓ Takehito Koganezawa Drawing
Book design
D: Bluemark Inc.

Colors

HEIWA PAPER

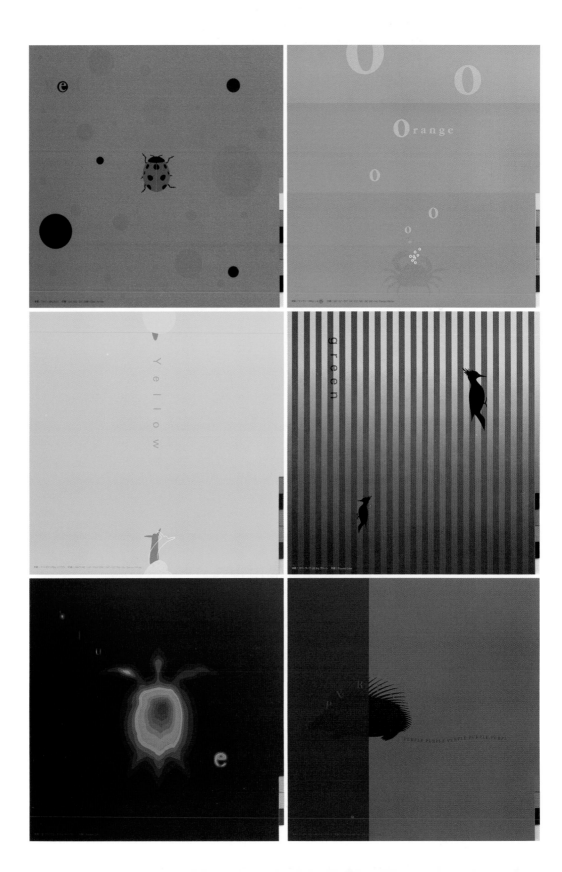

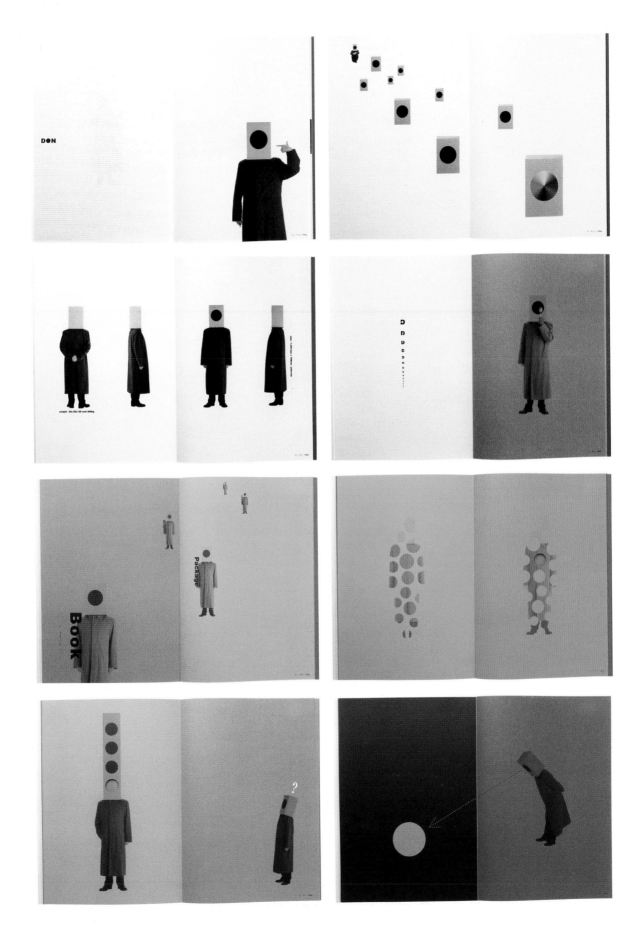

↓ IBM Design from Japan
→ Book design
D: Ken Miki

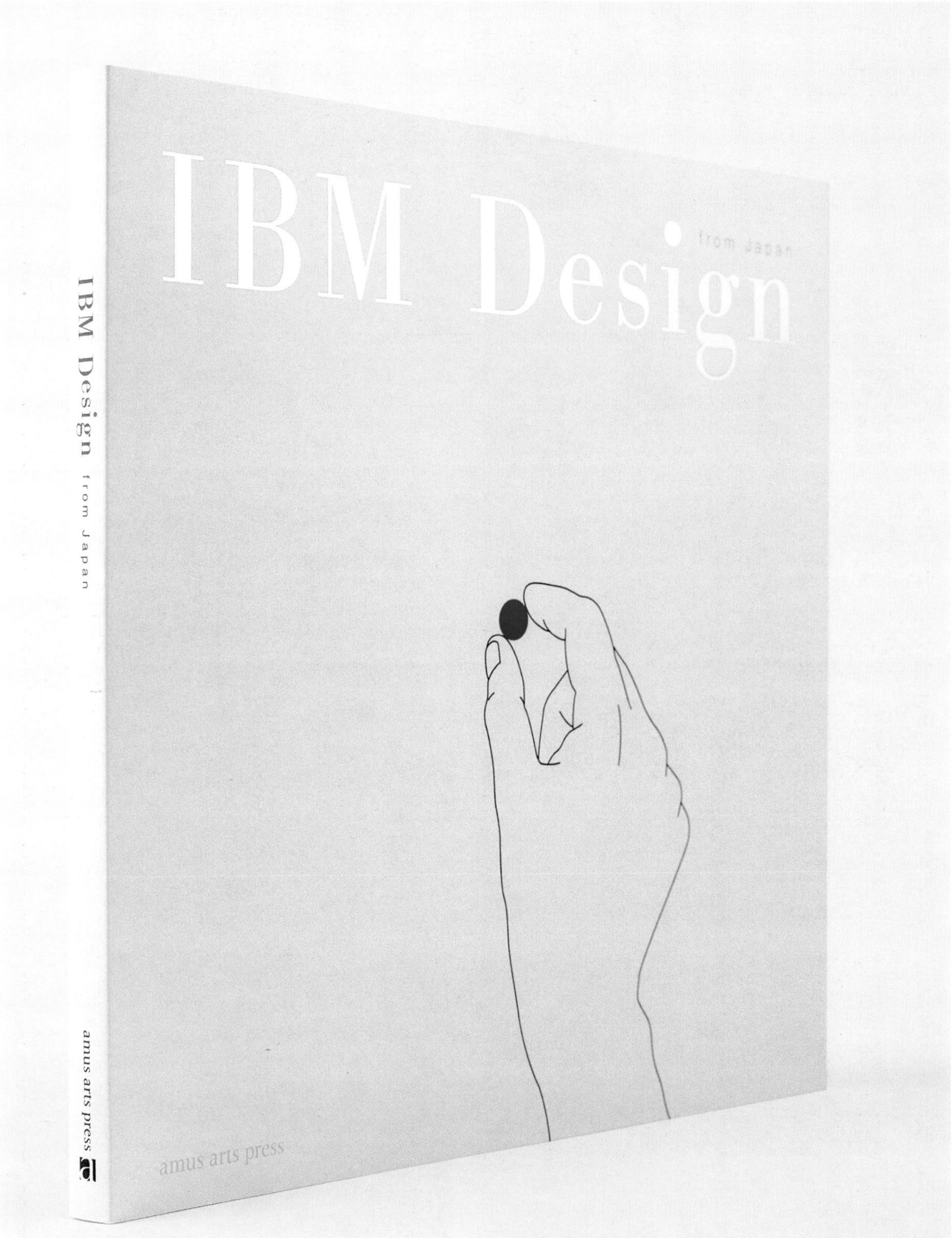

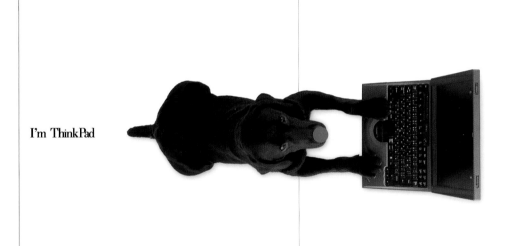

I'm ThinkPad

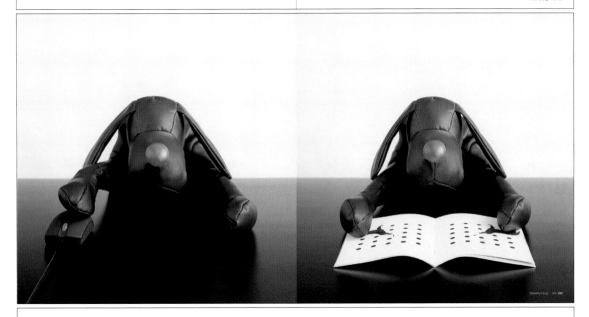

Sports Graphic Number

「スポーツ・グラフィック」
「ナンバー」

フクハラヒロシゲ — イラストレーション
Ilustration by Hiroshige Fukuhara

井本夏歩子 — 文
Text by Naoko Imoto（P75,78,81,97）

前田美保 — 文
Text by Miho Maeda（P72,88,91,94）

Chapter Two

32カ国完全ガイド
All About "The Korea/Japan"

↓ Brutus Nr. 518
Editorial design
D: Magazinehouse

BRUTUS

2002 8 15 特別定価 550円

ルイ・ヴィトンの謎。

BRUTUS

2002 11/1 特別定価 550円

安藤忠雄

ジャン・ヌーヴェル、
スティーヴン・ホールが
あなたのために
集合住宅を
建ててくれます

第2特集
ウイスキーの逆襲！

← Brutus Nr. 507 / 512
Editorial design
D: Magazinehouse

↓ Casa Brutus Nr. 5
Editorial design
D: Magazinehouse

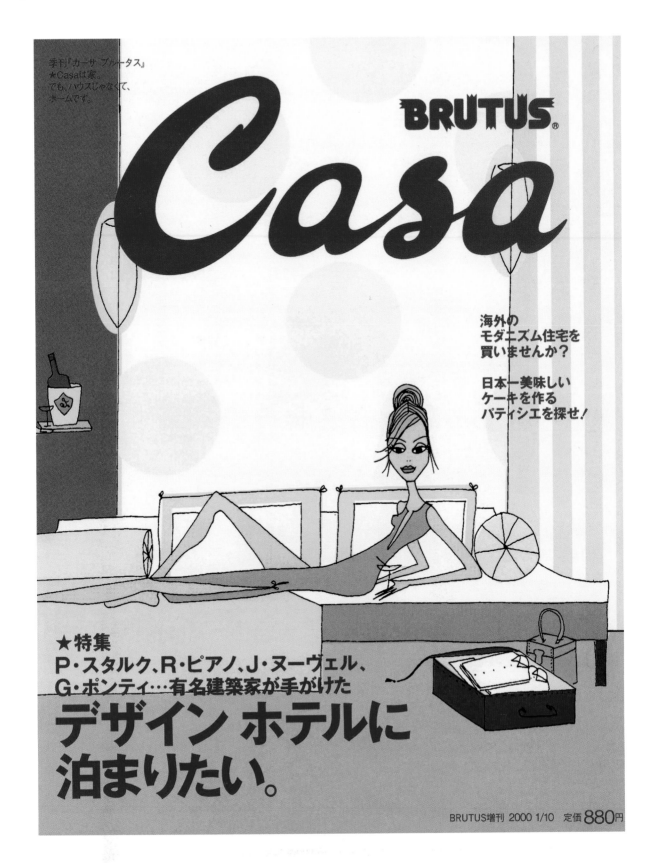

季刊『カーサ ブルータス』
★Casaは家。
でも、ハウスじゃなくて、
ホームです。

BRUTUS®

Casa

海外の
モダニズム住宅を
買いませんか？

日本一美味しい
ケーキを作る
パティシエを探せ！

★特集
P・スタルク、R・ピアノ、J・ヌーヴェル、
G・ポンティ…有名建築家が手がけた
デザイン ホテルに
泊まりたい。

BRUTUS増刊 2000 1/10 定価880円

Casa Brutus Nr. 7
Editorial design
D: Magazinehouse

Casa Brutus Nr. 16
Editorial design
D: Magazinehouse

Casa Brutus Nr. 20
Editorial design
D: Magazinehouse

Casa Brutus Nr. 21
Editorial design
D: Magazinehouse

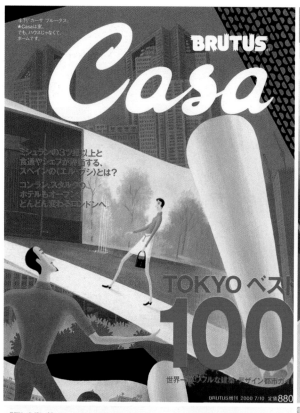

↓ Casa Brutus Nr. 14
Editorial design
D: Magazinehouse

Casa Brutus Nr. 27
Editorial design
D: Magazinehouse

Casa Brutus Nr. 22
Editorial design
D: Magazinehouse

Casa Brutus Nr. 31
Editorial design
D: Magazinehouse

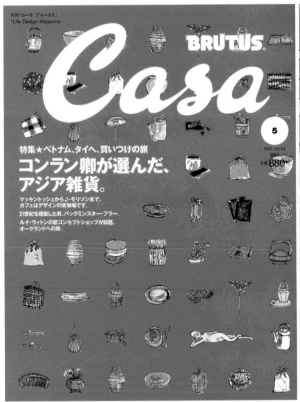

↓ Dream Design [Kitchen & Kitchen Tools] → Dream Design [Bath & Sanitary design]
Editorial design   Dream Design [Italian Mid-Century]
D: Magazinehouse   Dream Design [The Era of Design Shop]
                                            Dream Design [Joyful vs. Functional Kitchen]
                                            Editorial design
                                            D: Magazinehouse

プリント

516

MAGAZINE HOUSE MOOK

DREAM DESIGN

Dd

世界のキッチンツール。

KITCHEN & KITCHEN TOOLS

システムキッチンは、進化する。
SYSTEM EVOLUTION IN KITCHEN
デザインの国のキッチンメーカー。
CUCINA ALL'ITALIANA

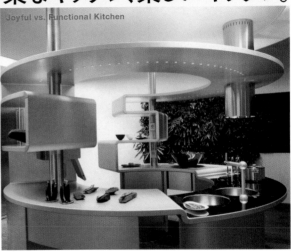

↓ Relax Nr. 49
Editorial design
D: Magazinehouse

→ Relax Nr. 62 / 68 / 66 / 67
Editorial design
D: Magazinehouse

518

プリント

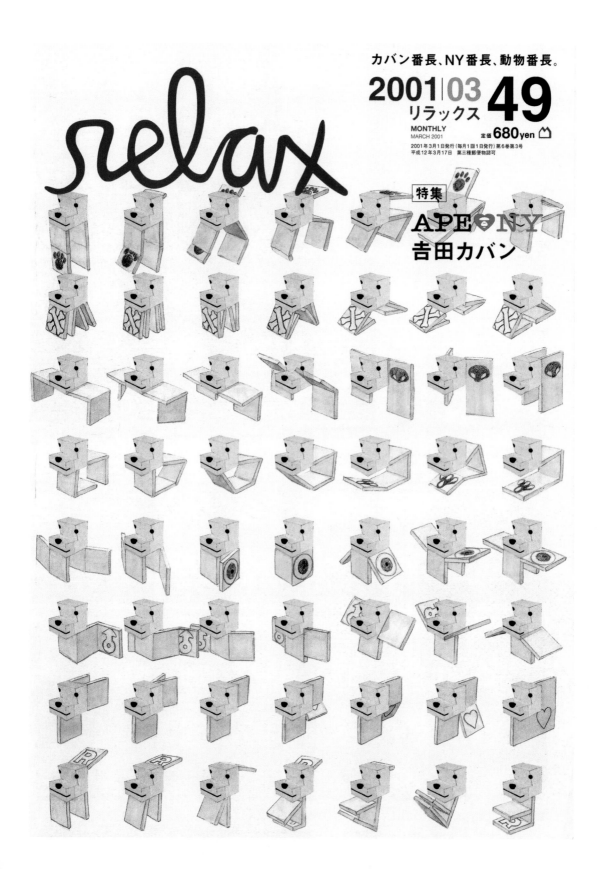

2003年2月12日発行（毎月第2・第4水曜日発行）第18巻第2号
昭和61年6月23日第三種郵便物認可

今年こそデブ・ズン胴から脱却を！

Tarzan ®

2 12 2003 No.389
450YEN 特別定価
http://tarzan.magazine.co.jp/

男と女の
年間トレーニング計画

男は自然なカラダが、
女は筋肉を感じさせる
カラダが断然いい！

このエクササイズで、
理想の
カラダに
なる！

← Tarzan Nr. 388
Editorial design
D: Magazinehouse

↓ Tarzan Nr. 389
Editorial design
D: Magazinehouse

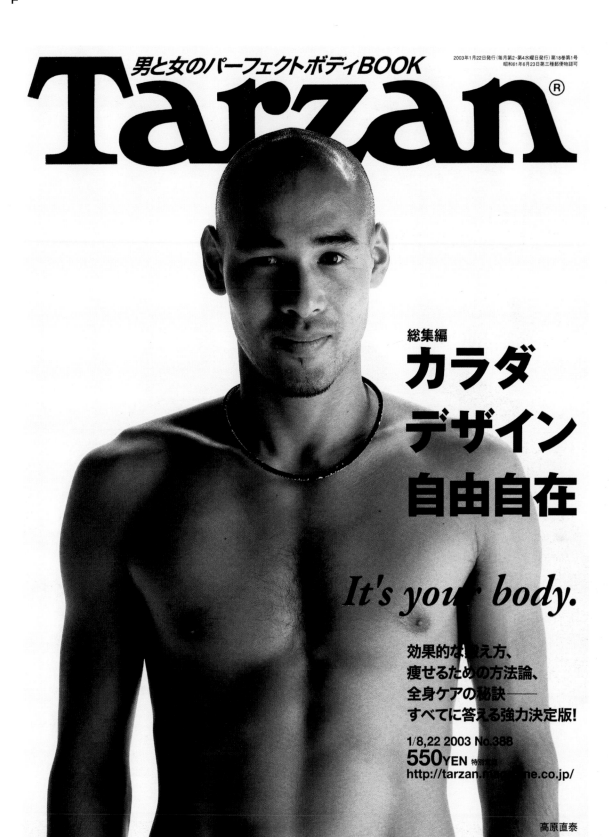

男と女のパーフェクトボディBOOK

2003年1月22日発行（毎月第2・第4水曜日発行）第18巻第1号
昭和061年6月23日第三種郵便物認可

Tarzan ®

総集編

カラダ
デザイン
自由自在

It's your body.

効果的な鍛え方、
痩せるための方法論、
全身ケアの秘訣——
すべてに答える強力決定版！

1/8,22 2003 No.388
550YEN 特別定価
http://tarzan.magazine.co.jp/

高原直泰

maomao

http://www.mao2.net/

● 2002 NOVEMBER

re-new volume 02

BUSHIDO

武士道

maomao

http://www.mao2.net/

2003 JANUARY

re-new volume 03

CARTA
いろはにほへと

2003 A HAPPY NEW YEAR !

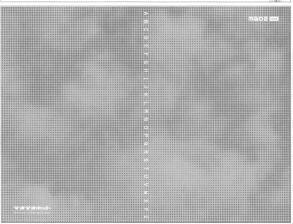

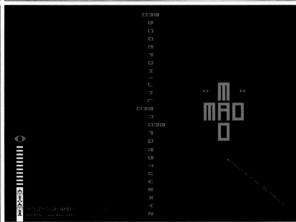

523 プリント

← Free magazine 'maomao'
vol.re02 / vol.01 / vol.re03 / vol.03
D: Osamu Sato / Outside Directors
Company Ltd.
ad+d: Osamu Sato
d: Shintaro Minami
cg d: Noboru Iizuka
c: Hiroko Nishikawa

↓ Hiroba 2001-2003
Magazine and layout design
D: Shinnoske Sugisaki

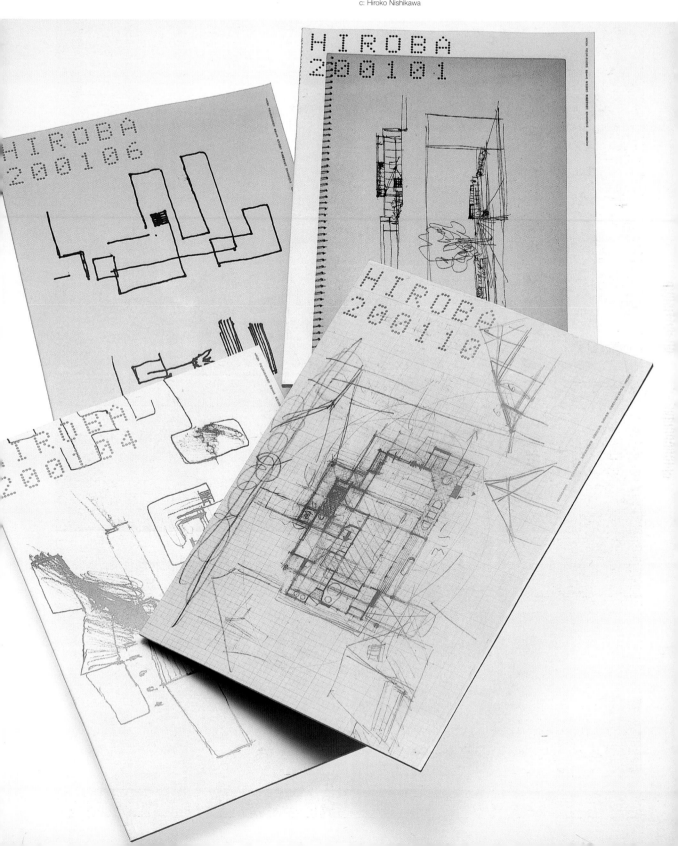

↓ Morisawa Font, 2nd version 1997   → Morisawa Font, 1st version 1997   プリント   524
   Booklet for digital font   Booklet for digital font
   D: Shinnoske Sugisaki   D: Shinnoske Sugisaki

文字の物語が画面を行き交う。ことばを映像化する力が、漢字にはある。

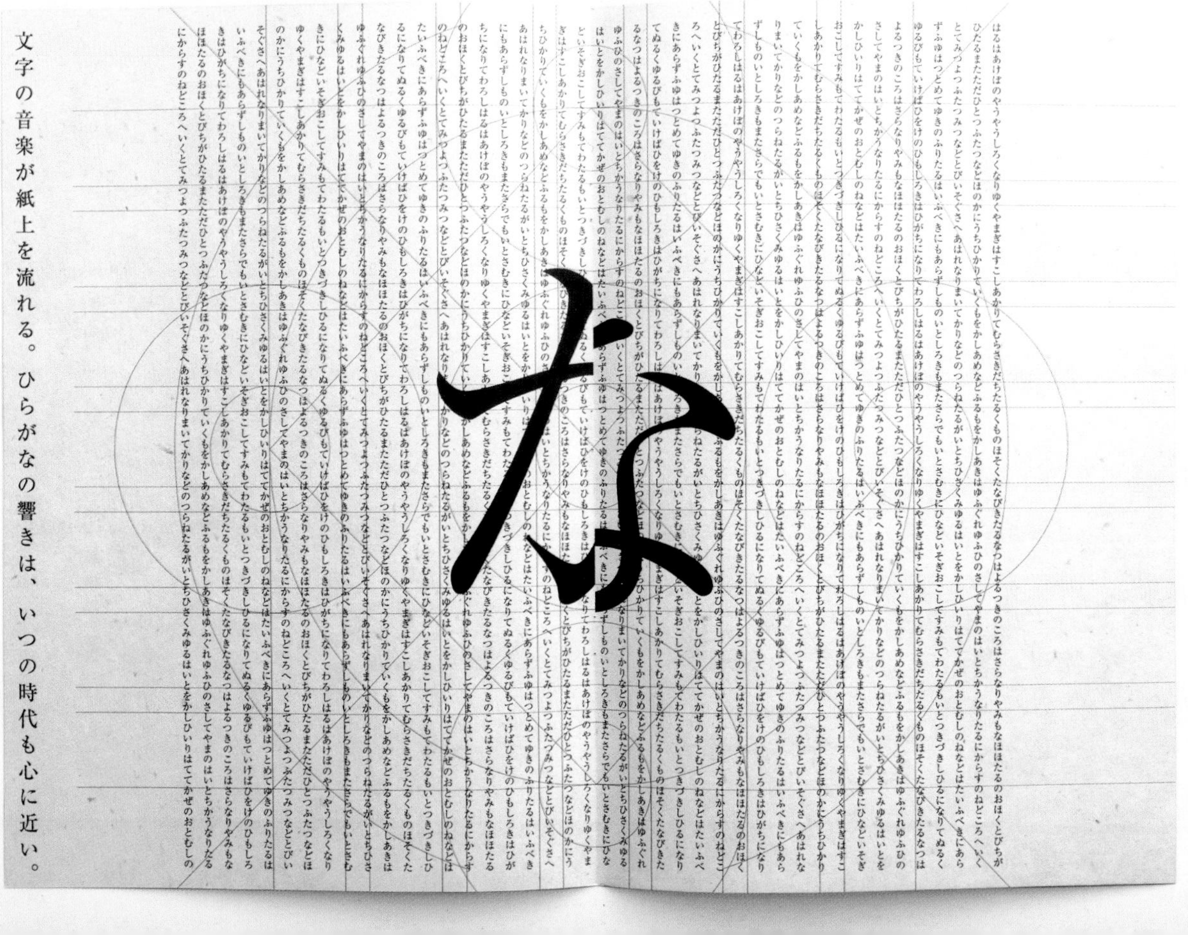

潔

文字の音楽が紙上を流れる。ひらがなの響きは、いつの時代も心に近い。

な

↓ Elementism
Mini book 2002
Mini-size book for a solo exhibition
D: Shinnoske Sugisaki

→ Yoshio Hayakawa Exhibition 2002
Collection of works for Yoshio
Hayakawa exhibition
D: Shinnoske Sugisaki

プリント

526

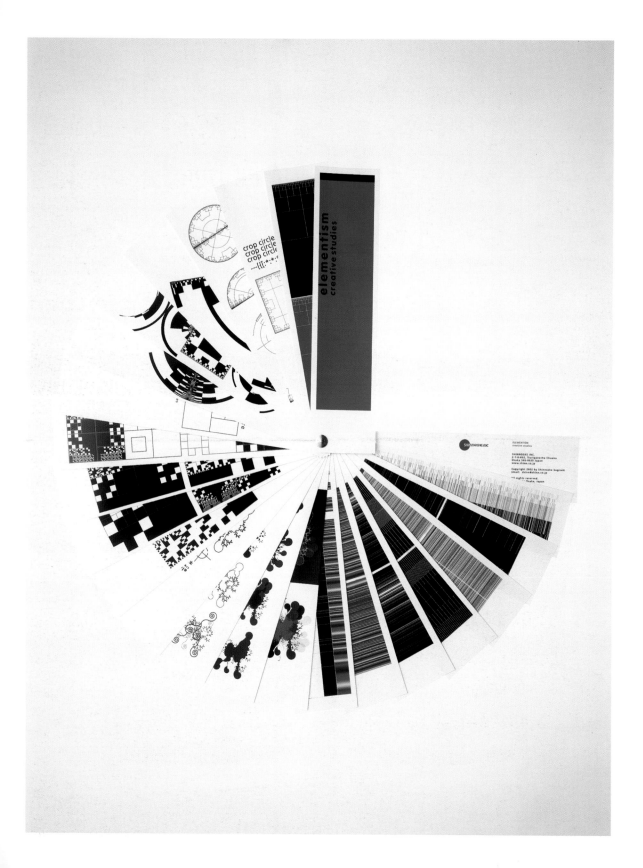

CAKE & COFFEE・G-SEN CONFECT

CAKE & COFFEE・G-SEN CONFECT

↓ **Tokyo ADC Annual**
Book design
D: Yoshie Watanabe

→ **Did God reply yet?**
Book design
D: Yoshie Watanabe

528

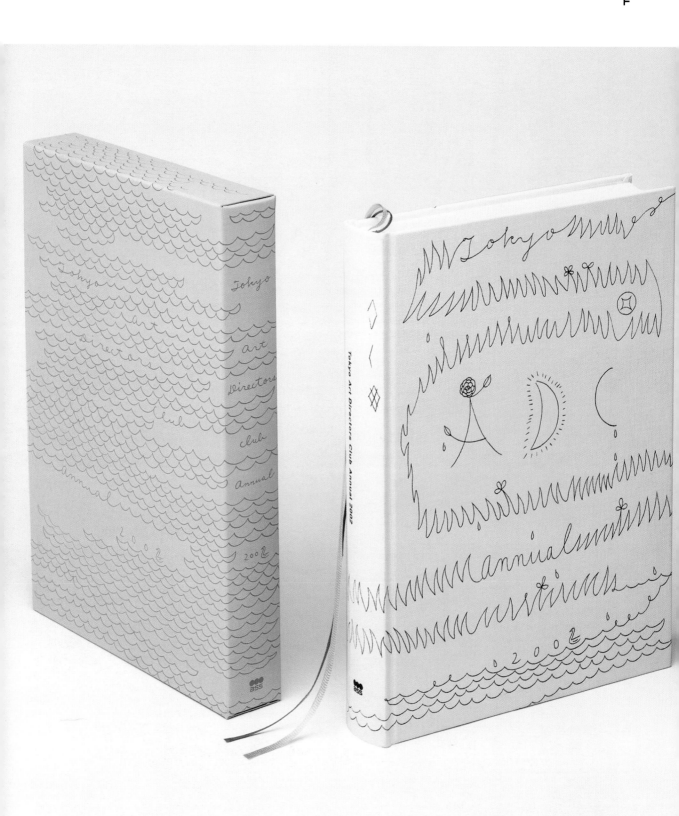

かみさま
どうして　このごろ
あたらしい　どうぶつを
はつめい　しないのですか？
もう　ずっとずっと
おんなじ　どうぶつ　ばっかり
　　　　　　　　ジョニー

かみさま
あなたは　きりんを
ああいうふうに　なればいいと
おもって　つくったの？
それとも　まちがって
ああなったの？
　　　　　　　　ノーマ

↓ Buch up and down
Book design
D: Yoshie Watanabe

Buch open
Book design
D: Yoshie Watanabe

→ Mine
Book design
D: Yoshie Watanabe

プリント

530

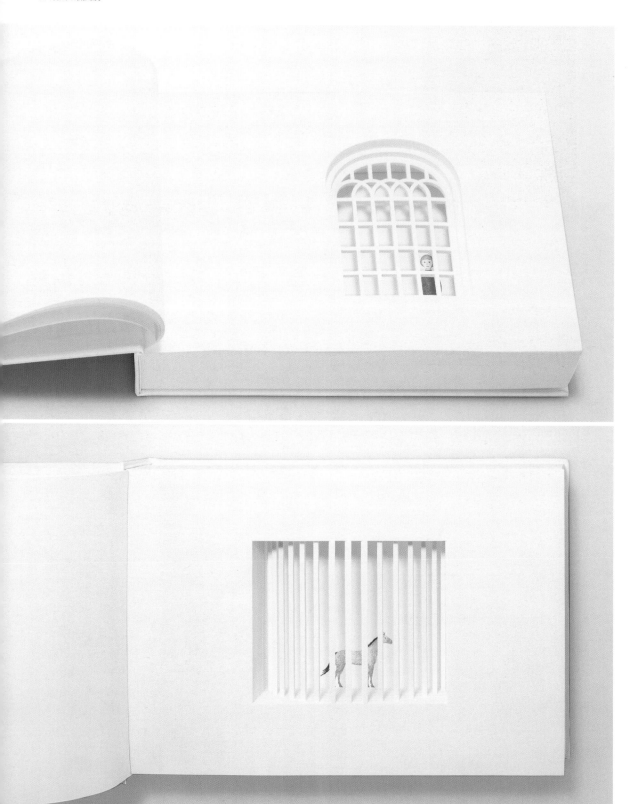

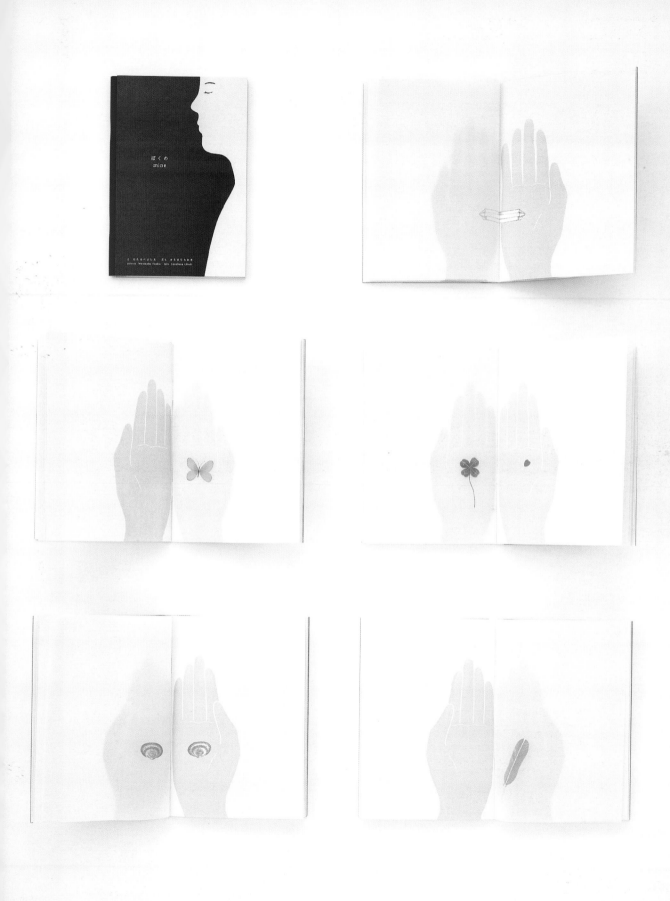

↓ Transfiguration of Steel: Kenichi
Kanazawa
Editorial design
D: Taku Satoh

→ Transfiguration of Steel : Kenichi
Kanazawa
Editorial design
D: Taku Satoh

プリント

532

Transfiguration of Steel : Kenichi Kanazawa

はがねの変相──金沢健一の仕事

川崎市岡本太郎美術館

Transfiguration of Steel : Kenichi Kanazawa

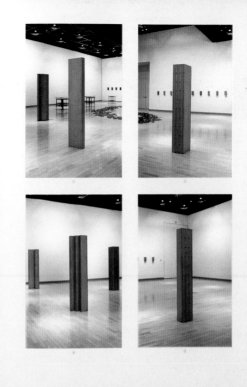

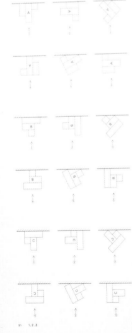

An Arbitrary Point P

Keio University Masahiko Sato Laboratory and Norio Nakamura

任意の点P

STEREO BOOK
48 stereoscopic graphics inside

慶應義塾大学 佐藤雅彦研究室 ＋ 中村至男

美術出版社

← An Arbitrary Point P
D: Kohji Yamamoto
cd: Masahiko Sato

↓ Tokyo Art Directors Club Annual 2000
D: Taku Satoh

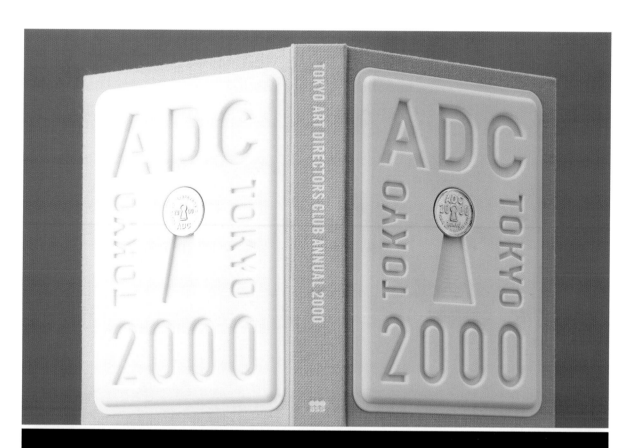

Licca

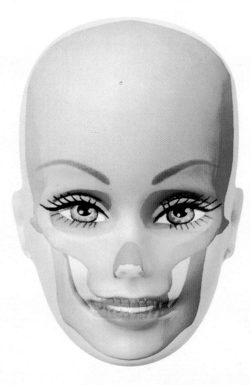

a Foreign Doll

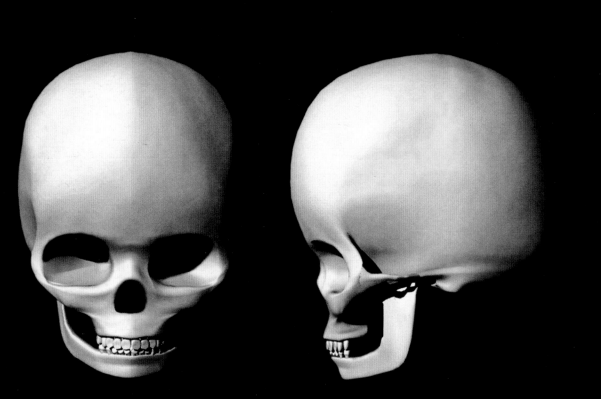

The Front Skull of Licca

The Left Skull of Licca

← Analysis of the Massproduct Design=
Takara [Licca]
Editorial design
D: Taku Satoh

↓ Analysis of the Massproduct Design=
Takara [Licca]
Editorial design
D: Taku Satoh

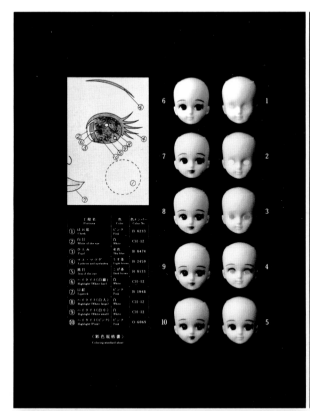

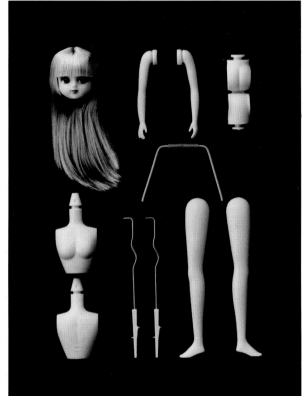

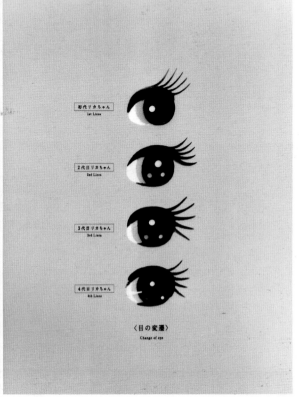

↓ Sampled Life
Editorial design
D: Hideki Nakajima

→ Revival
Editorial design
D: Hideki Nakajima

プリント 538

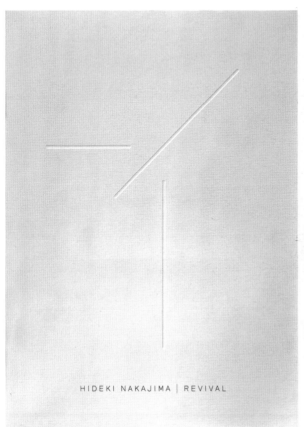

HIDEKI NAKAJIMA | REVIVAL

juliette
lewis

masatoshi
nagase

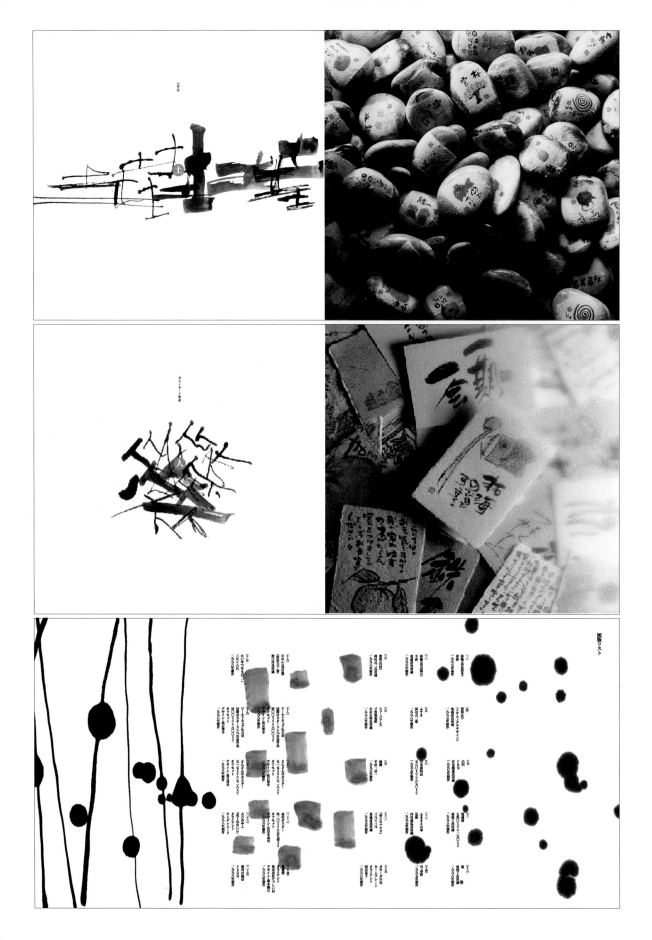

← Selected Works Youseki Miki
Editorial design
D: Hiroyuki Matsuishi

↓ Selected Works Youseki Miki
Editorial design
D: Hiroyuki Matsuishi

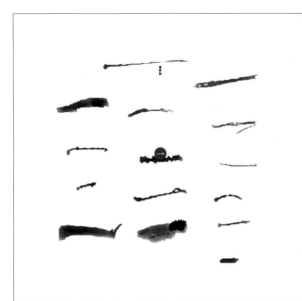

Strange Against Strange

You're strange and we like fur
Strange, walking down the avenue
You're strange just the way you are
Strange, always doing something new

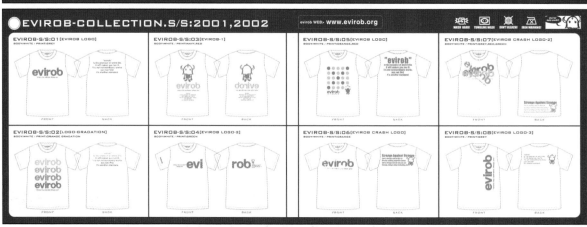

プリント

← Evirob-KIT
Booklet
D: Devilrobots Inc.

↓ Exposure
Free paper cover design
D: Devilrobots Inc.

↓ Paper and design
Book editorial design 2000
D: Kenya Hara
ad+d: Kenya Hara
d: Ike Maho

プリント 544

T-EOS
T-EOS

廣村正彰　バックグラフィックデザイン
Masaaki Hiromura

ハンマートーンGA

PAPER TALK カレンダー
PAPER TALK Calendar

成底良毛　アートディレクション
Yoshimoto Kato

マンダラ——西チベットの仏教美術
MANDALA——Buddhas in Western Way

秒速運平　ブックデザイン　グラフィックデザイン
Jugime Sakai

NT ラシャ

NT ラシャ・NT Rasha（1975〜）
ブックデザインの色彩表現の可能性を豊かにする——　杉浦康平
Kohei Sugiura

↓ MUJI Concept Book 2003
D: Kenya Hara
ad+d: Kenya Hara
d: Izumi Suge
p: Tamotsu Fujii

Each MUJI product entails a necessary consequence that has been discovered.　Naoto Fukasawa | Product designer

It is the Most Universal Japanese Idea.　Shigeru Ban | Architect

RE DESIGN
日常の 21 世紀

株式会社竹尾——編
原研哉＋日本デザインセンター原デザイン研究所——企画／構成

TAKEO
PAPER
SHOW
2000

朝日新聞社

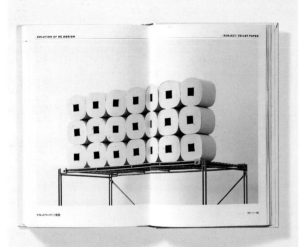

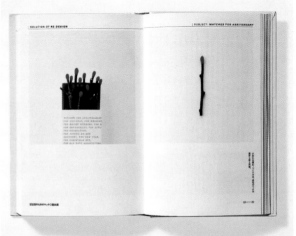

← Exhibition "Re Design" 2000
Book design
D: Kenya Hara
ad+d: Kenya Hara
d: Yukie Inoue

↓ Exhibition "Optimum" 2002
Book design
D: Kenya Hara
ad+d: Kenya Hara
d: Kaoru Matsuno

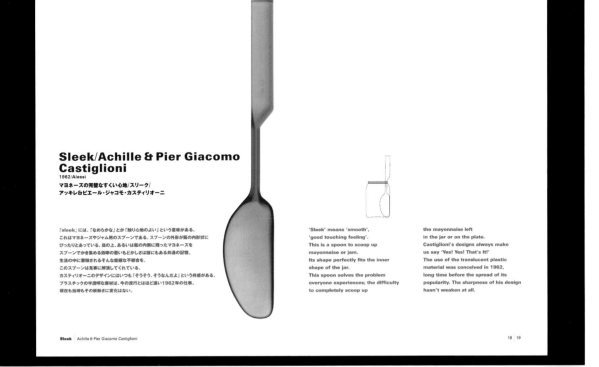

Sleek/Achille & Pier Giacomo Castiglioni

1962/Alessi

マヨネーズの完璧なすくい心地/スリーク/
アッキレ&ピエール・ジャコモ・カスティリオーニ

「sleek」には、「なめらかな」とか「触り心地のよい」という意味がある。
これはマヨネーズやジャム用のスプーンである。スプーンの外形が瓶の内形状に
ぴったりとあっている。瓶の上、あるいは瓶の内部に残ったマヨネーズを
スプーンでかき集める効率の悪いもどかしさは誰にもある共通の記憶。
生活の中に蓄積されるそんな些細な不都合を、
このスプーンは見事に解消してくれている。
カスティリオーニのデザインにはいつも「そうそう、そうなんだよ」という共感がある。
プラスチックの半透明な素材は、今の流行りとはほど遠い1962年の仕事。
現在も当時もその斬新さに変化はない。

'Sleek' means 'smooth',
'good touching feeling'.
This is a spoon to scoop up
mayonnaise or jam.
Its shape perfectly fits the inner
shape of the jar.
This spoon solves the problem
everyone experiences; the difficulty
to completely scoop up

the mayonnaise left
in the jar or on the plate.
Castiglioni's designs always make
us say 'Yes! Yes! That's It!'
The use of the translucent plastic
material was conceived in 1962,
long time before the spread of its
popularity. The sharpness of his design
hasn't weaken at all.

Sleek | Achille & Pier Giacomo Castiglioni   18 | 19

極限までシンプルなフォルムは高度な技術に支えられている。
薄く大きな天板を支える細い四本脚は繊細で絶妙のバランスを見せるが、
強度や天板の軽度などが本当にこの薄さで確保できるのかどうか不安になる。
この一見不可能とも思えるプロポーションは、天板の裏面から中心部に繋がる
なだらかな裏面の傾斜によって実現している。
すなわち中心部に向かって、天板が微妙に厚さを増しているのである。
厚みを増すための傾斜は、テーブルを見る視線から逃れている。
誰もが憧れてしまう形。それは具現化された透明。
他に替えがたい原点性を持つマジカルな魅力を放つのである。

Its simple but fine beauty is a fruit of
elaborated skills.
The four thin legs supporting the large
thin top table create an excellent
balance, but at the same time, you may
doubt if they can keep the strength and
the steadiness of the table board.
This seemingly impossible design is
made possible by changing

the thickness of the bottom surface
of the table board.
From the edge, the closer to the center,
the thicker it smoothly becomes.
This part is not visible from those who
look at the table. This form appeals
to everyone's heart. Its magical charm
is an embodied OPTIMUM QUALITY
impossible to replace.

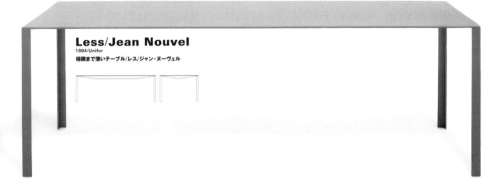

Less/Jean Nouvel

1994/Unifor

極限まで薄いテーブル/レス/ジャン・ヌーヴェル

Less | Jean Nouvel   12 | 13

↓ Chinese Star Sign

  Okumura's Design
  D: Akio Okumura

→ Japan Typography Association 2002
  D: Akio Okumura

プリント

550

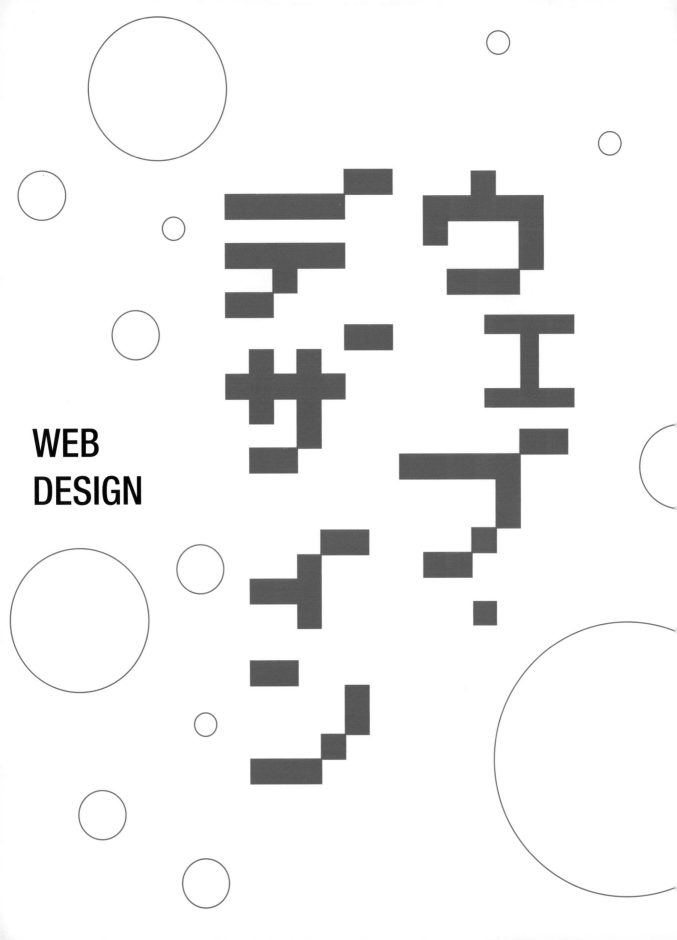

WEB
DESIGN

ウェブデザイン

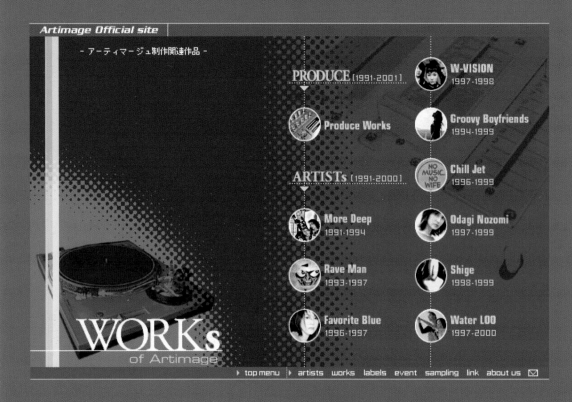

Artimage Official site

– アーティマージュ制作関連作品 –

PRODUCE [1991-2001]

Produce Works

ARTISTs [1991-2000]

More Deep
1991-1994

Rave Man
1993-1997

Favorite Blue
1996-1997

W-VISION
1997-1998

Groovy Boyfriends
1994-1999

Chill Jet
1996-1999

Odagi Nozomi
1997-1999

Shige
1998-1999

Water LOO
1997-2000

WORKs
of Artimage

▶ top menu ▶ artists works labels event sampling link about us ✉

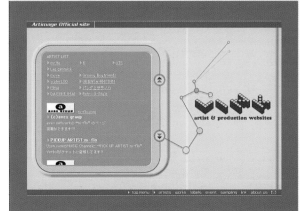

Artimage Official site

▶ top menu ▶ artists works labels event sampling link about us ✉

Artimage Official site

sAmpling
STREET & CLUB SOUND MAG

SHOP LIST   BACK NUMBER

INFORMATION

◀ latest issue!!

▶ top menu ▶ artists works labels event sampling link about us ✉

← Artimage inc
(C) Artimage Inc. / Kiwi Inc
D: 149design

↓ 149design.com
(C) 149design
D: 149design

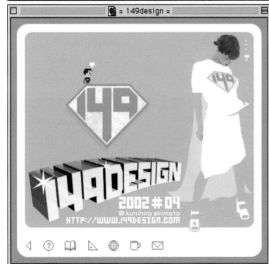

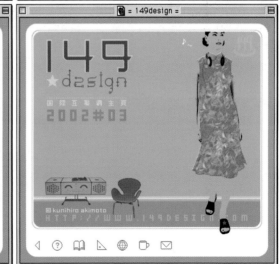

↓ Something Web magazine
(C) Edwin / Yomiko / Kiwi Inc.
D: 149design

→ Mariko Yoshida Official site
(C) BlueTurtle
D: 149design

556

MarikoYoshida
OFFICIAL WEBSITE

enter   **caution** : This site is optimised for Netscape4.0 & InternetExplorer4.0

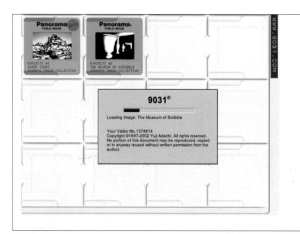

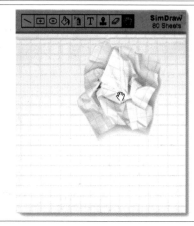

559

ウェブ・デザイン

← 9031.com
D: Yuji Adachi

↓ Berthier Associates Co., Ltd.
http://www.berthier.co.jp
D: Artless Inc.

Cover photograph : 1 2 3 4

Berthier Associates

designs attractive, functional, user-friendly workplaces...

Home

↓ Steelcase Inc. | LeapHD
http://www.leaphd.com
D: Artless Inc.

→ Steelcase Inc. | Let'sB
http://www.steelcase.co.jp/letsb/j/
D: Artless Inc.

560

ウェブ・デザイン

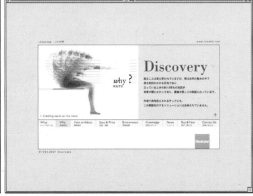

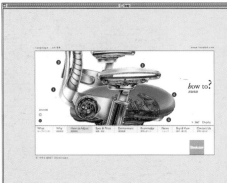

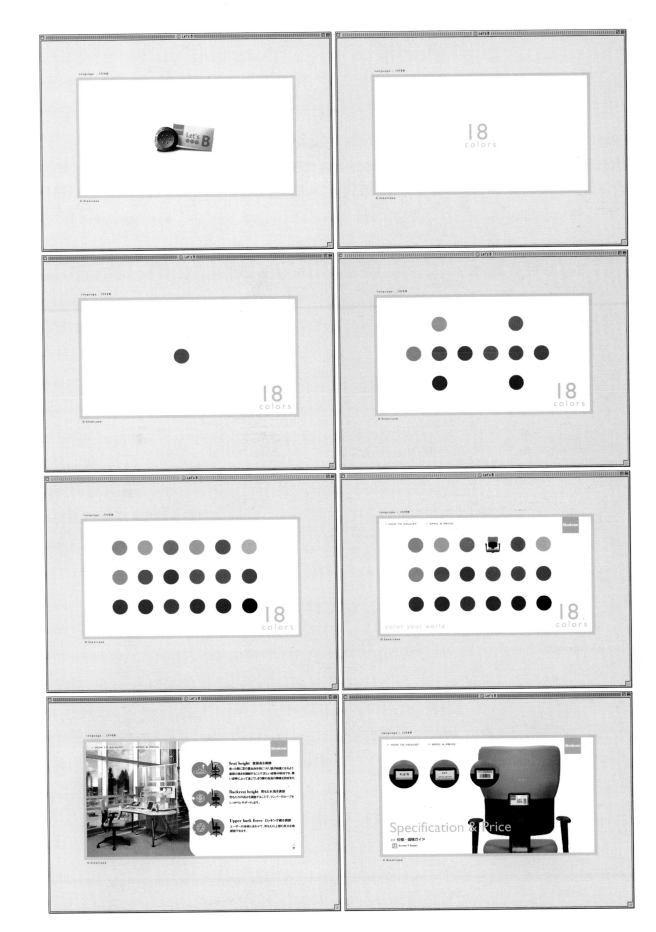

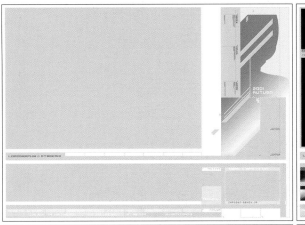

AT#REMIX LOVES VISUAL COMMUNICATION

AT#REMIX LOVES VISUAL COMMUNICATION

AT#R/NV.SYS

VERSION:0.9X BUILD_NO:XXXXX
PUBLIC PREVIEW

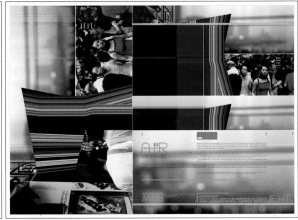

A#R

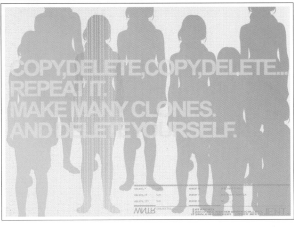

COPY,DELETE,COPY,DELETE...
REPEAT IT.
MAKE MANY CLONES.
AND DELETE YOURSELF.

← AT#REMIX
http://www.at-remix.jp
D: Air

↓ Bluemark Inc.
http://www.bluemark.co.jp
D: Bluemark Inc.

↓ Honda Fan Site
D: Drawing and Manual

→ Honda Fan Site
Asimo special site
D: Drawing and Manual

564

ウェブ・デザイン

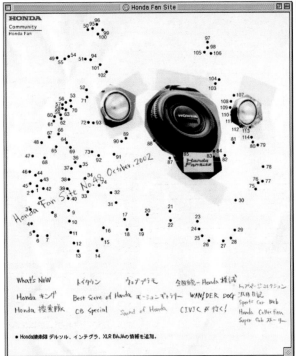

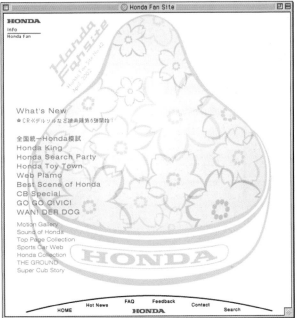

↓ ShotTV
Playbear
http://www.futureshot.com/
D: Yoshihito Kawata

→ Fresh
http://www.de-code.com/fresh/
D: Bluemark Inc.

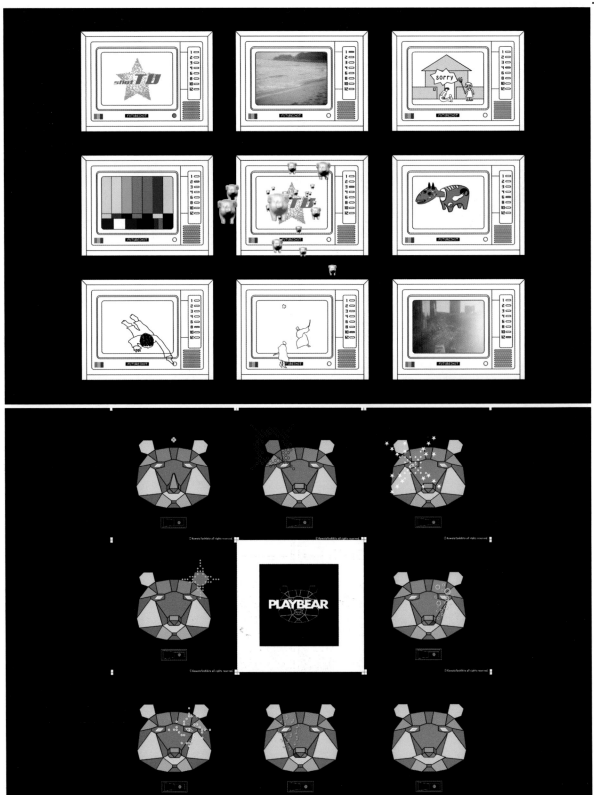

Back   1   Next ➡

09 Gloves

⬅ Back   Next ➡

Photography : Kenshu Shintsubo, assisted by Dai-Chan.
Hair and make-up : Kenji Ishida (Kiki).
Styling : Aomi, assisted by Machimi Kato.
Models : Shiho Ochiai (Soft M@chine), Kato.
Special thanks to Akihiro and Natsuko O.

01 02 03 04 05 06 07 08 09 00

10 Pajama

⬅ Back   Next ➡

Photography : Kenshu Shintsubo, assisted by Dai-Chan.
Hair and make-up : Kenji Ishida (Kiki).
Styling : Aomi, assisted by Machimi Kato.
Models : Shiho Ochiai (Soft M@chine), Kato.
Special thanks to Akihiro and Natsuko O.

01 02 03 04 05 06 07 08 09 10 00

Thursday, October 14th 1999,
Fondation Cartier pour l'art contemporain
Dramatics Nights.

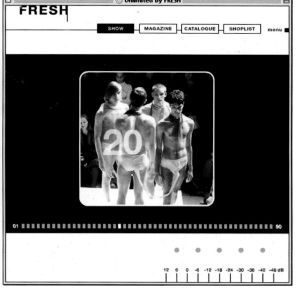

01 50

12 6 0 -6 -12 -18 -24 -30 -36 -42 -48 dB

- concept
- products
- faq
- shop list
- online shop
- links

自分 のためだから、お客様と同じものを。

GUEST & ME

What's New：ホームパーティの多い楽しい季節。ちょっとした贈り物にぜひお選びください。

Copyright 2003 GUEST & Me. All rights reserved.　Contact　Legal　Privacy

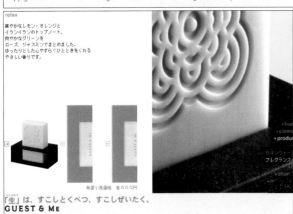

relax

華やかなレモン・オレンジと
イランイランのトップノート。
肉やかなグリーンを
ローズ、ジャスミンでまとめました。
ゆったりとした心やすらぐひとときをくれる
やさしい香りです。

希望小売価格　各800円

「生」は、すこしとくべつ、すこしぜいたく。

GUEST & ME

What's New：ホームパーティの多い楽しい季節。ちょっとした贈り物にぜひお選びください。

Copyright 2003 GUEST & Me. All rights reserved.　Contact　Legal　Privacy

誰かのために選ぶもの。それは自分なりのこだわりを表すもの。

GUEST & ME

What's New：ホームパーティの多い楽しい季節。ちょっとした贈り物にぜひお選びください。

Copyright 2003 GUEST & Me. All rights reserved.　Contact　Legal　Privacy

← Guest & Me
http://www.guestandme.com/
D: IMG SRC, Inc.

↓ IMG SRC
http://www.imgsrc.co.jp/
D: IMG SRC, Inc.

IMG SRC Meets The W3C

IMG SRC has joined W3C. There are fundamental, next generation technologies aimed at improving web interfaces and accessibility. XML, HTTP-NG, and more are there and waiting to be used. We are actively participating in standardizing those new technologies to make a better web environment for everyone.

One Show Interactive, 2002

for Corporate Image / Business to Consumer / WebSites

for IMAGINATION & REALIZATION
Corporate Image / Business to Consumer / CD-ROM

Golden Award of Montreux 2001

Gold Medal - online corporate information category

Stat-it2 has been Released

We've released a new version of our Access Log Analysis Program.

Communication Arts Web Site of the Week

was chosen as by Communication Arts.

Copyright(c)1998 IMG SRC, Inc.
All rights reserved.

In the world of web designing, it is not only the graphics in your web browser that must be designed. For a website to be functional, to be beneficial and to be outstanding, the supporting systems and programs must be crafted and designed as well.

We work with our customers on the fundamental levels of network and system development to create for them a truly beneficial internet environment.

System Integration

Our system engineers, mainly consisting of UNIX experts, will help with your system integration needs. We will offer you the best solution with open-source software in combination with UNIX-based OS, such as FreeBSD, Solaris, Linux, or MacOS X, and Apache to construct a durable and reliable system at a reasonable cost.
We also provide a hosting service for those customers who don't have the necessary resources to install their own network system.

Networking

The internet has been around for years, but the technology is still rapidly advancing and improving. As IP has become essential to our lives, so too have security issues. In the next few years, IPv6 is expected to expand in leaps and bounds. At IMG SRC, we introduced IPv6 in Fall 1998 and have continued working on research and experiment along with IPsec. Please consult with us about technologies supporting the internet, such as IPv6 or IPsec.

Software Development

At IMG SRC we also produce and develop software. Please refer to the product page for our latest products.

Copyright(c)1998 IMG SRC, Inc.
All rights reserved.

FORM FOLLOWS FUNCTION.
by Walter Gropius

Stat-it2

This is a program for analyzing access statistics - an essential for web servers. The interface is simple and designed for almost anyone to be able to operate. All the results are shown as graphs, so you can see the access numbers at a glance. Type "guest" for name and password to enter.

e-mail address (not Required)

[download]

Supported environment: We believe any Web server is supported if the logs are written in the 'common log format' but we've checked only Apache 1.3.x. Stat-it is a Perl script. We've checked that Stat-it works fine with both Perl 5.005_03 and Perl 5.6.0. Although there seems to be no reason why Stat-it would not work with other versions of Perl, please let us know the results if you try other versions.

Copyright(c)1998 IMG SRC, Inc.
All rights reserved.

It agrees very well with the new needs of decentralized team play in the electric age.

by M. McLuhan

Yusuke Koike	Ubiratan Ryuta Ohara		Moses Koizumi	Kazuo Soma	
Tatsuya Kubo	Yu Yamanaka	Koji Ito	Tomohiro Terashima	Jun Kuriyama	
Masafumi Nakane		Aki Nishina	Mikiko Ito	Yusuke Shibata	
Hiroyuki Hanai		Ryoji Tanaka	Hiroshi Sato	Toshiyuki Sugai	
Hitoshi Okazaki	Toshiyuki Ito		Tom Vincent	Emi Iwasa	
	Hisafumi Matsushita		Momoko Takaoka	Hisayoshi Tohsaki	
Toshiyuki Nagashima	Shino Komori		Takato Kanehara	Kenji Aragane	

Copyright(c)1998 IMG SRC, Inc.
All rights reserved.

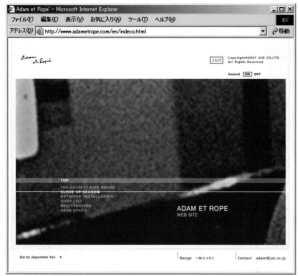

← Adam et Rope' 2003S/S
http://www.adametrope.com/
D: IMG SRC, Inc.

↓ Cover
http://www.sss.to/cover/
D: Kaiteki

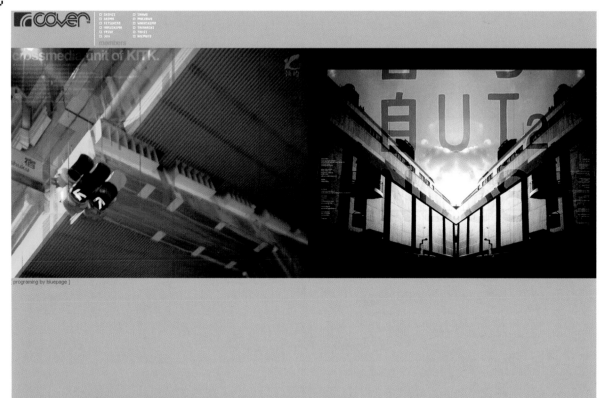

↓ Kaiteki
http://www.kitk.org/
D: Kaiteki

→ Cryogenicx
http://www.cryogenicx.com/
D: Kaiteki

ウェブ・デザイン

572

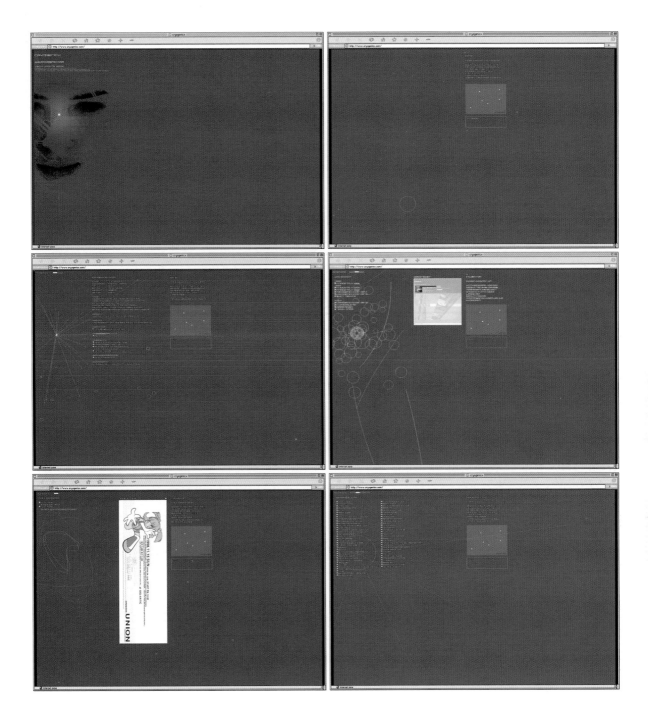

LET'S PLAY THE CLASSIC!
©2001 Chihiro Katoh All Rights Reserved.

CONTENTS
GO TO THE ZOO · CELEBRATE CHRISTMAS · PLAY THE DJEMBE ·
PLAY THE JAZZ · PLAY THE CLASSIC & PLAY THE PSYCHEDELIC ROCK
BBS · LINK · MAIL & NEWS
Sincerely,
Chihiro Katoh

Let's Play The Classic

Copyright(c)2000ChihiroKatohAllRightsReserved.
http://www.plala.or.jp/chihiro_/classic/LTSG-0055
Tribute To "GEMINI" 2001 Feb 16(Fri)
Please Play Your Classic Use [A]~[K] and [Space]Key

SPACE   K J H G F D S A   LET'S GO

LET'S PLAY THE JAZZ!
©2001 Chihiro Katoh All Rights Reserved.

CONTENTS
GO TO THE ZOO · CELEBRATE CHRISTMAS · PLAY THE DJEMBE ·
PLAY THE JAZZ · PLAY THE CLASSIC & PLAY THE PSYCHEDELIC ROCK
BBS · LINK · MAIL & NEWS
Sincerely,
Chihiro Katoh

LET'S PLAY THE JAZZ!

Copyright(C) 2000 Chihiro Katoh All rights reserved.
http://www3.plala.or.jp/chihiro_/jazz/ LTSG-0004
Tribute To [Gemini] 00.7.14(Fri)

L   K   J   H   G   D   F   S   A

LET'S PLAY YOUR JAZZ USE [A]-[L] and [SPACE]

LET'S PLAY THE PSYCHEDELIC!
©2001 Chihiro Katoh All Rights Reserved.

CONTENTS
GO TO THE ZOO · CELEBRATE CHRISTMAS · PLAY THE DJEMBE ·
PLAY THE JAZZ · PLAY THE CLASSIC & PLAY THE PSYCHEDELIC ROCK
BBS · LINK · MAIL & NEWS
Sincerely,
Chihiro Katoh

Let's Play The Psychedelic Rock

Copyright(c)2001 ChihiroKatohAllRightsReservea.
http://www.plala.or.jp/chihiro_/psyche /
Tribute To "GEMINI" 2001 Mar 24(Sat)
Please Play Your psychedelicRock
Use [A]~[K] and [Space]Key
LTSG-0006

[←]   K   J   H G F D S A   [→]

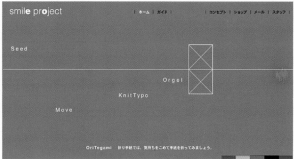

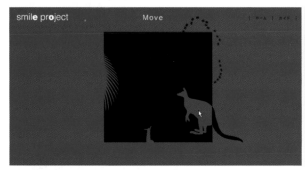

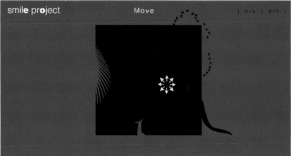

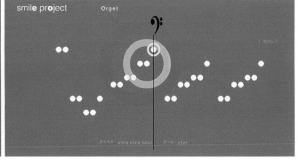

↓ s269
   TileGum.Compose();
   http://village.infoweb.ne.jp/~fwne4609/
   D: Yosuke Yasuda

→ Cowboybebop: Knockin' on heaven's door
   D: Masanori Sakamoto
   cl: Sony Pictures Entertainment (Japan) Inc.
   development firm: Frognation
   copyright: (C) Sunrise, Bones, Bandai Visual

ウェブ・デザイン   576

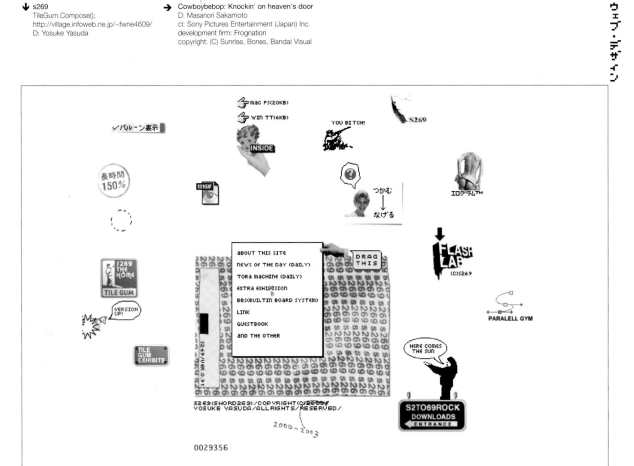

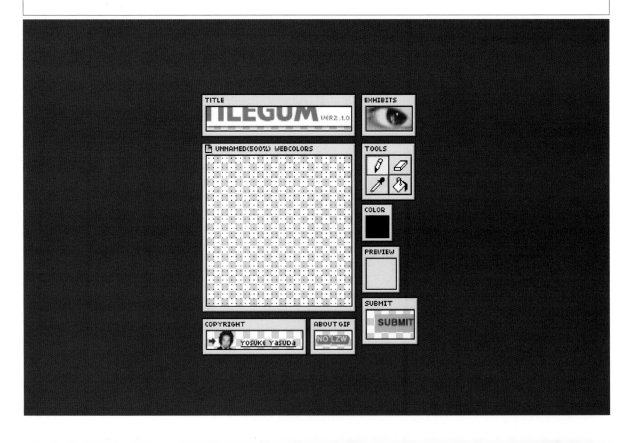

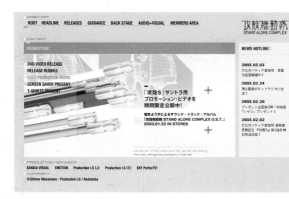

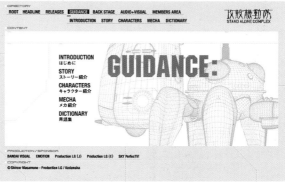

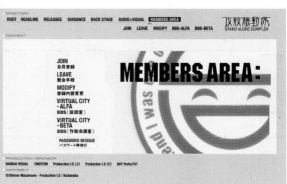

↓ Ghost in the shell: Stand alone complex
← http://www.bandaivisual.co.jp/kokaku-s/
D: Masanori Sakamoto
cl: Production I.G
development firm: Frognation
copyright: (C) Shirow Masamune
production I.G / Kodansha

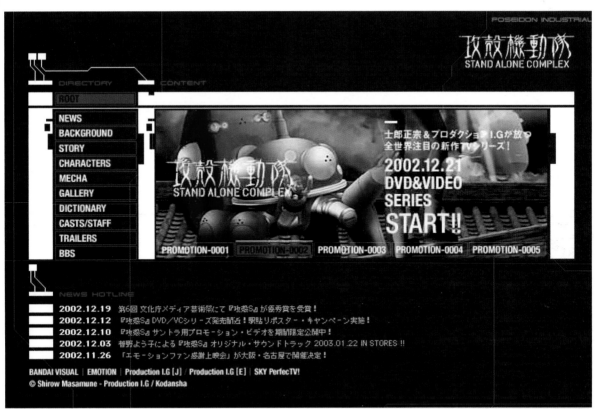

RMK
http://www.rmkrmk.com
D: Masanori Sakamoto
cl: RMK division E'quipe, LTD.
development firm: Whitewall
copyright: (C) 2003 RMK division E'quipe,
Ltd.

MotLa Archives+Grid systems
http://www.motla.com
D: Masanori Sakamoto

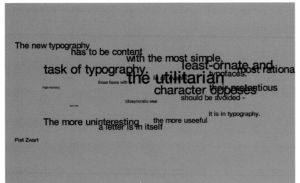

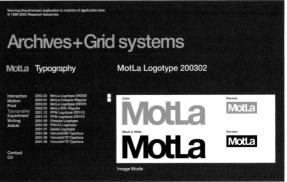
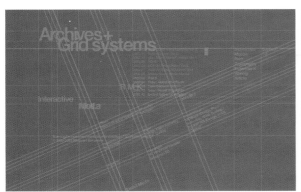

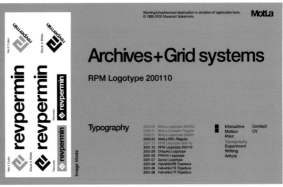

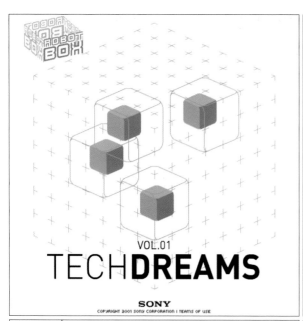

VOL.01

TECH**DREAMS**

SONY
COPYRIGHT 2001 SONY CORPORATION | TERMS OF USE

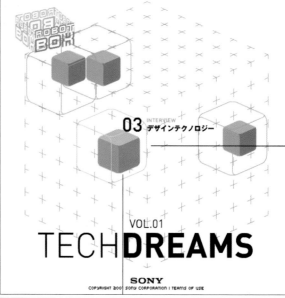

03 INTERVIEW
デザインテクノロジー

VOL.01

TECH**DREAMS**

SONY
COPYRIGHT 2001 SONY CORPORATION | TERMS OF USE

 VOL.01 TECH **DREAMS**

01 INTERVIEW WITH MOVIE
Tech in RoboCup2001
ロボカップで進化し続けるテクノロジーとは。

▶ 人間が操縦するAIBOと互角に戦う、ERS-2100
▶ プロのサッカープレイヤーが驚く程のレベルに達している！
▶ 「チームワーク」「チームマネジメント」で、もっと楽しくなる！
▶ 高度なテクノロジーが必要とされる、レスキューロボット
▶ ロボット達の認識力の鍵を握る「センサー」
▶ 来年はどうなる？
▶ 2050年のグランドチャレンジに向けて

ロボットに夢を見る人達が集まる、**RoboCup**。
「2050年、サッカーワールドカップの優勝チームに、ロボットのチー
ムが勝つ」という夢に向けて、ロボット研究者達は競い合っていま
す。この場所から、未来のロボットテクノロジーが生まれてくるのか
もしれません。

PAGE 1/9 ▶

SONY
COPYRIGHT 2001 SONY CORPORATION | TERMS OF USE

 VOL.01 TECH **DREAMS**

04 INTERVIEW
もう1つのロボット工学
もうひとつのロボット工学。その哲学的着眼点とは。

神経回路網、認知・自己意識など、
独特な観点でロボット研究に取り組む工学博士の谷淳氏。
ロボットに興味を持つきっかけや
認知の研究を始めるに至ったエピソードも
谷ワールドを感じさせる感性と切り口。
時代にながされることのないマイペースな探究心と
哲学に満ちたロボット学に見る認知の着地点とは。

PAGE 1/5 ▶

04 INTERVIEW
もう1つのロボット工学

SONY
COPYRIGHT 2001 SONY CORPORATION | TERMS OF USE

← Sony : Robot Box Vol.00 - 02
http://www.sony.co.jp/SonyInfo/dream/robotbox/
D: Masanori Sakamoto
cl: Sony Corporation
development firm: Drawing and Manual
agency: Frontage Inc.
copyright: (C) Sony Corporation

↓ Sony : Robot Box Vol.00 - 02
http://www.sony.co.jp/SonyInfo/dream/robotbox/
D: Masanori Sakamoto
cl: Sony Corporation
development firm: Drawing and Manual
agency: Frontage Inc.
copyright: (C) Sony Corporation

ROBODEX Information ～ パートナー型ロボット
FRIENDS
FFICIAL SITE
ROBODEX 開催情報
ROBODEX2002

About ROBODEX2002
ROBODEX2002について

ロボットはどこまで人間に「近づいた」のか？

パーソナルロボットの代名詞ともなったAIBOが発売されたのが1999年6月。以来、世紀を超えた3年の間に、ロボットはどこまで人間に近づいたのだろうか？

3月28～31日にパシフィコ横浜で開催されたパートナーロボット（人間共存型ロボット）の博覧会、ROBODEX2002。

今回の特集では、ROBODEX2002での出展作の紹介と開発者へのインタビューを元に、現在のロボットがどのような方向から人との距離を縮め続けているのかを、詳細にレポートします。

VOL.02 Friends
ROBOT BOX
SPECIAL FEAT. ROBODEX 2002

SONY
Copyright 2002 Sony Corporation l Teams of Use

FRIENDS
特集 Friends ～パートナー型ロボット

ロボットはどこまで人間に「近づいた」のか？

パーソナルロボットの代名詞ともなったAIBOが発売されたのが1999年6月。以来、世紀を超えた3年の間に、ロボットはどこまで人間に近づいたのだろうか？

3月28～31日にパシフィコ横浜で開催されたパートナーロボット（人間共存型ロボット）の博覧会、ROBODEX2002。

今回の特集では、ROBODEX2002での出展作の紹介と開発者へのインタビューを元に、現在のロボットがどのような方向から人との距離を縮め続けているのかを、詳細にレポートします。

OFFICIAL SITE
ROBODEX 2002

ROBODEX Information
ROBODEX 開催情報

About ROBODEX2002
ROBODEX2002について

VOL.02 Friends
ROBOT BOX
SPECIAL FEAT. ROBODEX 2002

SONY
Copyright 2002 Sony Corporation l Teams of Use

↓ Soul trash

Swatch
http://www.nicemix.com/
D: Asami Hirai

→ Berlin trash
http://www.nicemix.com/
D: Asami Hirai

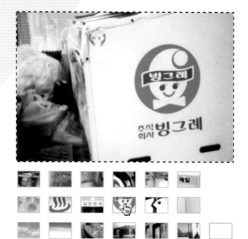

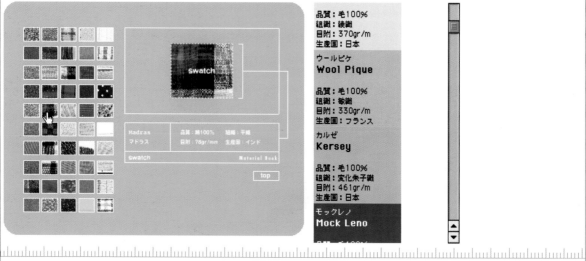

品質：毛100%
組織：綾織
目附：370gr/m
生産国：日本

ウールピケ
Wool Pique

品質：毛100%
組織：朱織
目附：330gr/m
生産国：フランス

カルゼ
Kersey

品質：毛100%
組織：変化朱子織
目附：461gr/m
生産国：日本

モックレノ
Mock Leno

ZOOM=CONTROL+CLICK

BACK

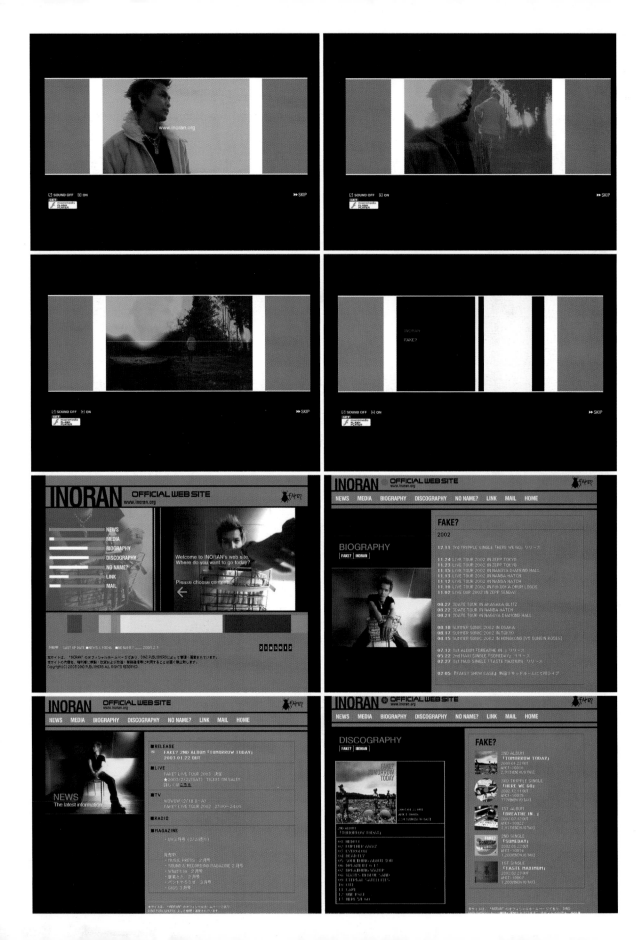

← Inoran / Official web site
http://inoran.org/
D: Sakaguchi Ken Factory Inc.

↓ Inoran / Official web site
http://inoran.org/
D: Sakaguchi Ken Factory Inc.

NO NAME?
MEMBERS SITE

NEWS ▶FAKE? ▶INORAN
▶ NO NAME? INFORMATION
▶ PREVIEW
▶ FROM STAFF
▶ DOWNLOAD
▶ HOME

webmaster@inoran.org

NO NAME?
MEMBERS SITE

NEWS ▶FAKE? ▶INORAN
▶ NO NAME? INFORMATION
▶ PREVIEW
▶ FROM STAFF
▶ DOWNLOAD
▶ HOME

webmaster@inoran.org

↓ Diesel Japan web site
D: Samohung

→ Nike Japan Football web site

Nike Japan ACG web site
D: Samohung

588

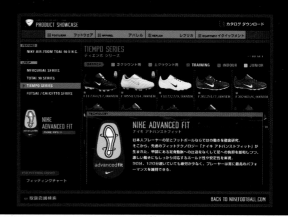

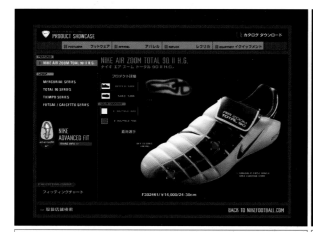

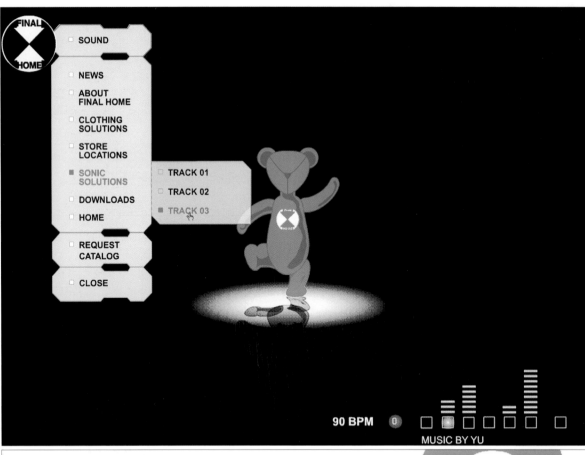

FINAL HOME

SOUND

NEWS

ABOUT
FINAL HOME

CLOTHING
SOLUTIONS

STORE
LOCATIONS

SONIC
SOLUTIONS

DOWNLOADS

HOME

REQUEST
CATALOG

CLOSE

TRACK 01

TRACK 02

TRACK 03

90 BPM

MUSIC BY YU

PLEATS
PLEASE

LOADING...

← Final Home website

Pleats Please website
D: Sayuri Studio, Inc.

↓ SH Digital Creations
http://www.sh-dc.com
D: Satoshi Hayakawa

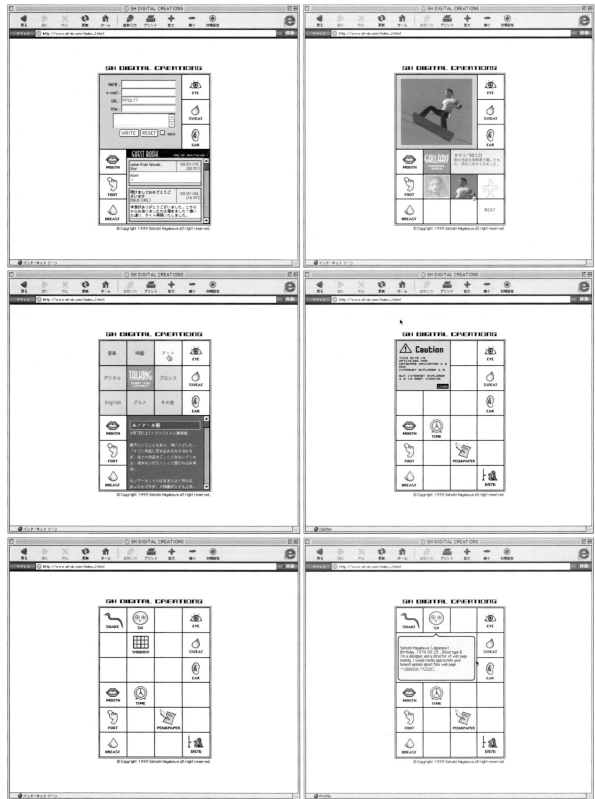

↓ http://www.sountain.com
D: Yosuke Abe

→ Morisawa Web
D: Shinnoske Sugisaki

592

ウェブ・デザイン

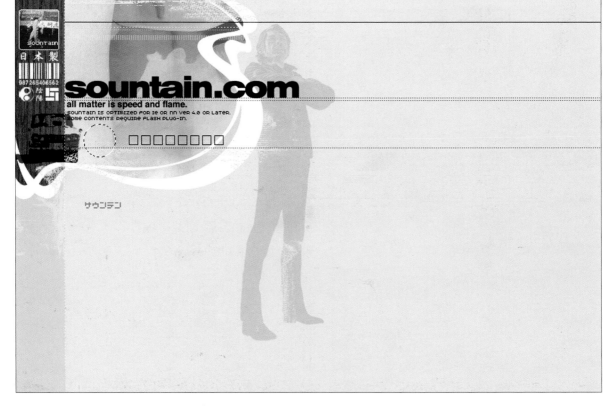

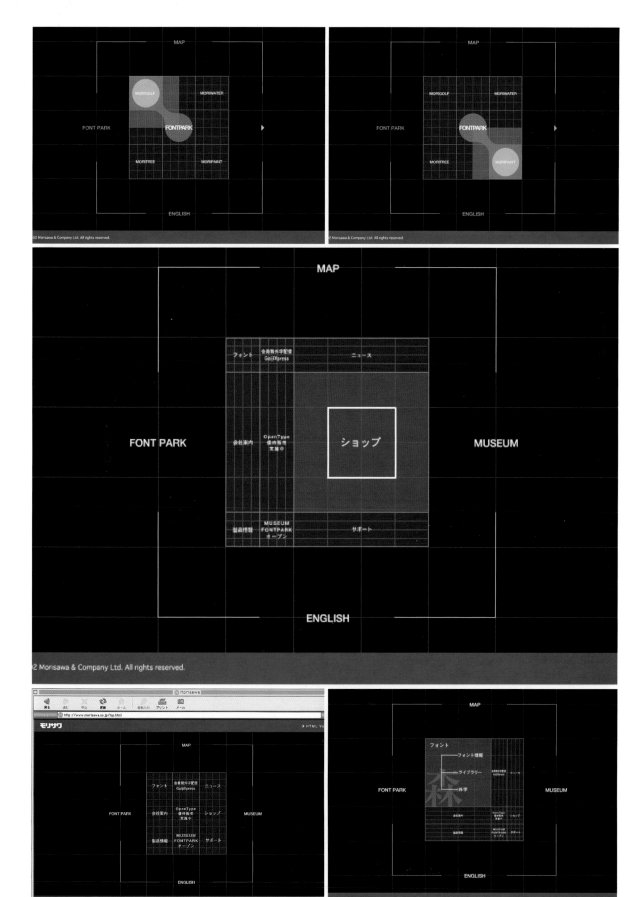

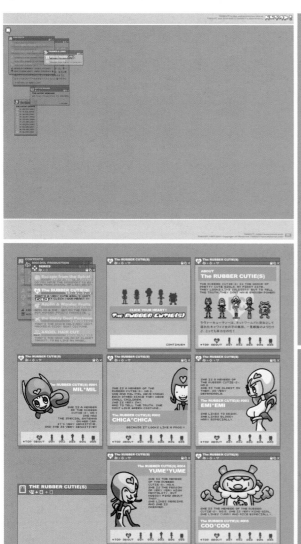

↓ Tarout!
← http://www.tarout.net
D: Tarout

↓ Kanebo "Woman's Beat Grand prix Words Forest"
D: Tarout

→ "My life as an ape"
http://39.img8.com/
D: +39 | Kay-ichi Tozaki

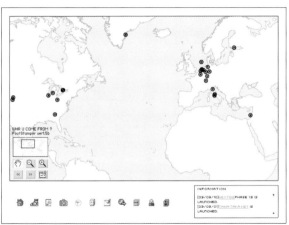

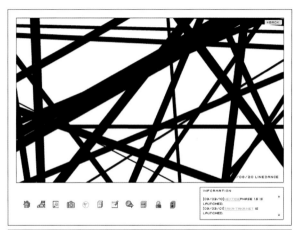

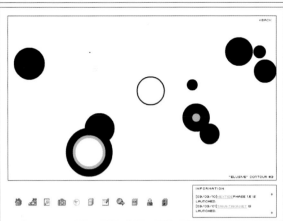

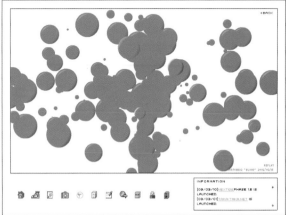

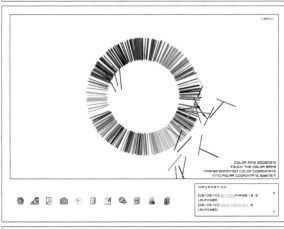

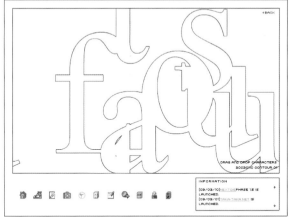

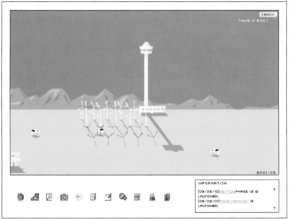

TYNY VOICE
COPYRIGHT 2001 TYNY VOICE. ALL RIGHTS RESERVED.

WHICH DO YOU LIKE?

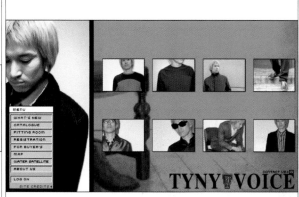

menu
WHAT'S NEW
CATALOGUE
FITTING ROOM
REGISTRATION
FOR BUYER'S
MAP
WATER SATELLITE
ABOUT US
LOG ON
SITE CREDITS

CONTACT US
TYNY VOICE

REVIEW

2001 AUTUMN AND WINTER COLLECTION
ITEM NO. Autumn and Winter #1
SIZE
COLOR
MATERIAL
PRICE

BACK

ネイビーブルーと言うのは一番気になる
色だし、VOICEには必ずある色です。ブラッ
クより、あえてネイビーブルーと言うの
は、黒のストイックさや人工的な感じが
あまり好きではないからです。もちろんブ

DO YOU LIKE THIS ?
SHOW MORE DETAILS

ITEM NO.   31212
SIZE   46 | 48
COLOR   BK
MATERIAL 絹100
PRICE   19,000yen

RELATED ITEMS

menu

SIZE SPEC

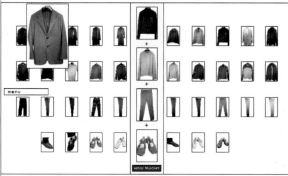

menu

HOW MUCH!

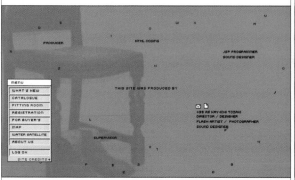

PRODUCER
HTML CODING
JSP PROGRAMMER
SOUND DESIGNER

THIS SITE WAS PRODUCED BY

menu
WHAT'S NEW
CATALOGUE
FITTING ROOM
REGISTRATION
FOR BUYER'S
MAP
WATER SATELLITE
ABOUT US
LOG ON
SITE CREDITS

439 AB KAY-ICHI TOZAKI
DIRECTOR / DESIGNER
FLASH ARTIST / PHOTOGRAPHER
SOUND DESIGNER

SUPERVISOR

menu

CONTACT US
TYNY VOICEは、

made
by
japan

で世界にも飛んでいきます。

← "Tyny voice"
http://www.tynyvoice.co.jp/
D: +39 | Kay-ichi Tozaki
cl: Water Satellite Inc.

↓ "Nextide"
http://www.nextide.co.jp
D: +39 | Kay-ichi Tozaki
cl: Nextide Inc.
direction: Yumiko Inoue
program: Hideyuki Takeya

ビジネスを**成功**に導く
エンタープライズ
ソリューションが
ここにある!

SOLUTIONS
Building Business Orchestration
▶ TERMS OF USE AND PRIVACY POLICY.
COPYRIGHT (C) 2002 NEXTIDE. ALL RIGHTS RESERVED.

新たなる企業価値を創造する
NExTideのビジネスオーケストレーション

↑ TOP
ⓘ INFO
🔒 OVERVIEW
⚙ **SOLUTIONS**
　ソリューションの概要
　コンサルティング
　インテグレーション
　システムマネージメント

　Infrastructure
　KM/EIP
　B2E

📄 .NET Showcase
🔲 PROFILE
📱 JOBS
✉ INQUIRY
◈ LINKS
🖨 PRINT

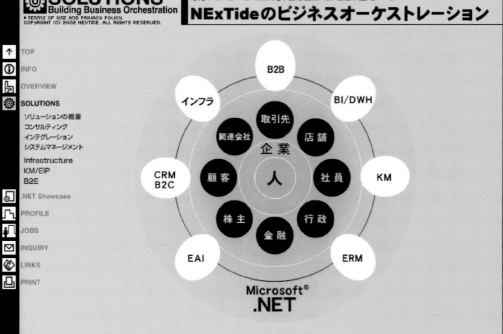

Presented by
MITSUI & CO.,LTD.

MAG·LITE
AMERICAN STYLE

TOP PAGE

NEWS
ニュース

HISTORY
マグライトヒストリー

LINE-UP
商品ラインナップ

STORE MAP
お取扱店地図

WARRANTY
REGISTRATION
保証登録

CONTACT US
お問合せ

アメリカ・カリフォルニア州オンタリオ。ひとりの女性
が地下室を修理中に、コンクリートの床に埋もれた化石の
ようなハンディライトを発見した。

6年前、家の修繕をした時に失くしたライトであること
を思い出しながら、彼女は何気なくスイッチを入れてみ
た。するとどうだろう。そのライトは当たり前のように
光を発したのだ。

そのハンディライトが『マグライト』。厳しい状況の中
で人が一番必要とするものは『光』、という信念に基づ
きアメリカで誕生したライトだ。

雨や雪、泥、砂塵など、どんなハードな環境で使われて
も弱音を吐かず、回りを明るく照らし出すそのクォリ
ティは、今や世界中で使われるほど愛され、信頼される
ハンディライトの代名詞になっている。

1955年	Mag Instrument社がロサンゼルスのガレージで創業開始
1970年代	Mag Instrument社創業者である アンソニー・マグリカ氏が 当時の懐中電灯に疑問を感じる。
1979年	初期モデル マグライト完成!! 警察官や消防士など懐中電灯の信頼性でみずからの生命が左 右されてしまう人々に、マグライトは絶大な信頼を受ける。 次第に消費者の間でもその信頼が話題に上りマグライトに注 目が集まっていった。
1982年	オンタリオに12万6000フィート四方の工場を新設。約80 人の従業員とともに移転。 移転後まもなく、充電式懐中電灯マグ・チャージャー充電可

MAG·LITE
AMERICAN STYLE

Presented by
MITSUI & CO.,LTD.

TOP PAGE

NEWS
ニュース

HISTORY
マグライトヒストリー

LINE-UP
商品ラインナップ

STORE MAP
お取扱店地図

WARRANTY
REGISTRATION
保証登録

CONTACT US
お問合せ

Welcome to MAG·LITE World

ようこそ、マグライトの世界に。
長年にわたる機械加工パーツの製造によって培われた世界最高水準の技術力、
そして妥協を許さない熟練職人たちの丹念な製品づくり。
すべての「マグライト」製品を製造するマグ・インストルメント社は、
その優れた開発力によって、斬新なアイデアをつぎつぎに具体化。
常に最高の製品を開発するために情熱を注いできました。
「マグライト」に搭載されている多彩な機能はすべて、
あらゆる角度からの研究、改良の積み重ねによって生み出された、
マグ・インストルメント社ならではのものです。
テクノロジーとクラフツマンシップの融合から生まれた「マグライト」。
いまだかつてない精密さと完成度で、これまでのハンディライトの常識を一変します。

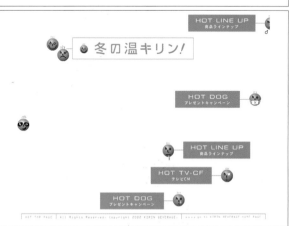

INDEX

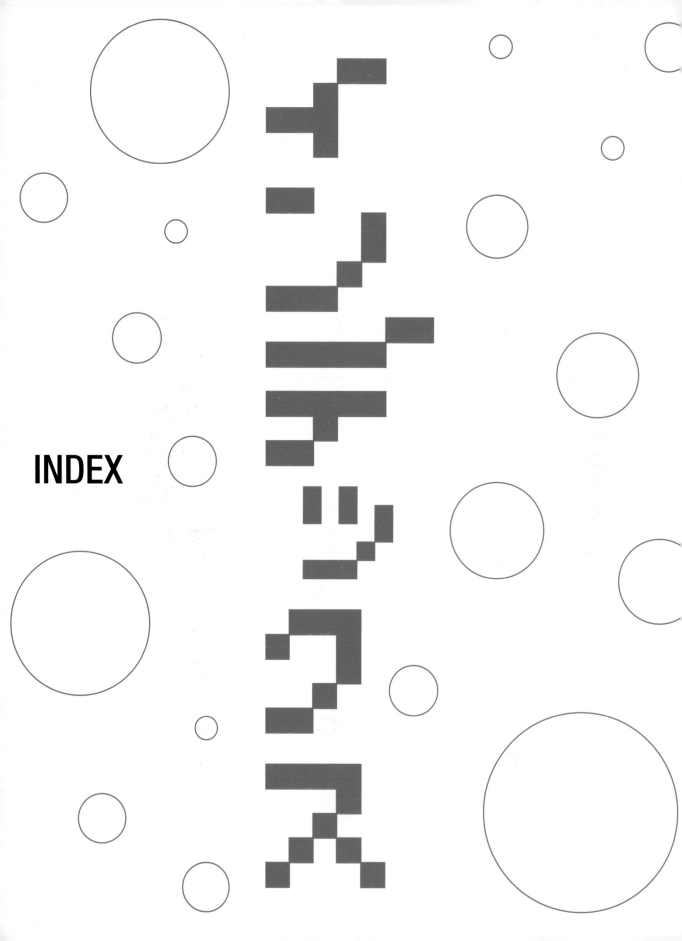

TORU ITO
1-15-22-412 Honcho, Nakano-ku,
Tokyo 164-0012 Japan (Tokyo Office)
Tel. 81-3-5350-5588
Fax. 81-3-5350-5588
158 Rue St-Jacques 75005 Paris, France
(Paris Office)
Tel. 33-1-5310-0967
Fax. 33-1-5310-0968
toruitodesign@ybb.ne.jp
http://mapage.noos.fr/toruitodesign

K NOTE
Kazuaki Okuda
502 New Aster House Morisaki 1-9-4
Itachibori Nishi-ku, Osaka 550-0012 Japan
Tel. 81-6-6543-7600
Fax. 81-6-6543-7601
k.note-okuda@titan.ocn.ne.jp

KINETIQUE INC.
Catty&Co.Division
D: t.o.L
4F Asahi Soko 1-14-7 Tsukishima
Chuo-ku, Tokyo 104-0052 Japan
Tel. 81-3-5548-5681
Fax. 81-3-5548-5684
info@kinetique.co.jp
www.tamala2010.com

KAITEKI
info@kitk.org
http://kitk.org

KATACHI
President: Hoshiba Kunikazu
7F Yowa bldg. 2-14-2 Tsukiji
chuo-ku, Tokyo 104-0054 Japan
Tel. 81-3-3544-5320
Fax. 81-3-3544-5321
6-7-15 Benten Minato-ku,
Osaka 552-0007 Japan
Tel. 81-6-6599-0210
Fax. 81-6-6599-0310
hoshiba@katachi.jp
www.katachi.jp

CHIHIRO KATOH
1-12-13 Nishiuragacho Yokosuka-shi,
Kanagawa 239-0824 Japan
Tel. 81-46-844-3140
Fax. 81-46-844-3140
Mobile. 81-90-9151-8356
works@chihiro.org
www.chihiro.org

YOSHIHITO KAWATA
3-26-12 Nakashirane Asahi-Ku
Yokohama-shi, Kanagawa 241-0004 Japan
Mobile. 81-90-7420-3074
info@futureshot.com
yosi_k@d4.dion.ne.jp
www.futureshot.com
www.d4.dion.ne.jp/~yosi_k

KENNY A INC.
Katsushi Ashida
8F Higobashi Park Bldg. 1-3-3
Kyomachibori Nishi-ku,
Osaka 550-0003 Japan
Tel. 81-6-6225-1067
Fax. 81-6-6225-1067

KATSU KIMURA
4-15-15-101 Nishiazabu Minato-ku,
Tokyo 106-0031 Japan
Tel. 81-3-3407-1719
Fax. 81-3-3499-1466
ad@packaging.co.jp

KOSÉ CORPORATION
Product Designing Dept.
AD: Fujio Hanawa
1-9-9 Hatchobori Chuo-ku,
Tokyo 104-0032 Japan
Tel. 81-3-3555-9199
Fax. 81-3-3555-9184
f-hanawa@kose.co.jp

MAGAZINEHOUSE
3-13-10 Ginza Chuo-ku,
Tokyo 104-8003 Japan
Tel. 81-3-3545-7130
Fax. 81-3-3546-6561
http://www.magazine.co.jp/english

HIROYUKI MATSUISHI
Axis Co.,Ltd.
208-1-16-6 Kazurugaoka Koga-shi,
Fukuoka 811-3104 Japan
Tel. 81-93-603-8714 (Office)
Tel. 81-92-943-0040 (Home)
matsuishi@axis.co.jp

KEN MIKI
Ken Miki & Associates
601, 602 Kiyosu Nakanoshima Plaza 1-3-4
Tenjinbashi Kita-ku, Osaka 530-0041 Japan
Tel. 81-6-6358-5270
Fax. 81-6-6358-1785
miki@ken-miki.net
www.ken-miki.net

HIROSHI MITSUISHI
Dai Nippon Printing Co.,Ltd.
Integrated Packaging Development Center
1-1-1 Ichigayakagacho Shinjuku-ku, Tokyo
162-8001 Japan
Tel. 81-3-5225-5867
Fax. 81-3-5225-5955
mitsuishi-h@mail.dnp.co.jp

RYOSUKE MIYASHITA
Dentsu Inc.
Creative Division 4
1-8-1 Higashishinbashi Minato-ku,
Tokyo 105-7001 Japan
Tel. 81-3-6216-1660
r.miyashita@dentsu.co.jp

MOON PROJECT
Yoshihiro Shibata
301 Park View Kyomachibori 2-3-1
Kyomachibori Nishi-ku,
Osaka 550-0003 Japan
Tel. 81-6-4803-7240
Fax. 81-6-4803-7240
Mobile. 81-90-3922-0821
cheva@moonproject.net

KAZUMASA NAGAI
Nippon Design Center, Inc.
Chuodaiwa Bldg. 1-13-13 Ginza
Chuo-ku, Tokyo 104-0061 Japan
Tel. 81-3-3567-3524
Fax. 81-3-3535-3569

HIDEKI NAKAJIMA
Nakajima Design
4F Kaiho Bldg. 4-11 Uguisudanicho
Shibuya-ku, Tokyo 150-0032 Japan
Tel. 81-3-5489-1757
Fax. 81-3-5489-1758
nkjm-d2@kd5.so-net.ne.jp

SHINYA NAKAJIMA
Tohokushinsha Film Corporation
4-8-10 Akasaka Minato-ku,
Tokyo 107-8460 Japan
Tel. 81-3-5414-0216
Fax. 81-3-5414-0407
tfshinya@tfc.co.jp
http://www.tfc.co.jp

NORIO NAKAMURA
7-1-12-602 Minami-Aoyama
Minato-ku, Tokyo 107-0062 Japan
Tel. 81-3-5468-2655
Fax. 81-3-5468-2662

MASAKI NEGISHI
Daiko Advertising Inc.
Art Director Group 2 Creative Division
Shuwa Shiba Park Bldg. B-kan 2-4-1
Shibakoen Minato-ku,
Tokyo 105-8533 Japan
Tel. 81-3437-8407
Fax. 81-3-3437-8482
masaki.negishi@daiko.co.jp

KOSHI OGAWA
Offbeat
1-7-7-7F Shintomi chuo-ku,
Tokyo 104-0041 Japan
Tel. 81-3-3555-1611
Fax. 81-3-3555-1622
koshi_ogawa@off-beat.co.jp

GAKU OHSUGI
702 Design Works Co.,Ltd
1-A Oak House 3-6-6 Uehara
Sibuya-Ku, Tokyo 151-0064 Japan
Tel. 81-3-3468-9702
Fax. 81-3-3468-9797
info@702design.co.jp
www.702design.co.jp

AKIO OKUMURA
Im-Lab
1F Commemorative Association
For The Japan World Exposition
1-1 Senribanpakukoen Suita-shi,
Osaka 565-0826 Japan
Tel. 81-6-4864-6380
Fax. 81-6-4864-6570
oku@okumura-akio.com
www.okumura-akio.com

OMURA DESIGN
Masaaki Omura
6-27-8 Jindaijihigasichou Chofu-shi,
Tokyo 182-0012 Japan
Mobile. 81-90-8892-0163
omura@kk.iij4u.or.jp
http://www.typo.or.jp/who/portfolio/omura_m

ROCKETDESIGN
14-1-1-104 Kita2jonishi Chuo-ku,
Sapporo-shi Hokkaido 060-0002 Japan
info@rocketdesign.org
http://rocketdesign.org

ROMANDO CO., LTD.
1-15-14 Jingumae Shibuya-ku,
Tokyo 150-0001 Japan
Tel. 81-3-5414 8211
Fax. 81-3-5414 8212
post@romando.co.jp
www.romando.co.jp

SAKAGUCHI KEN FACTORY, INC.
Staff: Ken Sakaguchi/ Izumi Honma/
Tomomi Takahashi
2-14-10 Misyuku Setagaya-ku,
Tokyo 154-0005 Japan
Tel. 81-3-3424-2304
Fax. 81-3-3424-2341
www.ken-factory.com

MASANORI SAKAMOTO
5-5-6-110 Kamikodanaka Nakahara-ku
Kawasaki-shi, Kanagawa 211-0053 Japan
Tel. 81-44-751-4335
masanori@motla.com
www.motla.com

SAMOHUNG
5c Tokiwamatsu Mansions 1-14-12
Higashi Shibuya-ku, Tokyo 150-0011 Japan
Tel. 81-3-3797-9071
www.samohung.jp

SAMURAI
Kashiwa Sato
7F Inoue Bldg. 6-7-13 Minami-aoyama
Minatoku, Tokyo 107-0062 Japan
Tel. 81-3-5766-0280
Fax. 81-3-5766-0281
etsuko@samurai.sh

OSAMU SATO
Outside Directors Company Ltd. (Osd)
3-13-2-3F Ginza Chuo-Ku,
Tokyo 104-0061 Japan
Tel. 81-3-3547-3404
Fax. 81-3-3547-3410
osamu@osd.co.jp
www.osd.co.jp
www.mao55.net

U.G. SATO
Design Farm Inc.
75 Yaraicho Shinjuku-ku,
Tokyo 162-0805 Japan
Tel. 81-3-3267-1267
Fax. 81-3-3267-1265
ugsato@kt.rim.or.jp

SAYURI STUDIO, INC.
Sayuri Shoji
6-7-5-308 Minami-aoyama
Minato-ku, Tokyo 107-0062 Japan
Tel. 81-3-3406-5003
Fax. 81-3-3406-5004
mail@ss-studio.com
www.ss-studio.com

EMIKO SHIBASAKI
Antenna Studio
802 Okada Bldg. 2-4-2 Sugamo
Toshima-ku, Tokyo 170-0002 Japan
emiko@antenna-studio.com
www.antenna-studio.com

NORITO SHINMURA
4F Seibido Bldg. 6-7-8 Ginza Chuo-ku,
Tokyo 104-0064 Japan
Tel. 81-3-3572-5042
Fax. 81-3-3572-5045
shinmura@kk.iij4u.or.jp

SIO DESIGN CO., LTD.
Yoshinori Shiozawa / London Tokura
2007 Chrysantheme 1-41-7 Tomigaya
Shibuya-ku, Tokyo 151-0063 Japan
Tel. 81-3-5478-1634
Fax. 81-3-5478-1635
sio-design@mtg.biglobe.ne.jp

SOEDA DESIGN FACTORY
Takayuki Soeda
101 T-House 3-6-7 Minami-azabu
Minato-Ku, Tokyo 106-0047 Japan
Tel. 81-3-3442-3989

SHINNOSKE SUGISAKI
Shinnoske Inc.
2-1-8-602 Tsuriganecho Chuo-ku,
Osaka 540-0035 Japan
Tel. 81-6-6943-9077
Fax. 81-6-6943-9078
info@shinn.co.jp
http://www.shinn.co.jp/

SAYAKO TAKASAKI
302 Guresu Nakamachi 2-10-8 Nakamachi
Meguro-ku, Tokyo 153-0065 Japan
Tel. 81-3-3791-9840
Mobile. 81-90-8477-1123
sayacot@hotmail.com

TAKU SATOH
Taku Satoh Design Office Inc.
4F Ginsho Bldg. 1-14-11 Ginza
Chuo-ku, Tokyo 104-0061 Japan
Tel. 81-3-3538-2051
Fax. 81-3-3538-2054
tsdo@tsdo.co.jp

TAROUT
Taro Yamakawa
2-17-7 -402 Wakabayashi Setagaya-ku,
Tokyo 154-0023 Japan
tarout@tarout.net
www.tarout.net

TCD CORPORATION
TCD bldg. Kasugacho 7-19 Ashiya-shi,
Hyogo 659-0021 Japan
Tel. 81-797-34-4300
info@tcd.jp
www.tcd.jp

TUGBOAT
5-6-24-4F Minami-aoyama
Minato-ku, Tokyo 107-0062 Japan
Tel. 81-3-5485-7475
Fax. 81-3-5485-7476
mail@tugboat..jp

GANTA UCHIKIBA
607 Harajuku corp. annex 1-10-34
Jingumae Shibuya-ku,
Tokyo 150-0001 Japan
Tel. 81-3-5786-2460
Fax. 81-3-5786-2465
ganta@grounder.jp

HIROYUKI UENO
Hiroyuki Ueno Design
Office Limited Company
2-9-5 Shinnezukamachi Toyama-shi,
Toyama 939-8205 Japan
Tel. 81-76-421-3507
Fax. 81-76-491-6210
ueno-des@tateyama.or.jp
www.tateyama.or.jp/~ueno-des

TOSHIHIRO WATANABE
1-9-5-412 Tamagawa Setagaya-ku,
Tokyo 158-0094 Japan
Tel. 81-3-3708-2774
Fax. 81-3-3708-2774
Mobile. 81-90-3092-2079
wata@d-gall.com

YOSHIE WATANABE
Draft
2-14-6 Higashi Shibuya-ku,
Tokyo 150-0011 Japan
Tel. 81-3-3498-5281
yoshie@draft.jp

KOHJI YAMAMOTO
kohji@sfc.keio.ac.jp

YOSUKE YASUDA
y@mosless.com
village.infoweb.ne.jp/~fwne4609/
www.mosless.com

YOSHIE YOKOYAMA
Alfa Eyes Design Inc.
2-13-10-404 Ebisunishi Shibuya-ku, Tokyo
150-0021 Japan
Tel . 81-3-5459-3436
lynx@alfaeyes.com
www.alfaeyes.com

TADANORI YOOKO
www.tadanoriyokoo.com

We would like to thank for the brilliant cooperation we have had from all the designers during all the production process and for their willingness to help us to make this publication a significative showcase of how graphic design has developd in Japan. Moreover we would like to thank also Yoshiyuki Sakaguchi, Director/Curator of the Advertising Museum Tokyo, Sayuri Shoji, President/Art director of Sayuri Studio Inc., Taku Satoh, Graphic Designer of Taku Satoh Design Office Inc., Shinya Nakajima, CM Director of Tohokushinsha Film Corporation and Seijo Kawaguchi, Art Director of TUGBOAT for their time, patience, support and wisdom, and their contribution to the DVD with interviews.

We would like to thank of course all the professionals and friends that contributed to make this publication better, among them Yasuo Satomi, Taschen`s director in Japan and Kiyonori Muroga, editor from IDEA Magazine in Tokyo, that in the last minutes have helped us do much. Also the great effort of Ricado Gimanes who almost alone produced the DVD that comes together with this book. We thank also the people and institutions that have helped us to find all the designers we were willing to feature in the book, such as Naoki Kondo, from JAGDA (Japan Graphic Designers Association), Tokuzo Ito from Dentsu Inc. for his help and introduction to the Japanese advertisement business, Junko Fujii also from Dentsu Inc. for her intense collaboration, Noriko Iwamoto from the ADMT (Advertising Museum Tokyo), for introducing the Museum collection, Leila Kozak-Gilroy for the comments on the introduction, and special thanks to Takashi Tsurumaki for his support and invaluable help all along the process. At last, but not at least, we would like to thank all the staff at TASCHEN Japan, specially Yuko Aoki and Mari Omura, who has done so much for us during the whole production.

DVD - Intreview with Shinya Nakajima, CM Director of Tohokushinsha Film Corporation/film credits: Suntory, Dentsu, Frontage, Shingata, Tohokushinsha. Interview with Yoshiyuki Sakaguchi, Director/Curator: Advertising Museum Tokyo. Sayuri Shoji, President/Art director: Sayuri Studio Inc. Taku Satoh, Graphic Designer: Taku Satoh Design Office Inc. Seijo Kawaguchi, Art Director: TUGBOAT. All subtitle translations by Tamami Sambonmatsu, Tokyo. Japanese questions` translation: Ms. Mari Omura.

Film Credits - Dakara: Suntory, Dentsu, Frontage, Shingata, Tohokushinsha. ISAO: isao.net, Break up, Dentsu, Engine Film, Yuya Furukawa, Grand Funk (James Shimoji, Yuka Goto-Singer, James Shimoji-Singer). ISAO: isao.net, Wife and mother-in-law, Dentsu, Engine Film, Yuya Furukawa, Grand Funk (James Shimoji, Yuka Goto-Singer, James Shimoji-Singer). ISAO: isao.net, Club, Dentsu, Engine Film , Yuya Furukawa, Grand Funk (James Shimoji, Yuka Goto-Singer, James Shimoji-Singer). Staff Service Corporation: Oh personal affairs, Dentsu, Nitten Alti, Yoshikazu Tanaka Nobutake Sera. Staff Service Corporation: Nice putt, Dentsu, Nitten Alti, Yoshikazu Tanaka Nobutake Sera. Staff Service Corporation: Hole in one + Dump in pond, Dentsu, Nitten Alti, Yoshikazu Tanaka Nobutake Sera. Wowow: Wowow, The Birdman, Dentsu, Jeff / Yarra Films, Yoshimitsu Sawamoto, Grand Funk, Toyohiko Kanehashi. Mitsubishi Pencil Uni: power tank, Marriage registration, Dentsu, C.M.N, Takuma Takasaki, Boogie Box, Eric Zay (Composer).

© 2003 TASCHEN GmbH
Hohenzollernring 53, D-50672 Köln
www.taschen.com
Design: Julius Wiedemann, Cologne
Layout: Julius Wiedemann, Cologne & Gisele Kozak, Tokyo
Production: Ute Wachendorf
Editors: Gisela Kozak & Julius Wiedemann
DVD Design, Edition and Production: Ricardo Gimenes
German Translation: Anke Caroline Burger
French Translation: Marc Combes
Japanese Translation: Ritsuko Hiraishi, Tokyo
Spanish Translation: Rosa Plana Castillón
for LocTeam, S. L., Barcelona.
Italian Translation: Quirino Di Zitti for LocTeam, S. L., Barcelona.
Portuguese Translation: Vera Maia Rocha
for LocTeam, S. L., Barcelona.

ISBN: 3-8228-2589-1
Printed in Spain

IMPRINT